'A fasc...
well i...
discov...
to rush off and reread Anne's novels and poetry'
Juliet Barker, *Mail on Sunday*

...ous and direct . . . a timely reappraisal'
Johannah Thomas-Carr, *Evening Standard*

'You will find insights aplenty here'
Lucasta Miller, *Sunday Times*

'Genuinely revisionist'
Margaret Drabble, *Times Literary Supplement*

'Anne has been in her sisters' shadows for too long and the time has
come to give "the other Brontë" her proper due'
James Walton, *Daily Mail*

'Samantha Ellis skilfully reclaims Anne as a truly modern, feminist
writer whose work is just as relevant today'
Red

'Her personal approach is the source of both the book's immense
charm and also its considerable power . . . Ultimately the book is a
deeply moving depiction of how reading and writing allows us to
forge an emotional and intellectual connection with someone
who died over a century before we were born . . . Brilliant'
Anna Carey, *Irish Times*

'Ellis – who is, it should be noted, as intelligent and perceptive a
reader as she is an evocative storyteller – truly writes from the heart,
which isn't to say she hasn't done her research . . . A deeply sympathetic
and interesting re-evaluation of a woman ahead of her time who
has much to teach us all about living courageously'
Lucy Scholes, *Independent*

SAMANTHA ELLIS

Samantha Ellis's first book *How To Be A Heroine* was published in 2014. Her plays include *Cling to Me Like Ivy* and *How to Date a Feminist*. She has written prefaces for Persephone Books and for the Vintage Classics edition of *Agnes Grey*, and she reviews for the *Guardian*, *Observer*, *TLS*, *Literary Review*, the *Pool* and more. She lives in London.

ALSO BY SAMANTHA ELLIS

How To Be A Heroine

SAMANTHA ELLIS

Take Courage

Anne Brontë and the Art of Life

VINTAGE

For Jude

1 3 5 7 9 10 8 6 4 2

Vintage
20 Vauxhall Bridge Road,
London SW1V 2SA

Vintage is part of the Penguin Random House group of companies
whose addresses can be found at global.penguinrandomhouse.com

Penguin
Random House
UK

First published in Vintage in 2018
First published in Great Britain by Chatto & Windus in 2017

www.vintage-books.co.uk

A CIP catalogue record for this book is available from the British Library

ISBN 9781784701116

Printed and bound by Clays Ltd, St Ives plc

Penguin Random House is committed to a sustainable future
for our business, our readers and our planet. This book is made
from Forest Stewardship Council® certified paper.

MIX
Paper from
responsible sources
FSC
www.fsc.org
FSC® C018179

CONTENTS

INTRODUCTION

Until I found myself holding Anne Brontë's last letter in my hands, I thought I knew all I needed to know about her. I thought she was a virginal Victorian spinster, sweet and stoic, selfless and sexless, achieving very little before wasting away at twenty-nine. Emily had always been my top Brontë. I'd come to appreciate Charlotte's toughness and spirit. I'd sometimes thought it might be fun to have a drink with Branwell. But Anne had always seemed a bit, well, boring. Gentle. Pious. Meek. The less talented Brontë, the one in her sisters' shadow, the *other* Brontë.

I'm in Yorkshire, giving a reading from my last book, which pitched *Wuthering Heights* against *Jane Eyre*. While I'm here, Ann Dinsdale, the collections manager at the Brontë Parsonage Museum in Haworth, offers to show me some Brontë treasures – and no Brontë fan could refuse.

It's my first time meeting Ann Dinsdale but I have often seen her on TV; every time there's some new Brontë discovery, she appears, white-gloved, dressed in black, with a fierce dark bob and a slash of red lipstick. It's a blowy May morning and the Parsonage is empty except for us; this is the lull before it opens to the public.

Ann leads me through the kitchen, which is kept as if the Brontës have just popped out for a moment. A book leans against an old-fashioned set of scales, the black range gleams like it has just been polished, tea towels have been hung up as if to dry and a red tea cosy sits ready to warm a pot. Undoing the cordon, careful not to set off the alarms, Ann opens a heavy wooden door, and then we are in the annexe added after the Brontës' time, which is now the library, lined with glass-fronted, floor-to-ceiling bookcases in dark wood, full of everything you ever wanted to know about the Brontës and quite a lot you didn't. There are three desks squashed up by the windows, which look out onto the moors, rain spattering the glass, sheep shivering. A yellowing newspaper clipping taped to a filing cabinet reads, 'In Austen, sex is just a kiss on the hand. In the Brontës, everything happens.' I assume it refers to *Wuthering Heights*, but Ann says no, it is about Anne's second novel, *The Tenant of Wildfell Hall*. Then, as I sit at the long table, and put on latex gloves, she asks if I want to see Anne's last letter. I'm more interested in looking at some of the other treasures – Emily's drawing of a fist smashing a mullioned window (whose fist? whose window?), and the book Charlotte and Branwell made, on scraps of paper and sugar bags, in writing tiny enough for their toy soldiers to read – but when I actually read Anne's letter, I get a shock.

I had read a lot about Anne's death, more than about her life. The accounts of it ooze high-Victorian sentiment. As a death scene it has everything: a virtuous heroine, piteous coughing, heartfelt prayer, sledgehammers of pathos and mawkish hints of a glorious ascent to heaven. In the books I'd read, poor consumptive Anne slipped out of life on a couch in Scarborough in May 1849, as Charlotte wept beside her. They both knew she was Going To A Better Place, and although she was only twenty-nine, she was ready, because, as Charlotte said, 'Anne, from her childhood, seemed preparing for an early death.'

Anne's death was quiet, like a death Charles Dickens had imagined eight years earlier. In *The Old Curiosity Shop*, his heroine, Little Nell, dies in silence. Not just any silence: 'Angel hands have strewn the ground deep with snow, that the lightest footstep may be lighter yet; and the very birds are dead, that they may not wake her.' Yes, that's right: *birds have been killed*, or maybe sacrificed themselves, or died of broken hearts, so Nell can die in perfect quietness. 'She was dead,' Dickens intones, again and again, his noisy grief eclipsing his dull, wan heroine. Nell is almost an angel herself. So is another dying Victorian heroine; in Louisa May Alcott's 1868 weepie, *Little Women*, Beth's sister can see, just by looking at her, that 'the mortal was being slowly refined away, and the immortal shining through the frail flesh with an indescribable pathetic beauty'.

Alcott felt very connected to the Brontës. She also had a father with strong beliefs (hers was a transcendental philosopher who almost killed his family by making them live on a vegan commune which didn't use 'noxious' manure or oppress animals by making them plough the fields). She also grew up poor and burned to write. She was also intensely close to her siblings. In 1857, while her sister was dying, Alcott devoured Elizabeth Gaskell's biography of Charlotte Brontë and wrote in her diary, 'Wonder if I shall ever be famous enough for people to care to read my story and struggles.' When she wrote her 'story and struggles' into *Little Women*, she cast herself as conflicted, clever Jo while Beth was a mix of her own sister and Anne Brontë, as portrayed by Gaskell; a sweet, passive girl who never dreams of the future or makes plans because she is convinced she was never intended to live long. She's so resigned and insipid that she is hard to like.

Reading Anne's last letter, I feel Alcott has got her wrong, and Gaskell too, and maybe even Charlotte. It's like meeting a completely different woman.

Anne wrote the letter five weeks before her death, on 5 April 1849. The paper is bordered in black because Anne was in mourning for Branwell and Emily, who had died seven and four months before respectively. The letter is cross-written. To save paper, and postage, after writing each page, Anne turned it ninety degrees and wrote over ('crossed') the words she had written already. It took skill to cross-write; you had to space out the first lines so that the crossed lines could fit into the spaces between words. You had to be achingly neat. Although Anne was very ill, and weak, her writing is elegant, slanted and clear. The letter was a physical effort to write, and it took courage too, because it was an act of defiance. Anne was writing to ask Charlotte's lifelong friend Ellen Nussey to go to Scarborough with her, a place she loved, in the hope that it would cure her tuberculosis. Nussey was up for it, but Charlotte had written behind Anne's back, to tell her to refuse. Charlotte didn't think Anne was well enough to travel, she didn't think the cure would work, and maybe in the back of her mind, too, was her idea that Anne was preparing for an early death. But in Anne's letter, she is full of hope and spirit. She wants to live, because 'I long to do some good in the world . . . before I leave it. I have many schemes in my head for future practise – humble and limited indeed – but still I should not like them all to come to nothing, and myself to have lived to so little purpose.' This catches at my heart, and makes me breathe hard suddenly. I put the letter down. This Anne knew what she wanted. She had published two novels and many poems. She didn't want to have to stop. She was courageous, she was tough, and she wanted more life.

As the Parsonage opens for business, I go back through the cordons, eavesdropping on visitors chatting about the Brontës, and no one mentions Anne, and then I'm in the shop, among the fridge magnets and the mugs, and then I'm slip-sliding down the wet cobbled lane, and I'm choking back tears, because Anne *didn't* want to die. Of course she didn't.

I remember how in her phenomenal group biography *The Brontës*, Juliet Barker said Anne had 'a core of steel'. Most of the volunteers at the Brontë Parsonage, passionate Brontë fans who spend their days among the Brontës' intimate objects (Charlotte's darned stockings, Emily's paper knife, Branwell's walking stick) and call them all by first names (even the servants, even the hangers-on), say Anne is their favourite. So as I try to get a hold on myself, I wonder: why is she ignored, or written off as boring? Why isn't she read as much as her sisters? Why was her work suppressed, why is it underrated even now, and what does that say about what women still are and aren't allowed to say? And what can I learn from her life and from her afterlife?

Walking down Haworth's steep Main Street, I spot a cartoon pasted in a bookshop window. In *Dude Watchin' With the Brontës*,

Kate Beaton draws Charlotte and Emily lusting after various dark, brooding Heathcliff-types. Anne bursts their bubble, saying these men are all right 'If you like alcoholic dickbags!' Charlotte snaps back, 'No wonder nobody buys your books.' Maybe *this* is why Anne isn't read: she is too radical. In *The Tenant of Wildfell Hall*, she takes a heroine who starts out like all the other Brontë heroines, charmed by a sexy dangerous man, but she sees the light and leaves him. It's very refreshing. And it wasn't what anyone wanted to hear in 1848.

Later, on the bus to the nearest town, Keighley, bumping along and squinting at my phone, I read the preface Anne wrote to the second edition of the novel – published after the first edition sold out in just six weeks. 'I wished to tell the truth,' she writes, and truth 'hides at the bottom of a well, it needs some courage to dive for it, especially as he that does so will be likely to incur more scorn and obloquy for the mud and water into which he has ventured to plunge, than thanks for the jewel he procures'. The image of her emerging triumphant from the well, covered in mud, drenched, but grasping a jewel, decides me. I am going to dive into mud and water too, to see what I can find.

I know it won't be easy. Anne says that diving for the truth takes courage. And she will be hard to get to know. She wasn't hungry for fame like Charlotte, who carefully managed her public image. She wasn't unconventional like Emily, who tramped the moors in odd clothes and learned to shoot. Even Branwell, who never got anywhere as a writer or an artist, leaves a stronger impression – maybe because he was a man, encouraged to stomp messily through the world, while Anne was taught to tread carefully, and cover her tracks. Or were they covered for her?

But I want to try. After years of reading and rereading Charlotte and Emily, I want to spend some time in Anne's company, to find out who she really was, and what she had to say. On the train, speeding south, I make a list of things to read, places to go, people to talk to.

It's late now, and the dark is seeping in at the windows, and everyone else on the train is asleep, but I'm wide awake. Maybe because I'm a year off turning forty, and single, and not a parent, and maybe because much of the writing I have done has been for the theatre, which is so heartbreakingly ephemeral, I've recently started to think about what mark I might make, what I might leave behind. Now the words of Anne's last letter are going round in my head. I long to do some good in the world too. But I don't know how. I feel stuck, somehow; limited, boxed-in, uneasy about where to go next, an anxiety sharpened by the fact that, having suffered from seizures for just over twenty years, I am also facing the future with all the challenges and complications of a chronic condition. How did Anne find her purpose? Did she feel she'd left enough of a mark, and what does it mean that so much of that has been erased? I read that Anne began her first novel with the promise that 'All true histories contain instruction'. If, despite the sparse record, and the encrustation of myth, I can arrive at any kind of truth about Anne, what will I learn?

Later, I'll study a photograph of the flyleaf of Anne's Bible, which is now in the Morgan Library & Museum in New York. When she turned twenty, Anne decided to read and study the

Bible right through, to make up her own mind about what was in it. This is, it turns out, a very Anne-ish thing to do. Serious and searching, fearless in her pursuit of the truth, she is the best companion I could have found for trying to work out how to live a more considered life. In her Bible, she wrote in pencil what I am asking myself as the train pulls into London: 'What, Where, and How Shall I Be When I Have Got Through?'

1

MARIA
or how to know who you come from

At the crisis of Anne Brontë's second and last novel, *The Tenant of Wildfell Hall*, her heroine Helen finally decides to leave Arthur Huntingdon, her drunk abusive husband. She's put up with a lot. But now he's trying to ruin their son, teaching him to swear and be horrid to his mother and pouring booze down his throat; he is *four*. It's supposed to 'make a man of him'.

When Helen flees her marriage, she has to make a woman of herself. She moves into Wildfell Hall, which is half in ruins, like her life. She swaps her hateful married surname for her mother's maiden name, and the ostentatious clothes her husband liked in favour of the 'plain, dark, sober' clothes she likes. This is useful, too, because in these dark clothes she can disguise herself as a widow. She is killing off her husband in her mind. She is remembering who she was before she married him. Knowing this day would come, she's secretly taught herself to paint. She finds a dealer in London, adopts another pseudonym and starts turning out commercial landscapes. She works out how to evade the village's prying gossips. She learns not to let anyone get too close, not even her brother, Frederick Lawrence, who has helped her find this place of safety, and especially not the handsome young gentleman farmer, Gilbert Markham, who keeps popping round. Helen becomes self-sufficient. She won't owe anyone anything, not again. She won't be vulnerable, not again. She learns how to mother her son, Arthur, teaching him that being a man is not about liquor and swearing, but about intelligence and kindness. And when Gilbert's mother Mrs Markham criticises her mothering, she lets rip. Why should girls be brought up like hothouse flowers, while boys are encouraged to go out in the world to get 'experience'? Experience only means boys are encouraged to be bad, and when men are bad, women get hurt. This line of argument doesn't win Helen any friends. But she doesn't care. She works hard, and gains independence (financial, emotional, creative). Most courageously of all, when Huntingdon gets ill, she risks everything to go and nurse him, to be with him when he dies. And when she decides she might like to marry again, she chooses Gilbert, who is worthy of her love – and this time, *she* proposes to *him*.

Helen has made a woman of herself.

Back home in London, working my way through a tottering stack of Brontë biographies, I become convinced Anne knew how to write about Helen making a woman of herself because she did it too, transforming herself from the baby of the family, a delicate, gentle girl who grew up full of fear, never thinking she'd amount to anything, into a talented teacher, a bold thinker and an extraordinary writer.

In the past fortnight I've read every word Anne left behind. I had hoped it would take longer, but Anne really hasn't left many traces. I'm a bit stunned by how much of what she said has been lost. Only five of her letters survive, though she wrote many more. This is bad. Trying to work out just how bad, I open a biography of Virginia Woolf and find that she left nearly four thousand letters. Even Charlotte left around 950. All the prose Anne wrote as a child is gone. Many of her poems are missing too, as well as, possibly, the start of a third novel. If she wrote a diary, it no longer exists. But she and Emily wrote a 'diary paper' every four years, a brief update on their lives which they would fold up and squirrel away in a tin box like a time capsule, to look at when it was time to write the next. If they were together, they wrote them jointly; if apart, they wrote one each. Two of Anne's are left, and two of the joint ones. Four pieces of paper. Compared with Woolf's fat volumes of diaries, it's not much. Even Sylvia Plath's journals make up an impressively chunky book, and she only lived a year longer than Anne did, *and* some of her journals were destroyed. Of course there are also letters *about* Anne, and reminiscences of her; there are some of her books with her revealing marginalia; there are her things, which are surprisingly eloquent; and there are heaps and heaps of scholarship about her family. Yet Juliet Barker writes that the known facts of Anne's and Emily's lives 'could be written on a single sheet of paper; their letters, diary papers and drawings would not fill two dozen'. It's very discouraging. How can so little be known about a member of one of the most famous families in history? The library shelves are groaning with books about the Brontës. Some biographers daringly follow their own hunches (sometimes into wild and dubious conjectures), while the so-called 'laundry list' biographers scrutinise all the tiny, daily details (sometimes missing the big picture). And no one agrees on anything. Even the colour of Anne's hair!

All the biographers rely heavily on a few contemporary sources, so I go back to those. Charlotte's school friends, Ellen Nussey and Mary Taylor, actually knew Anne. But they both seem to have axes to grind. And they don't agree either. The first biography was written by Elizabeth Gaskell who was friends with Charlotte, but they only met after Anne had died. Anne's father outlived her, but he wasn't chatty. Nor was Arthur Bell Nicholls, the curate who became Charlotte's husband. Maybe this is reassuring. Would I want people poking about in my stuff 170-odd years after I died? Absolutely not. By most (but not all) accounts Anne was a private person. So maybe I should be pleased for her. But I'm not. I'm frustrated. Because I'm nosy and because I feel quite ardently about her, and I wish she would stop slipping out of view.

I'm on safer ground with Anne's work. When I reread her two novels, the blistering preface she wrote explaining *The Tenant of Wildfell Hall* to its hostile critics, and her fifty-nine poems, Anne speaks out loud and clear. It can be dangerous to assume anything about a writer from her work, but Anne did write autobiographically. Charlotte said *Agnes Grey* was 'the mirror of the mind of the writer', while *The Tenant of Wildfell Hall* was an attempt 'to reproduce every detail (of course, with fictitious characters, incidents, and situations)' of what happened to their brother.

A lot of stories have been told about Anne, and the more I learn about her, the more I dislike the way she was forced into particular roles, both in her life and in her afterlife. Her work has such clarity, such vigour, that it feels like an act of resistance, a way of pushing back against being turned into a character in someone else's story, especially a minor character who doesn't have many lines and makes an early exit. I want to try to see Anne through the stories she told, not the stories told about her. Anne's fiction reveals a lot about how she saw the world. Sometimes she wrote to fulfil wishes. Sometimes she tried out lives she might want to live. Sometimes she turned difficult experiences to good use. Sometimes she defied fate. One afternoon in the library, with dusty books stacked around me like a fort, I realise what upsets me most about Charlotte saying Anne was always preparing for early death is that it dooms her, it traps her in one story, and not a good one. Can her story be told another way?

I decide to look at Anne through the women and men who shaped her, and the women she shaped, on the pages of her books, to try to find out how she made a woman of herself, how she ripped up the story she was supposed to live and became the artist of her own life.

Anne never knew one of the women who shaped her most: her mother, Maria Brontë, née Branwell, died when she was just twenty months old. Twenty months is very young to remember anything, but a life-changing event can sometimes stick. My seventies childhood is a haze of brown and orange, but I remember my brother being born, when I was twenty-one months old. When I imagine what it might have been like if my first big event was a death, not a birth, I start to get a sense of the weight of Anne's loss, its unbearable heft. Every Sunday, in church, Anne saw her mother's memorial stone, with its stark, ominous line from Matthew – 'Be ye also ready: for in such an hour as ye think not the Son of Man cometh' – warning that death could come for her at any moment. Anne was the baby, the one who needed a mother most. Did she already suffer from asthma? She certainly had it later on in life, but no one knows when it began. If she was a child who sometimes found it hard to breathe, she might have seemed, as Charlotte later said, 'delicate all her life', and maybe that's one of the reasons Charlotte thought it couldn't be long before Anne stopped breathing altogether.

I look at pictures of Anne next to pictures of Maria and I'm struck by how alike they look. They both have the same cherubic faces, the same curls, the same rosebud mouths. When Anne was very young, Charlotte said she saw an angel at Anne's cradle, and from then on, Anne's role in the family was fixed; she was sweet, lost and ethereal, halfway to being an angel herself.

Anne's mother also comes over as a saint in the early biographies. In the very first, published in 1857, *The Life of Charlotte Brontë* by Elizabeth Gaskell, Maria is a 'little, gentle creature' who was 'gentle, delicate', full of 'tender grace', 'feminine modesty' and 'deep piety' and 'always dressed with a quiet simplicity of taste, which accorded well with her general character'. Gaskell had an agenda. She wanted to tell the critics who called Charlotte's books coarse and unwomanly that they were wrong, that Charlotte wasn't a bad woman but a martyr whose life was so tough that she couldn't help it if some of it ended up on the page. Gaskell started by giving Charlotte a suitably angelic mother.

It's only one of the ways Gaskell skewed the story. Now I see why everyone who writes about the Brontës has to grapple with her *Life*: it didn't just come first, it's also fantastic. I speed through it like a novel. Which it more or less is, because Gaskell never lets facts get in the way of a good story. When a visitor asked Patrick, the Brontës' father, how much was true, he said, 'Mrs Gaskell is a novelist, you know, and we must allow her a little romance, eh?' The publishers of the mighty Shakespeare Head edition of the Brontës' works agreed; in 1859 they reprinted it alongside the novels, as though it was fiction too.

The *Life* reveals as much about Gaskell as it does about Charlotte. Because although Gaskell looked like a domestic goddess (she was a minister's wife, a mother of four and an active philanthropist, always rolling up her sleeves to help someone in need), she wrote out of a welter of grief and guilt. She turned to fiction after her baby son died of scarlet fever and she 'took refuge in invention to exclude the memory of painful scenes'. She wasn't just grieving her son, but her other losses, starting with her mother, who died when she was a baby, and the six brothers and sisters who died before she was born. Gaskell always knew life was fragile. Her aunt brought her up in Knutsford (basically Cranford) and it was all very loving and cosy and chocolate-boxy (except when her aunt had to deal with her violent husband, and when Gaskell had to make painful visits to her father and his new family). She had a good education, and married a good man. But her brother drifted. Without money or support, he found his options so viciously limited that all he could do was risk his life at sea. He never returned. Just vanished, off the coast of India. No one knows if he drowned, had an accident, killed himself or just decided to disappear. Gaskell's novels are full of dead mothers, dead children and thwarted men, so for her, Charlotte's story was catnip.

But as I learn more about the real Maria Brontë, she seems gutsier, more interesting and much less sweet than Gaskell makes out.

She was born Maria Branwell, in sunny, fun Penzance, into a big family. They were comfortable and well off; her father was a grocer and tea merchant, and one of her brothers became town mayor. Pale, petite and clever, Maria wasn't in any hurry to marry. Her parents died when she was in her twenties, and she and two sisters stayed on in the family home until their uncle, who owned the house, died, and they had to find somewhere else to live. Maybe Maria wanted to shake up her life, because instead of appealing to any of her ten siblings, she bravely travelled four hundred miles, from balmy Cornwall to cold, rugged Yorkshire, to help run her aunt and uncle's school. Her pluck was rewarded; she met Patrick Brontë, a young, ambitious, Cambridge-educated clergyman, tall and handsome, with a husky Irish accent. He wooed her strenuously. Who wouldn't be impressed by a man who walked ten miles to take you out for a walk, then walked ten miles back? Whether Maria liked Patrick's moral stamina, or his leg muscles, when he proposed, in the romantic ivy-covered ruins of medieval Kirkstall Abbey, she said yes. She was twenty-nine.

Gaskell compares Maria's love letters to Juliet's speeches to Romeo, but Maria wasn't an innocent, smitten teenager; she was an independent woman who knew her own mind and she warned her fiancé, 'For some years I have been perfectly my own mistress, subject to no *control* whatever.' She prepared for marriage by reading a book called *Advice to a Lady*, by making a wedding cake, by flirtatiously threatening 'My Dear Saucy Pat' with 'a real downright scolding' and by declaring her love as candidly as her daughters' heroines ever did:

> you possess all my heart. Two months ago I could not possibly have believed that you would ever engross so much of my thoughts and affections, and far less could I have thought that I should be so forward as to tell you so.

Maria knew love was a leap of faith and she was ready to jump:

> I am certain no one ever loved you with an affection more pure, constant, tender, and ardent than that which I feel. Surely this is not saying too much; it is the truth, and I trust you are worthy to know it.

He was. They married on 29 December 1812, and they were happy. When she turned thirty, Patrick wrote her a tender birthday poem, opening with the alluring invitation, 'Maria, let us walk, and breathe, the morning air', where birds sing and 'The primrose pale, / Perfumes the gale.' They had a girl, Maria, in 1813, and a year later, another girl, Elizabeth, named after Maria's older sister. That year, they moved to Thornton, a lively town in West Yorkshire.

Their little house is still there; it's now an Italian cafe called Emily's. I visit it one cold bright day. Sun streams through the windows, into the drawing room where, by the fireplace, Maria gave birth to four more children in four years – Charlotte in 1816, Branwell in 1817, Emily in 1818 and finally Anne on 17 January 1820. I check with the waiters.

Is this hearth The One? It is. I sink into a squishy sofa, exactly where Anne was born. Over the years, the house has been a butcher's shop and a restaurant. It was lovingly restored by the crime novelist Barbara Whitehead, then sold again, rented out, flooded, renovated again, and through all this, the fireplace survived. As I drink my cappuccino, and eat my tiny, perfect cannoli, sweet with ricotta and vanilla, it feels wonderful that the house is alive, a family home (the couple who own it live upstairs), full of books and chatter. I imagine Maria sitting where I am sitting, her baby in her arms, when Patrick told her he'd got a new job. It came with a bigger house, and Haworth was only six miles away, so they could still see their friends. In April 1820, they set off in a convoy of horse-drawn carts. Patrick walked, sometimes lifting one of the children out for fresh air, and Maria held three-month-old Anne in her lap.

But they'd barely got settled into the Parsonage at Haworth when Maria collapsed with a pain in her stomach. It was cancer of the uterus, probably made worse by all the pregnancies. She was ill for seven and a half horrific months during which, Patrick said, 'Death pursued her unrelentingly'. In her love letters, she'd worried that 'My heart is more ready to attach itself to earth than heaven'. Nine years of marriage and six children hadn't made her a more quiescent clergyman's wife, and she refused to slip serenely away. She questioned her fate and her faith, and it hurt Patrick to admit that 'the great enemy . . . often disturbed her mind in the last conflict', and when she died it was 'not triumphantly'. Of course it wasn't. She was only thirty-eight, and she was terrified of what would become of her family; her anguished last words were, 'Oh God, my poor children!'

I wonder if Anne heard her say it. She was at her mother's deathbed after months of being told to creep around the Parsonage and play quietly, starved of attention as her mother lay dying and Patrick nursed her, when he wasn't working at his demanding new job. Anne wrote about her early childhood when she was twenty-seven, in a long, intense autobiographical poem called 'Self-Communion', composed over five months of unflinching reflection. I go to the British Library to have a look at the manuscript. I have to request it in advance, I have to be vouched for, and once I have it in my hot little hands, I have to sit at a desk where I can be watched while I read it. None of this prevents me becoming enchanted. It wasn't published in Anne's lifetime; in fact it wasn't published at all until 1900, in a limited edition of just thirty copies. Which seems appropriate, as it is so raw and exposed, a distillation of Anne's life rather than a straightforward story. Anne remembers being 'a helpless child', 'feeble', frightened, gullible, timid and frantic for 'protecting love', which is her 'only refuge from despair'. Her earliest memories must have been of her father poleaxed by grief; of her oldest sister, seven-year-old Maria, bravely trying to stand in for their mother; of her aunt Elizabeth coming to help but hoping to get back to Penzance as soon as she could. In 'Self-Communion', Anne describes wanting to be loved and wanting *to* love, overwhelmed by a 'love so earnest, strong, and deep / It could not be expressed'. She pictures herself, as a toddler, as a 'Poor helpless thing!' whose loss has left her utterly disorientated: 'Where shall it centre so much trust . . .?' Like ivy that 'clasps the forest tree', she wonders, 'How can it stand alone?'

As Anne got older, she would drive herself to stop being the ivy and to become the tree. She would struggle for independence, creating an imaginary world with Emily. She would force herself to work hard at school. She would battle with asthma and with deep gloom. She would leave home at nineteen and get a job before any of her siblings, and when she lost it she would refuse to be daunted and get a better post, at double the salary, and stick at it and succeed. She would write and write and push herself to find out what kind of writer she was. She would get Branwell a job and he would mess things up so badly she would have to resign. Back in Haworth in her twenties, she would work at her poetry and get it published, along with her sisters. At twenty-six, she would write her first novel, *Agnes Grey*, an exposé of what it was like to be a governess, before Charlotte covered the same ground in *Jane Eyre*. Both novels would be published in 1847, along with Emily's *Wuthering Heights*. Then Anne would tackle Branwell's drinking and drug addiction in *The Tenant of Wildfell Hall*, published in 1848.

Anne did become the tree, not the ivy. But she also worked hard to understand her roots. Virginia Woolf said it best: 'We think back through our mothers, if we are women.' Woolf also lost her mother when she was young, and she also found it hard to understand who she came from. She brought her mother back to life in *To the Lighthouse* in the character of Mrs Ramsay, a matriarch who nurtures everyone, her husband, her children, her household and her guests, with food, with advice, with knitwear, with love. At first Mrs Ramsay seems to be the heroine.

But as Woolf wrote the novel, she was beguiled by another character, Lily Briscoe, who rebels against Mrs Ramsay because she wants to be an artist. The book changes, then, from an ode to Woolf's mother into an argument with her. Woolf's sister Vanessa said it was like meeting their mother again, but grown up and equal, so she could argue with her. Woolf said that after writing it she finally stopped seeing her mother's ghost. She found it incredibly liberating. She became more confident about pursuing a different path to her mother's, and she was able to write her vivid, searing polemic, *A Room of One's Own*, which could almost be Lily's manifesto.

Anne didn't know her own mother as well as Woolf did hers. She never got to read Maria's letters – only Charlotte did that, in 1850, when she was the only one of Maria's children left alive. The letters were 'yellow with time', and she read them 'in a frame of mind I cannot describe'. She found them 'sad and sweet' and her mother's mind 'fine, pure, and elevated' and most of all, she wrote, 'I wish she had lived, and that I had known her'. Anne pieced together a sense of her mother from scraps and stories – just like I'm doing now, except Anne *had* to do it because you have to know who you come from so you know who you want to be.

On the pages of her novels, Anne thought back through her mother. *Agnes Grey* follows Anne's life as a governess fairly closely. At Agnes's first job the children are violent and unmanageable. Her second set of pupils are a tomboy, Matilda, and a flirt, Rosalie, who tries to thwart Agnes's romance with the lovely, clever curate Edward Weston. Agnes's father dies, and Agnes sets up a school with her mother, Alice. Then Weston reappears, just in time for a happy ending.

Alice Grey is a lot like Maria. She has also married a man with very little money – declaring that 'she would rather live in a cottage with Richard Grey than in a palace with any other man in the world' – and she also has six children. She is sweet and practical and so affectionate that when Agnes is trying to keep her pupils in line, she thinks the worst she can do is to threaten not to kiss them goodnight. She's astonished that they don't care. This passage just aches with Anne's longing for a mother to kiss her goodnight.

But it isn't all sweetness and light. Agnes has to muster all her courage to fight her mother for independence. She wants to go away and earn her own living. Her parents think she's too young. She only gets her way because they need her earnings. Her father's made a dodgy investment and they've become very poor. Agnes feelingly describes how, 'Our clothes were mended, turned, and darned to the utmost verge of decency; our food, always plain, was now simplified to an unprecedented degree . . .; our coals and candles were painfully economised'.

Anne's family got suddenly poorer too, when Maria's annuity of £50 a year ended with her death. Anne was writing on paper scrounged from any which where, wearing clothes that were hand-me-downs from her sisters or gifts from her godmothers, and so cold that she always sat (as Agnes does) with her feet on the fender to keep warm.

All this would have upset Maria, had she lived. Maybe it would even have changed her mind, and made her rewrite the one thing she ever wrote for publication. I was excited when I found out Maria had written an essay. It was never published but it proved she had literary ambitions, and it set an example for her daughters, showing women *could* write. I hoped the essay would be brilliant. Then I read it.

'The Advantages of Poverty in Religious Concerns' isn't just bad prose; it's pious cant about how poverty is good because the poor don't have the same temptation to sin, and because, unable to afford a proper education, they're more open to the Bible's simple truths. Maria thinks 'poverty . . . will tend to increase and strengthen our efforts to gain that Land of pure delight, where neither our souls nor bodies can possibly know pain or want'. Ugh. What if you're stuck in a land of pure *un*delight where your body knows pain and want all too well, and your soul does too, because who can think of God and grace on an empty stomach? Maria admits it is 'an evil to hear the heartrending cries of your children craving for that which you have it not in your power to give them', but she thinks Christian charity will step in if things get really bad. It's true that Patrick's friends helped him with the debts he'd piled up paying for medicine and nursing for Maria, and with his children's education, so, yes, she was right; charity does step in. But for the Brontës it just wasn't true that 'poverty which is sanctified by true religion is perhaps the state most free from care and discontent'. Patrick was full of care and discontent as he made himself badger his friends for handouts and beg his employers for more money. Anne had enough religion for ten women, but she could have been a lot more carefree and contented (and useful to society, for that matter) if she hadn't had to worry about money every day of her life. I think she was disappointed by her mother's essay too, and when she wrote about what it was like to be poor, *actually* poor, she was arguing with Maria. She was telling her there was nothing good about poverty. And her book, which starts as a portrait of a perfect mother, becomes instead the story of a heroine who has to argue with her mother to become her own woman, to become the tree, not the ivy. It's hard not to see in this Anne robustly disagreeing with her mother, too.

Maybe we never stop arguing with our mothers. Maybe it's how we know who we are. It's easier to argue with your mother if she's around, and up for it. It's much harder if she is unloving and inadequate, or if, as with Anne and Woolf, she is gone. Woolf realised – and perhaps Anne did too – that if you lose your mother, you also lose the chance to argue with her. The danger is that instead you spend your life trying to live up to a mother who is both dead and perfect.

Charlotte's novels are haunted by perfect mothers. In her 1849 novel *Shirley*, she writes a heroine, Caroline Helstone, who is motherless and desperate for love. Caroline gets her heart broken, pines and declines. On the verge of death she is (spoiler alert) reunited with her long-lost mother. She swiftly recovers, as if her mother has literally kissed her better. Charlotte wrote this part of the novel after Anne died. Caroline is supposed to be Anne, virtuous and untainted, like the baby who was visited by angels. Charlotte even gives Caroline's mother the maiden name of Grey, as if setting a trail from Caroline to Agnes to Anne. Writing in the depths of her grief, Charlotte thought that bringing their mother back from the dead was the absolute best present she could give Anne. Unfortunately, the plot twist ruins Caroline. She's not the most vital character to start with, and after the reunion, she dies on the page. My heart goes out to Charlotte, but I wish she hadn't done it.

I also wish Charlotte hadn't summoned up her mother again in *Jane Eyre*. Jane is a *much* better character than Caroline, more conflicted and audacious, but even she loses vividness when she encounters her lost, seraphic mother. It happens when she is in crisis. She's found out – at the altar – that her fiancé, Rochester, is already married. He's dragged her home to meet the mad wife he's been hiding in the attic. And now he wants her to run away with him. And maybe she should. She loves him. She fancies him. She's got no family to be ashamed of her living in sin, she's already decided she doesn't want to be a martyr like her (dead and perfect) friend Helen Burns, and she hates the hypocritical faith she was taught at school. Maybe it's time to throw off the shackles of religion and move into Rochester's love nest on the shores of the Mediterranean. But then she sees her mother.

It's not actually her mother. It's the moon.

I watched her come . . . She broke forth as never moon yet burst from cloud; a hand first penetrated the sable folds and waved them away; then, not a moon, but a white human form shone in the azure, inclining a glorious brow earthward. It gazed and gazed on me. It spoke to my spirit: immeasurably distant was the tone, yet so near, it whispered in my heart –

'My daughter, flee temptation.'

'Mother, I will.'

And off Jane goes. She doesn't leave because she's solved her moral dilemma herself, but because her mother's sprung out of the moon to tell her what to do. It's very weird, and maybe Charlotte knew that, because a few pages later she fudges it by saying Jane's real mother is Nature. But Jane's not interested in nature worship. She's stumbling about the dark, cold moor, homeless and desperate, and she's going to take any steer she can get. If Charlotte had written this scene so that Jane *wished* so hard for her mother that she saw her in the moon, it would be moving and Jane would still have some agency. But Charlotte couldn't resist a supernatural voice. For me, this takes away some of Jane's power.

I don't think Anne liked it either. When she and her sisters wrote their novels, they competed as much as they collaborated. They talked to each other on the pages of their books, reworking each other's stories, shaping the same raw material into different forms, working at the same problems and trying out different solutions. Anne's take on Charlotte's mother-in-the-moon episode is in *The Tenant of Wildfell Hall*. Anne's heroine, Helen, is motherless too, and when she leaves her husband, she also wants her mother. But unlike Charlotte, Anne doesn't give her heroine any visions or voices. Helen reaches for her mother in a very practical way; she takes her mother's maiden name. It's a good idea, because she's a fugitive now, from her husband and from the law. But it's also risky because it's a name her husband surely knows, and might make her easier to find. She takes the risk because she wants something of her mother's with her as a talisman, to keep her safe. I find this tiny moment of Helen aching for her mother, like a child reaching up to grab her mother's hand as she crosses a road, incredibly poignant.

It's only one of the ways Anne thinks back through her mother in the novel. Her most innovative decision is to make the heroine a mother. The popular novels of Anne's day most often ended at the altar. They didn't follow their heroines into marriage or motherhood. And mothers were often absent or dead. But the swooning, virginal, helpless heroines of Gothic novels like *The Castle of Otranto* and *The Mysteries of Udolpho* were giving way to characters like Becky Sharp and Oliver Twist who managed to make themselves up from scratch, make their own homes, find their own place in the world. Novelists wrote motherless protagonists because so many women died young (in 1850, the average life expectancy in Haworth was twenty-six), but also because killing off a character's mother was a shortcut to throwing them into terrifying dangers and exhilarating freedoms. All Charlotte's heroines are orphans. Almost every child in *Wuthering Heights* loses at least one parent. Anne was the only Brontë who wrote protagonists with families. Helen has lost her mother but is close to her aunt and uncle, and forges a relationship with her brother, and marries a man with a comfortable, bustling home life. Agnes grows up with both her parents, and her mother – a rare survivor! – is still alive at the end of the book. Most of all, Anne dared to put a mother centre stage and, even better, she didn't make her perfect. 'I am no angel,' says Helen. She has faults, she has desires, and it takes her a while to grow into becoming a mother. But when she does, it emboldens and empowers her. Motherhood *makes* her a heroine.

When I get out my battered hardback of the novel, I'm struck by the way Helen's motherhood is the first thing you notice. She's on the cover, a pen-and-ink wash in muted reds and greens. Helen ignores dashing Gilbert and gazes at her son. Her eyes are chips of coal, her dress is black and black hair flies out of a black veil. She is mesmerising. I was given the book by my aunt, who was a gifted painter, which might have been one reason she wanted me to read the book. But I like to think it was because she was rigorously honest, and *The Tenant of Wildfell Hall* is, as much as anything, a novel about telling the truth. I got the book at twelve, too young to appreciate it, but I remember the heroine on that cover, and the way she stared at her son as if he was literally pulling a string that tied him to her heart.

Helen's adventures in motherhood are all the more intrepid because she doesn't have a mother of her own. Like Anne, she lost her mother when she was very young, and she doesn't remember her. She invokes her when she's trying to persuade her aunt to let her flirt with debonair Mr Huntingdon. 'All the mammas smile upon him,' she wheedles. Her aunt isn't moved. 'Unprincipled mothers *may* be anxious to catch a young man of fortune without reference to his character' but she won't let Helen fall into that trap. Helen seizes on the mention of unprincipled mothers, because she believes Huntingdon had a *terrible* mother. If he's bad, it's because she spoiled him, so it's not his fault. When she marries him, 'his wife shall undo what his mother did!' Helen has a lot to learn. Huntingdon doesn't want to be mothered by his wife. When Helen tries it, he rebels and gets more dissolute than ever, and she finds she's backed herself into a corner and can only get more prim and joyless. When their son is born she tries so hard to stop Arthur turning into his father that she becomes a 'cross mamma', who is 'too grave to minister to his amusements and enter into his infantile sports'. His 'bursts of gleeful merriment' alarm her. 'I see in them his father's spirit and temperament,' she writes, 'and . . . too often damp the innocent mirth I ought to share.' Unable even to enjoy playing with her son, on her fourth wedding anniversary, she feels 'weary of this life' and wishes she could die but knows that 'I cannot wish to go and leave my darling in this dark and wicked world alone'.

But then something shifts. Huntingdon starts trying to wreck little Arthur, amusing himself by encouraging him 'in all the embryo vices . . . and . . . all the evil habits'. He tries to spin this as a criticism of Helen's parenting, saying 'he was not going to have the little fellow moped to death between an old nurse and a cursed fool of a mother', so Helen is forced to watch her son learn 'to tipple wine . . . to swear . . . and to have his own way like a man, and [send] mamma to the devil'. Huntingdon cruelly tells her she is 'not fit to teach children, or to be with them', that she has 'reduced the boy to little better than an automaton . . . broken his fine spirit with [her] rigid severity; and [will] freeze all the sunshine out of his heart'. It's the darkest moment of the book because she knows he is not entirely wrong. But she resolves that 'this should not continue; my child must not be abandoned to this corruption'. She can suffer, but she doesn't want her son to. Because she's a mother, she makes the heroic decision to leave.

That's when Helen starts to become a good mother – and that's what makes Gilbert Markham fall for her. He watches her argue with his mother over how to bring up boys (Mrs Markham is yet another character who claims a stiff drink will put hairs on little Arthur's chest), and he wonders if maybe he was 'a little bit spoiled'; he starts to question himself, and soon he's head over heels in love.

In writing about motherhood (and especially about single motherhood), Anne was plunging into one of the biggest controversies of the 1840s, and setting out her stall as a feminist. For early-Victorian women activists, motherhood was the front line. Their reluctant poster girl was Caroline Norton, a society beauty who got married at nineteen to George Chapple Norton, who hoped she'd be a docile and decorative wife. But she was tempestuous and clever, and an ambitious writer. Maybe the eleven-year-old Anne saw the portrait of 'Fair Mrs Norton!' printed in *Fraser's* magazine in 1831. 'We display her,' said *Fraser's* proprietorially, 'as the modest matron making tea in the morning for the comfort and convenience of her husband'. I'm not sure about *modest*; Caroline looks languid and stunning, her hair coaxed up elaborately, her dress just slipping off her shoulders. *Fraser's* fawned over her sparkling prose and glittering salons but they also warned that 'a lady ought to be treated, even by Reviewers, with the utmost deference – except she writes politics, which is an enormity equal to wearing breeches'.

Caroline would end up writing a *lot* of politics. Her husband was jealous of her fame, and he was violent. Caroline stuck it out for eight years, until in 1835, when she was pregnant with her fourth child, Norton beat her so brutally that she had a miscarriage, and she left. In the years when Anne was incubating *The Tenant of Wildfell Hall*, the collapse of the Nortons' marriage was reported, pruriently, in all the papers. Caroline found herself in a hellish fix. She wanted a separation and custody of her children. But in English law, married women didn't exist. They were *femmes couvertes*, women 'covered' by their husband's protection. This only worked if their husbands actually did protect them. Norton was doing the opposite. He accused her of having an affair. With the prime minister. Then he sued the prime minister. Because Caroline didn't legally exist, she couldn't defend her name in court or get anyone to do it for her. If someone *else* had slandered her, she could have got her husband to defend her. But he was on the attack.

Norton was laughed out of court. But he still had the children. Like Helen in *The Tenant of Wildfell Hall*, Caroline might have suffered silently if it was only her happiness at stake. But she couldn't abandon her sons. It was motherhood that emboldened her to take on the whole vast monolith of English law. She campaigned for a bill that would give mothers the right to appeal for custody. Long before anyone said the personal was political, she told people her story, over and over, until they started to listen. The Infant Custody Act was passed in 1839. But cruel, wily Norton took their children to Scotland, out of reach of English law, where one child died. In a fiery campaign letter Caroline appealed to Queen Victoria as a fellow mother, to try to understand how it hurt to see her son in his coffin: 'I believe *men* have no more notion of what that anguish is, than the blind have of colours.'

Caroline carried on campaigning. She had to, when women like her were being told that if they left their husbands they would be 'plunged into a yawning abyss of horror, from which there was never more any escape – never more, never more', as Ellen Wood put it in her 1861 potboiler *East Lynne*. 'Oh, reader, believe me!' she implored. 'Lady – wife – mother! Should you ever be tempted to abandon your home, so will you awake.'

In 1863, Caroline wrote a novel she hoped would support her campaign. In *Lost and Saved*, Beatrice Brooke elopes with dastardly, moustache-twirling Montagu Treherne. When she falls ill, she begs, 'let me die married . . .!' so he marries her and she rallies. But when it turns out that she's pregnant, Treherne admits their marriage was a sham – conducted by a fake priest – and scarpers. Beatrice's father disowns her, so she has to fend for herself and her son but she can't get a job because she has no 'character'. Up to this point, Beatrice is so gullible and clueless that she lacks character in other senses too. But motherhood gives her the courage to get work, support her son, make up with her father and even find new love.

Yet *Lost and Saved* is not half as bold as *The Tenant of Wildfell Hall*. While Caroline's experience showed that an innocent woman could marry in good faith, suffer abuse, lose her children and find no help from the law, she didn't tell that story in her novel. Beatrice is not innocent (she elopes), Treherne doesn't try to take her child, and if he did, she could fight him in court because their marriage isn't real, so she still exists in English law. It was Anne who had the nerve to write about the very real predicament of women like Caroline.

As Anne tried to feel her way into writing Helen, to understand why she fought so hard to save her child, she must have remembered a story closer to home. Her mother's eldest sister, Jane, had emigrated to America with her husband but found their marriage unbearable. After nine years, she returned to Penzance with her baby, but had to leave behind her four older children. As Maria lay dying, worrying about what would happen to her children, maybe she wondered how her sister could have done it, crossed the Atlantic and left her children to the mercies of a man she couldn't go on living with herself. No one knows why the marriage broke down, but Jane must have felt pretty desperate to make that painful choice. Maria couldn't choose. She had to leave her children to the perils of life without her. And her last words, 'Oh God, my poor children!', cast a shadow over every page of *The Tenant of Wildfell Hall* and its story of a woman who is terrified for her son in a dangerous world, and who risks everything to take him to a place where she can mother him better.

2

ELIZABETH
or how to do the right thing (and how to
know what that is)

I'm going to call Anne's aunt by her name: Elizabeth. Everyone –
even biographers and literary critics – calls her 'Aunt Branwell',
but she was more than just an aunt. And before she dropped
everything to come to Haworth, she had a life. I feel strongly
about her because history is not always kind to spinsters and
it has not been kind to Elizabeth. For much of my twenties
and thirties I've been single myself, so I am sensitive to the
ways she has been misunderstood, and to what they reveal about
how single women are slighted, even now.

In the biographies Elizabeth comes over as spiky, sharp, unloving
and unloved. May Sinclair called her a 'small, middle-aged,
early Victorian spinster . . . dragging out her sad, fastidious
life'. Gaskell said she was respected but not loved by her nephew
and nieces. When Charlotte imagined a heroine being brought
up by her aunt it wasn't a loving portrait. Jane Eyre's Aunt Reed
sees her niece as an irksome responsibility, sends her to a terrible
school and leaves her there. But if *The Tenant of Wildfell Hall*
is anything to go by, Anne did love Elizabeth. Helen is brought
up by an aunt too, but she loves Peggy Maxwell, and when she

and Gilbert get engaged, she immediately says she wants her aunt to live with them.

Peggy tells Gilbert bluntly, 'Could she have been contented to remain single, I own I should have been better satisfied.' It's quite a thing to say to your niece's fiancé. It is not welcoming. But it is wonderfully honest. Peggy knows it would be safer for Helen to stay single. She is refusing to pretend that the engagement is anything other than a risk. She's giving Gilbert a warning. And she's saying there is more than one way for a woman to live her life. Helen doesn't have to marry. She *could* stay single. After all, Elizabeth did. And after seeing her sister Jane get stuck across the Atlantic with the wrong man, and her sister Maria die of a disease exacerbated by so many pregnancies so close together, maybe she was glad to be single.

I hope Elizabeth knew Anne loved her. I hope when she was on her deathbed in October 1842, when she was sixty-six, Branwell said aloud some of the things he wrote in a letter to his friend, about how Elizabeth had 'been for twenty years as my mother' and 'the guide and director of all the happy days connected with my childhood'. I hope Elizabeth knew that Patrick thought she 'afforded great comfort to my mind . . . by sharing my labours and sorrows'. He makes it sound as though she committed to the Brontës with her whole heart.

When Elizabeth swept into the Parsonage from Penzance in May 1821, her sister was dying, and all six children had scarlet fever, and Patrick couldn't cope. Elizabeth was forty-five then, skinny, austere, beautifully dressed, with a string of admirers back home. She wasn't planning to stay, but she kept finding she couldn't leave. First she nursed the children, then she nursed Maria, then she held the fort as she waited for Patrick to find a way of looking after his family. He tried to find the children a stepmother. When that didn't work he decided to send the girls away to school. He would educate Branwell, while the servants, Nancy and Sarah Garrs, would run the house, and Elizabeth could go back to Penzance. So in 1824, the two oldest girls, ten-year-old Maria and nine-year-old Elizabeth, went off to the Clergy Daughters' School at Cowan Bridge. Eight-year-old Charlotte followed and then Emily, who was six. Anne would be next.

But Anne never made it to Cowan Bridge. It was a lucky escape. The school was shameful. Charlotte said that when she wrote about it in *Jane Eyre* she toned it down, because no one would believe the truth. The girls were often hungry (and the food was cooked by a 'whalebone and iron' woman who burned porridge and kept a filthy kitchen). They were cold. They were forced to walk miles to church in wet shoes. One teacher picked on clever, kind, untidy eleven-year-old Maria. She bullied her, and beat her, even after Maria became ill, but Maria didn't complain. In February 1825, the school sent for Patrick because she was dying. Even then, she didn't tell him how grim it was, and he didn't notice anything wrong himself, so he left his other daughters there. After three agonising months, Maria died in May. While his wife had died full of anger and doubts, this time Patrick could say proudly that little Maria 'exhibited during her illness many symptoms of a heart under Divine influence'.

Years later Charlotte echoed this when she talked about Maria to Ellen Nussey, whom she met at the second, better, school she went to, and who became her steadfast friend. Much of what we know about the Brontës comes from Nussey – and is filtered through her holier-than-thou perspective. Nussey was, it seems, a bit of a prig. Her thoughts on little Maria make for particularly queasy reading; 'most touching of all, were the revelations of her sufferings – how she suffered with the sensibility of a grown-up person, and endured with a patience and fortitude that were Christ-like'. Nussey was speaking as an adult, about a child she never met, a child who might not have suffered so much if she'd only spoken out about what was happening at school. But Maria forced herself to silently endure and now there's nothing left of her but her amazing suffering, and her tattered, faded sampler. I wish she'd told Patrick about the neglect and cruelties of Cowan Bridge, I wish she'd made him bring her sisters home. I wish she'd made him expose the school in the press. If Patrick thought something was wrong, he felt it his duty to shout about it. He wrote vitriolic letters to the papers opposing everything from capital punishment to the Poor Laws. With testimony from his daughter, Patrick could have dragged the school through the mud. But Maria never said anything because she believed she should be a martyr.

Maria felt this way because of the unforgiving religion she was force-fed at school. It's all there in a magazine written by the school's founder, William Carus Wilson, who inspired *Jane Eyre*'s Brocklehurst. *The Children's Friend* is entirely unfriendly, full of ghoulish stories of naughty children dying. Some sickeningly pious ones die too – luckily they 'die happy in the Lord Jesus!' The magazine is rammed with inappropriate exclamation marks, as if Wilson was positively thrilled by the deaths of children. He lovingly details the dangers that face them – fires, floods, freak waves, diseases and even shark attacks. He likes nothing more than a child in great peril. He warns children who dare to laugh, 'All your happiness is only like the crackling of thorns under a pot. You make a noise, and seem very merry, and all the time your souls are in danger of burning for ever in hell.' In case they don't get it, he adds, 'You dance and play, and all the time you are in danger of dropping into a place of torment so deep, that nobody will ever be able to pull you out again, except God, and he will not do it.' No wonder Maria didn't complain. No wonder Charlotte battled guilt her whole life. Emily didn't, but then Emily was very good at ignoring things.

Branwell poured his grief about Maria into a poem he wrote when he was twenty-eight. In 'Caroline' he remembers being taken to see Maria in her coffin where

> She lay with flowers about her head –
> Though formal grave-clothes hid her hair!
> Still did her lips the smile retain
> Which parted them when hope was high.

He describes touching her 'marble cheek', being lifted up (that's how small he is) to see her, feeling a 'voiceless gasp', a 'sickening chill', and hiding his white face. He was seven when he lost his sister, but twenty-one years later, the wound is still fresh.

A few weeks after the funeral, a stranger knocked at the Parsonage front door. It was a servant from Cowan Bridge, bringing ten-year-old Elizabeth home. She was so ill that the school hadn't written to Patrick to collect her, just packed her off in a rush. In a panic, Patrick brought back Charlotte and

Emily. Anne, only five, had to watch her second sister die. Elizabeth only lasted two weeks. There are no stories about her faith or her death. Which is a relief because as I try to understand what Anne went through, I can't face reading any more about the angelic deaths of neglected children.

Many years later, Anne wrote about this painful time, remembering, in 'Self-Communion',

> kneeling on the sod,
> With infant hands upraised to Heaven,
> A young heart feeling after God,
> Oft baffled, never backward driven.
> Mistaken oft, and oft astray,
> It strives to find the narrow way.

Her poem is very different from her brother's; as Branwell writes, every feeling, every sensation, comes rushing back, and almost overwhelms him. There's no relief, no release, no room to think. In Anne's poem she is thinking as much as feeling. She's trying to understand what has happened, what it means. There is a sturdy confidence to her striving. She might get baffled, but she's never driven back. She keeps advancing, however uncertainly, walking into the unknown, 'feeling after God' because only God knows about her 'inner life of strife and tears, / Of kindling hopes and lowering fears'. She wants comfort, she wants someone to listen, and (these stanzas glimmer with optimism) she gets both.

But I struggle with the idea of 'the narrow way', which comes from Matthew 7:14. 'Because strait is the gate, and narrow is the way, which leadeth unto life, and few there be that find it.'

Anne must have liked the verse a lot because in April 1848 she also wrote a poem called 'The Narrow Way'. It has been set to music many times, and it contains Anne's most quoted lines:

> But hc, that dares not grasp the thorn
> Should never crave the rose.

When I type the couplet into Google, I find it engraved on jewellery, tattooed in prickly thorn-like lettering, tweeted over images of falling petals, chalked on blackboards on Pinterest, used to illustrate a lookbook for an Islamic fashion studio, advertising a florist, captioning a recipe for rosewater tarts, and printed on inspirational cards, in swirly letters over swirly roses. Out of context, the lines form the perfect sweet yet spiky mantra. In context they have more weight; they are about Anne's fight to keep to the narrow way.

I'm in Cardiff, producing a feminist theatre festival, which somehow involves putting up a tent (our temporary stage) and taking it down, three times, on concrete, in the freezing rain. I feel like I'm grasping the thorn, but the bag of Brontë books I have hoicked to Wales doesn't even get opened and Anne seems more distant than ever. I feel disgruntled about 'The Narrow Way'. Why do I have to be limited to a narrow way? Why can't I be free to roam? And surely I have to find my own path? I grew up with Judaism, and have felt the push-and-pull of faith all my life, but the idea of having to follow anyone else's route (let alone a narrow one) makes me rebellious. I wonder what I'm doing investigating this woman who was so secretive (I spill my heart out), so neat (I'm a slattern), so meticulous (so not), so dejected (well, sometimes). I can't make her out.

And then I start seeing her. Or, all right, dreaming her, but they don't feel like dreams. She is sitting on my bed in a blue dress, like in every portrait ever made of her. (The Brontës drew and painted each other often, so there are a surprising number of images of Anne.) She leans against the iron frame, a piercing look in her eyes which are violet blue, and have something else in them, something of a grey dawn. Astonishingly, she deadpans, 'Why aren't you writing my book?' And before I can reply, still less defend myself, she says, 'I've been neglected for a hundred and fifty years.' This Anne isn't nice. She is difficult. She is prickly. She is a thorn. A thorn I really want to, need to, grasp.

I have bought myself some earrings cast from thorns from Scottish rose bushes. When I put them on, I feel harder, edgier. I read 'The Narrow Way' again and again, and I realise it's not about following a route mapped out by God. Anne wrote the poem when she was trying not to let the depressing response to her first book stop her writing her second. She tells herself not to be cowed by 'The World's dread scoff' because

> What matters who should whisper blame,
> Or who should scorn or slight?
>
> What matters – if thy God approve,
> And if within thy breast,
> Thou feel the comfort of His love
> The earnest of his rest?

Writing 'thy God', not just 'God' or 'my God', Anne opens the poem up to anyone, not just people of her faith, or any faith. God isn't telling her where to go, but cheering her on as she finds her own way. This poem is really about Anne sticking to her guns, pushing herself to 'Arm – arm thee for the fight!'

As for the much-quoted couplet, I notice something odd. Anne has reversed the usual phrase, 'Every rose has its thorn'. I haven't (willingly) listened to Poison's power ballad since the eighties but now I put it on. As Bret Michaels belts out the chorus in his heartbreak-ravaged voice, the difference is clear. For Michaels, the rose comes first. It is the rose he wants, and he wants it to be perfect. He is dismayed to discover it has a thorn. So dismayed that he dumps her. His girlfriend, that is. The story goes that one day on tour, at a launderette, watching his washing go round, he called her, and heard a male voice in the background.

But Anne is not saying that every exotic-dancer girlfriend is unfaithful. Nor is she saying that if you want roses you might have to put up with the odd thorn. For Anne, the thorn comes first. Anne is positively encouraging herself (and us) to grasp the thorn. She's saying we shouldn't expect a rose. We shouldn't even hope for a rose. And if we aren't daring enough to grasp thorns then we have no business craving roses in the first place. She's saying we have to dare to do the right, hard thing, and not expect any reward. I can't see this becoming a glam-metal hit any day soon. Anne's couplet makes me grumpy. I would like to say I put up a tent in Cardiff and took it down, three times, on concrete, in the rain, purely because I believe in feminist theatre. I do. But afterwards, I wanted wine, applause, and ideally a roaring fire. The satisfaction of doing the right thing wasn't enough. I am not as good a person as Anne.

I am certainly not as good a person as Elizabeth. She really grasped the thorn when, after her namesake, little Elizabeth, died, she decided to stay in Haworth. It meant giving up her independence, and her life in Penzance, and she never saw Cornwall again. She didn't do it because she wanted to; she did it because it was right. Maybe that's why she has been seen as the epitome of grim, joyless duty. But what if we didn't call what she did dutiful; what if we called it altruistic? And what if her altruism laid the groundwork for all Anne's writing and for her radical agenda too?

The biggest criticism flung at Elizabeth was that she filled the children with religious gloom, scared them with talk of hellfire, especially Anne, because she was the youngest and most sensitive, and because she and Elizabeth almost certainly shared a bed. It's true that Elizabeth had a teapot inscribed 'To me to live is Christ, to die is gain'. But can you really judge a person by their teapot? How about their shoes? Elizabeth wore wooden pattens (strap-on overshoes) indoors and, according to Gaskell, she 'went about the house . . . clicking up and down the stairs'. This has been taken up in book after book about the Brontës. And I'm sure it was annoying, but my goodness, if I thought that nearly two centuries after my death I'd be criticised for the noisiness of my shoes, I'd never wear anything, or do anything, or even get out of bed, let alone leave my home and friends and everything I knew to live hundreds of miles away in a place I didn't like and bring up my sister's six grief-stricken children.

Also, Elizabeth wore pattens because she was cold. The Parsonage was freezing, what with being on top of a hill, edging the moors, with the winds raging, and no carpets or curtains because Patrick was scared of fire.

It's still not warm. Researching in the Parsonage archive, I wrap a shawl over my jumper and wear an extra pair of socks. If I get there before they open up, I have to pace the lane outside, stamping my feet to keep warm. If I thought pattens would make a difference, I would gladly get some. On the one sunny day when I don't feel like the wind is tearing through me, the woman at the admissions desk sighs. 'The visitors won't like it,' she says. 'They don't like it to be sunny; they like it to be wind and rain and gloom.' I remember this when, rootling through the library, I find the Irish novelist Rosamond Langbridge gleefully exclaiming in a 1929 study of Charlotte, 'What a feast of exploration for the modern psycho-analyst is here in these harrowing records of suppressed and crippled childhood!' Stormy weather is what we want from the Brontës.

Elizabeth doesn't sound gloomy to me. Nussey sourly said that when Elizabeth talked a lot about Penzance, 'she gave one the idea that she had been a belle'. But maybe Elizabeth was a belle. She always wore silk and 'caps large enough for a half a dozen of the present fashion'. This is Nussey again, sounding personally offended by Elizabeth's dated, extravagant clothes. I quite warm to a woman who insisted on silk (and after all, she was paying for it herself; she never took a penny from Patrick). And maybe she clung to the fashions of her young and carefree days to remind herself that she *had* been young, that she hadn't always been responsible for six children.

I have a picture pinned up above my desk of myself, age four, with my mother and brother, riding a Ferris wheel. Next to it is my driving licence. When I was eighteen I started having seizures, and I haven't been on a Ferris wheel or behind the wheel of a car since. But I like remembering that I once did both. Elizabeth shocked Nussey by offering her snuff out of a gold box, and maybe that's why Nussey was so prissy about her later. She sounds like a girl who was teased and still feels stung.

As for Elizabeth's religion, she was a Methodist. In *Shirley*, Caroline reads her aunt's 'mad Methodist magazines', 'full of miracles and apparitions, of preternatural warnings, ominous dreams, and frenzied fanaticism'. The Brontës did have a stash of Methodist magazines, but they probably belonged to their mother, not their aunt. Their mother had also had several copies of the *Lady's Magazine* sent over from Penzance. Caught in a shipwreck en route, they were stained by salt water. Charlotte read them 'as a treat . . . by stealth' until 'One black day my father burnt them because they contained foolish love stories'. If Elizabeth was a fanatic, she would have approved, but instead she insisted the *Lady's Magazine* love stories were 'infinitely superior to any trash of Modern literature'. She thought for herself. Even Nussey had to admit that Elizabeth was 'very lively and intelligent, and tilt[ed] arguments against Mr Brontë without fear'. Living with the Brontës did give Elizabeth some rewards. She could enjoy family life, and the company of a clever, interesting man. Their good-natured arguments set the tone for a household that was surprisingly open to different kinds of beliefs. As soon as she was grown up, Emily refused to teach Sunday school, rarely went to church, and rejected conventional Christianity in favour of the 'God within my breast'. Branwell wrote several startlingly atheist poems. Charlotte could be savagely satirical about curates. And I find Anne's religious writing bracingly critical, angry about hypocrisy and never static: a record of struggle, of a brilliant mind wrestling with complex ideas.

Not everyone agrees. A fellow Anne fan (I keep finding them, like members of a secret society) tells me she skips the religious bits of Anne's novels because, as an atheist, she finds them irrelevant. I read an influential essay the novelist Ernest Raymond wrote in 1949, arguing that religion cramped Anne's writing, drained the blood from *Agnes Grey* and turned *The Tenant of Wildfell Hall* into a glorified temperance tract. He concludes with a backhanded compliment; piety ruined Anne's art but it made her a beautiful person.

Raymond was ordained, served on six fronts in the First World War, and then resigned holy orders, which maybe influenced his thoughts on religion, and on Anne. But was he right? Did piety ruin her art? Did it make her writing boring? Did she fill her pages with records of arid wrangling about burning issues for Victorian clerics which no one cares about now? I don't think so. In *Agnes Grey*, Anne writes, 'The end of Religion is . . . to teach us . . . how to live.' It seems to me that Anne tried so hard to work out what she believed because she wanted to *act* on those beliefs. None of it was hypothetical for her, none of it was airless. It wasn't even only about religion. Anne was trying to work out how to do the right thing. And how can you do the right thing until you know what the right thing is?

Anne's faith was not blind. It was not her opium, as the critic Margaret Lane argued in her powerful essay 'The Drug-Like Brontë Dream', equating it with Branwell's laudanum (and with the drug of fantasy she thought Charlotte and Emily overdosed on). For Lane, Anne's tragedy was that she was addicted to an 'uncomforting' faith. But Anne didn't want to be lulled into easy comfort. She wanted to keep her eyes open, to keep asking questions. In 1843, when she was twenty-three, she wrote a hymn which asks,

> What shall I do if all my love,
> My hopes, my toil, are cast away,
> And if there be no God above
> To hear and bless me when I pray?

These are valiant questions to ask in a hymn. Anne prays, in wrenching italics, for God to '*give me – give me Faith*', but the verse is full of *if* as she says she doesn't know if she's praying to anyone, if anyone can hear. Her belief is slippery – 'I often feel it slide away' – and then she feels cold and dark, sinking and anguished, and tormented by 'cruel doubts'. The hymn is called 'The Doubter's Prayer', and maybe faith has no value unless it is tested, and maybe the only proper prayers are doubter's prayers.

Anne knew this was not the conventional view. In *Agnes Grey*, the poor widow Nancy Brown tries to ask serious, thoughtful questions about the Bible and the rector, Mr Hatfield, threatens her with hell. He blasts 'the reprehensible presumption of individuals who attempted to think for themselves in matters connected with religion'. Instead of finding her own path, he thinks Nancy should come to church where he can tell her what to do. It's a reminder that it took courage for Anne to write about faith at all, in an era when women weren't allowed to preach, when John Ruskin derided women who 'dare to turn the Household Gods of Christianity into ugly idols of their own; – spiritual dolls'.

But Anne clearly felt she couldn't leave faith to men, especially men like Hatfield who she describes 'sailing up the aisle . . . with his rich silk gown flying behind him' to 'mount the pulpit like a conqueror ascending his triumphal car', who gabbles the prayers, but lingers over the theatrics, like drawing off his bright lavender gloves to show off his sparkling rings. Hatfield deprives his parishioners of harmless pleasures and gives 'sunless and severe' sermons but Agnes caustically notes that minutes later, he is 'laughing at his own sermon, and hoping that he [has] given the rascally people something to think about'. A hypocrite, then, and Anne hated hypocrites. Agnes sums him up as a man who loads up other people with heavy burdens, while not lifting a finger himself.

In contrast, the gentle curate Weston explains tricky Bible passages to Nancy 'clear as the day' so that 'it seemed like as a new light broke in on my soul'. While Hatfield butters up his rich parishioners, Weston preaches from the heart, on the text, 'Come unto me all ye that labour and are heavy laden, and I will give you rest', which makes sense to working women like Nancy and Agnes. The sermon makes Nancy '*so* happy!' that it inspires her to start knitting for her neighbours. There's something so warm about this, so kind, so *cosy*. In Anne's world, there is no point in going to church unless it prompts you to try to make your world a better place.

So Anne may well have taken exception to the way Charlotte wrote about religion. When they wrote their novels, the sisters read their work aloud to each other, night after night, after Patrick had gone to bed and Branwell had gone out, pacing round and round the dining table, sharing pages.

This table has just returned to the Parsonage, years after it was sold in 1861 at an auction held after Patrick's death. It was brought back to Haworth on a snowy day in 2015, swathed in blankets to protect it as it was carried out of a van, up the steps and put back where it belongs. (Afterwards, Ann Dinsdale was deluged by calls from people hoping their old furniture needs saving for the nation.) The mahogany drop-leaf table is dark and heavy – and big. Once it is opened out, there's not much room for pacing, even in skinny jeans, let alone in a Victorian dress and all the layers underneath. It's a real writers' table, marked with Anne and her sisters' ink blots, a candle burn and even a small, carved 'E'.

As they were pacing and reading, reading and pacing, and Charlotte read from *Jane Eyre*, Anne must have found the story of Helen Burns very troubling. Helen was based on little Maria, who Charlotte kept trying and failing to live up to, and Charlotte's sadness and guilt cling to her. Helen Burns doesn't fight injustice but looks forward to 'putting off our corruptible bodies', losing her 'cumbrous frame of flesh' and becoming 'only the spark of the spirit'. She tells Jane, 'I live in calm, looking to the end' – terrifying words to come out of the mouth of a small girl. Jane ultimately rejects this hardline faith. By the time

Rochester asks her to be his mistress, Jane has found her own principles to live by. She doesn't refuse because of religious zeal, or because of what people will say, but because her heart sings out, '*I* care for myself. The more solitary, the more friendless, the more unsustained I am, the more I will respect myself.'

Jane does the right thing. But then she meets St John Rivers who makes her feel she doesn't know what the right thing is. Rivers is 'a cold, hard man', 'icy', a 'glacier'. Even his sister, who adores him, calls him 'inexorable as death'. After his bile-filled, doomy sermons Jane finds that 'instead of feeling better, calmer, more enlightened by his discourse, I experienced an inexpressible sadness'. Anne must have bristled at Rivers telling Jane 'the fearful, the unbelieving . . . shall have their part in the lake which burneth with fire and brimstone'; Anne thought fear and doubt were vital elements of a robust faith.

Rivers's 'narrow path' is *too* narrow. He is rejecting 'the world and the flesh', leaving behind his sisters, his home, and the woman he loves, to become a missionary. His sister calls this 'right, noble, Christian; yet it breaks my heart', as if doing the right thing always involves sacrifice. When Rivers asks Jane to join him, she is sure that 'God did not give me my life to throw away', but she finds it hard to resist. When Rivers talks, she feels as if 'Religion called – Angels beckoned – God commanded' and she is about to 'rush down the torrent of his will into the gulf of his existence, and there lose my own' when she is saved by a device straight out of a sensation novel. Rochester cries out for Jane, miles away, and, somehow, she hears him and leaves. But maybe Charlotte wasn't sure Jane was doing the right thing, because she made the odd decision to end the novel with an update on this minor character. In the closing paragraphs, Jane piles on the praise for Rivers, calls him 'a giant', compares him to Christ and feels 'divine joy' at the thought that when he dies (soon, because being a missionary has made him ill) he'll get 'his sure reward, his incorruptible crown'.

When Jeanette Winterson's evangelical mother read *Jane Eyre* to her as a child, she changed the ending so Jane married Rivers and became a missionary. It seems a travesty, but reading the novel again, I can see that it is not that far from what Charlotte wrote herself. The image of Rivers eagerly preparing to meet Jesus reminds me of all the pious children going happily to death in *The Children's Friend*, and how that book is creepily obsessed with missionaries, and especially with converts in India. Maybe Charlotte never escaped the warped ideas she learned at school. Maybe *she* was the morbid, gloomy one.

Both Brocklehurst and Rivers call Jane 'a castaway'. Charlotte derived the horribly powerful idea of being cast away by God from the poet William Cowper. He is mostly now known for writing 'Amazing Grace', and the line, 'God moves in mysterious ways', but when the Brontës were growing up, he was wildly popular and younger poets were inspired by the way he investigated his heart on the page. He was also famously miserable.

Cowper found God in a lunatic asylum. It should have helped him regain his equilibrium but Cowper's faith was as cold and hard as Rivers's. He thought God couldn't wait to send him to hell. Convinced he should speed things up, he attempted suicide more than once. Writing mostly kept the demons away, but sometimes they burst into his poems and danced. In 1798, when he was sixty-seven, he wrote 'The Castaway', his best and bleakest poem.

It was inspired by a true story about a violent storm at sea. Although Cowper was often too scared to leave his house, he liked reading tales of wild travel. In this storm, winds ripped apart a ship's sails and rigging, and the sailors were ordered to 'man the shrouds' – to climb up the rigging to give the ship wind resistance, to get it moving. One sailor slipped and fell into the frozen ocean. The waves were too strong for the others to turn the ship around and rescue him, so they had to watch, as they got further and further away, knowing he could only battle the waves so long and would soon drown. When Cowper read this, he recognised his own predicament. He felt God had cast him away, and now he was in the icy seas, and however hard he swam he'd never be able to get back on board with all the happy people, the saved people. At the end of the poem, he lurches from the sailor's story to his own, saying they have both drowned, 'But I beneath a rougher sea, / And whelm'd in deeper gulfs than he.'

This terrible, turbulent poem stayed with Charlotte and Anne. Anne even addressed a poem to Cowper in 1842, thanking him for articulating 'The language of my inmost heart', and asking,

> Yet should thy darkest fears be true,
> If Heaven be so severe
> That such a soul as thine is lost,
> O! how shall I appear?

It sounds anxious but it is also a hypothetical question: if Cowper is doomed then how can anyone else escape? Anne's 'should' and 'if' make me think she doesn't think we are doomed. She is reassuring Cowper his fears can't be true, reaching out to him, across the dark water, drowning soul to drowning soul, hoping faith and empathy can save them both.

In the same poem Anne said she'd never experienced Cowper's 'wilder woe'. But Charlotte disagreed. Convinced, after Anne's death, that religion 'subdued her mood and bearing to a perpetual pensiveness', that her 'sincere though sorrowing piety' made her fear a 'pomp of terrors' as if 'her whole innocent life had been passed under the martyrdom of an unconfessed phys-ical pain', Charlotte decided to edit Anne's 1844 poem 'A Prayer' by changing 'Unless Thou hasten to relieve, / I know my heart will fall away' to 'Unless Thou hasten to relieve / Thy suppliant is a castaway'. It distorts the meaning. In Charlotte's version, all is lost; in Anne's, there is hope.

Anne disagreed with Cowper about election, the idea that it didn't matter what you did in life, how good or bad you were, because some people were going to hell and some (the elect) were going to heaven, and it was all fixed – predestined – before you were born. Elizabeth Branwell is supposed to have believed this. And yes, some Methodists did believe in election, but Elizabeth was a Wesleyan Methodist, and John Wesley thought election was blasphemy, and Elizabeth might even have heard him say it, when he preached in Penzance, when she was a girl. It's hard to find an early Victorian who *didn't* hear Wesley preach, because, armed with the conviction that 'The world is my parish', he travelled over four thousand miles a year, *before* the railways came, preaching two or three times a day. Elizabeth must have agreed with Wesley's stance on election or she couldn't have sat happily through decades of Patrick's sermons, where he railed against 'the appalling doctrines of personal Election and Reprobation'.

Anne's angriest poem, 'A Word to the Calvinists' (sometimes also called 'A Word to the Elect'), begins by mocking those who believe they are the lucky few: 'You may rejoice to think *yourselves* secure,' she says, accusing the self-styled Elect of having 'black hearts' and a massive failure of empathy. She asks,

> Say does your heart expand to all mankind?
> And would you ever to your neighbour do,
> – The weak, the strong, the enlightened, and the blind –
> As you would have your neighbour do to you?

It is a manifesto about how to live. Elizabeth expanded her heart to her sister's family. And on a smaller scale, in *Agnes Grey*, Weston's sermon inspires Nancy to expand her heart and take up her knitting needles for a neighbour.

Anne's poem takes a sudden turn at the end, contracting from pentameters to ballad metre, becoming brisk, even jaunty, as Anne reveals that she has long nursed a 'cheering' hope, 'That even the wicked shall at last / Be fitted for the skies'. Everyone can be saved by doing good in their lives and even those who do go to hell won't stay there forever. Everyone will get to heaven eventually. This radical poem did not go unnoticed. A Liverpool minister called Dr David Thom wrote to congratulate Anne for speaking out, and she replied that she'd come to her beliefs 'with a trembling hope at first, and afterwards with a firm and glad conviction of its truth. I drew it secretly from my own heart and from the word of God before I knew that any other held it.' She also tells him that in her new novel, 'I have given as many hints in support of the doctrine as I could.'

This new novel was *The Tenant of Wildfell Hall* and it goes much further. The debate about whether people can be saved, in this life or the next, starts early on, when Helen first falls for Huntingdon. Helen knows in her heart that he is a rake. She is in danger of believing, as empty-headed Rosalie does in *Agnes Grey*, that 'reformed rakes make the best husbands, *everybody* knows'. Helen's aunt Peggy tells her that even if they do marry, and even if Huntingdon is the first rake in the history of rakes to reform and they are happy together, 'how will it be in the end, when you see yourselves parted for ever; you, perhaps, taken into eternal bliss, and he cast into the lake that burneth with unquenchable fire – there for ever to –' And Helen cuts her off, exclaiming, 'Not for ever.' She's been reading the Bible for herself (just as Anne did) and she's decided that when God says 'everlasting' or 'eternal' he only means until the sinner has purged their sins. Huntingdon might have to go to hell for a bit, but after that he can join her in heaven. 'I don't know the Greek,' she says, 'but I believe it strictly means for ages, and might signify either endless or long-enduring.' This is the kind of sparky discussion about faith I think Anne must have had with her own aunt.

Peggy thinks Helen's views are dangerous and false – and Anne's critics agreed. *Sharpe's London Magazine* called the novel 'repugnant to Scripture, and in direct opposition to the teaching of the Anglican Church'. But Helen goes on believing staunchly that Huntingdon will be saved. On his deathbed, he accuses her of nursing him purely to 'gain a higher seat in Heaven for yourself, and scoop a deeper pit in hell for me'. He imagines himself 'howling in hell-fire' while she stands by, an 'immaculate angel'; 'Catch you lifting a finger to serve me *then*? – No, you'll look complacently on, and not so much as dip the tip of your finger in water to cool my tongue!' He's at his most vivid here, and his predicament is very real. Anne gave him good arguments, but she also gave Helen the compassion to believe he will be saved, because she can't 'endure to think that the poor trembling soul was hurried away to everlasting torment'. It would drive her mad. 'But thank God,' she says, 'I have hope.'

All the hope in Anne's writing makes me wonder if Charlotte was projecting when she said Anne suffered from the 'tyranny of too tender a conscience'. Because Charlotte did feel guilty about writing. In one story, 'Four Years Ago', she imagines magicians conjuring up 'scenes so gorgeous and so polluted' that they come to seem a 'monument of their own guilt'. Was this how she saw her novels? Was Gaskell drawn to Charlotte's writerly guilt? In the *Life*, she interrupts the story to say,

When a man becomes an author, it is probably merely a change of employment to him . . . But no other can take up the quiet, regular duties of the daughter, the wife, or the mother, as well as she whom God has appointed to fill that particular place: a woman's principal work in life is hardly left to her own choice; nor can she drop the domestic charges devolving on her as an individual, for the exercise of the most splendid talents that were ever bestowed. And yet she must not shrink from the extra talents. She must not hide her gift in a napkin.

Although Gaskell references Jesus's parable of the talents to argue that if you have talents, you have a moral imperative to use them, she sounds too guilty to be convincing. Anne sounded much more sure of herself when she made the same point in her preface to *The Tenant of Wildfell Hall*. 'Such humble talents as God has given me I will endeavour to put to their greatest use,' she writes. Her only doubt came in the word 'endeavour'; Anne knew it was right to use her talents for good, but she wasn't so arrogant as to think it would be easy.

Anne was specific about the 'greatest use' of her talents too, asking, 'Is it better to reveal the snares and pitfalls of life to the young and thoughtless traveller, or to cover them with branches and flowers?' She decides it definitely is, that 'if I have warned one rash youth from following in their steps, or prevented one thoughtless girl from falling into the very natural error of my heroine, the book has not been written in vain'. It is not just God who can save people. She can do it too. Maybe Anne wasn't tyrannised by conscience; maybe conscience spurred her on. In rejecting the idea that only God can decide, unfairly and randomly, who will be saved, Anne found the radical idea that anyone can save themselves, now, in this life, and that her writing could help them do it.

Elizabeth undoubtedly saved Anne and her siblings from many snares and pitfalls. She even went on helping her nieces after she died; the money she left them transformed their lives – it paid for the publication of their poems, and of *Wuthering Heights* and *Agnes Grey*. Most of all, she taught Anne to be the opposite of a 'thoughtless girl', to strive to be both considerate and considered.

3

TABBY

or how to find solace in nature

Tabby was the Brontës' cook and housekeeper – Tabitha Aykroyd, to be exact, but she stayed so long, and got so knitted into their lives, that in Haworth people called her Old Tabby Brontë.

There's so little definite information about Tabby that in *At Home with the Brontës*, Ann Dinsdale wrote, 'it's almost as if her life didn't begin until she walked through the door of Haworth Parsonage'. She was almost certainly born in Haworth, and brought up there, and was in her fifties when she came to work for the Brontës. At least one brother (a woolcomber like their father) and a sister, Susannah, still lived in the village. Tabby almost certainly never married. Nussey said she was 'faithful', 'trustworthy', 'very quaint in appearance' and (ironically, given how much Nussey liked to bang on about the Brontës) discreet. When questioned about the family she worked for, Tabby was 'invincible and impenetrable'. And when asked, in the village, if the children 'were not fearfully larn'd', she left in a huff but told Anne and her siblings, because she knew it would make them laugh.

Gaskell met Tabby for herself and found her 'a thorough specimen of a Yorkshire woman of her class', praising her 'strong practical sense and shrewdness', her plain speaking, and her grasp of local lore. Tabby had always worked near Haworth, as a housekeeper and at a farm. She had the deep knowledge of the village and the moors that came from generations spent in one place, and because she shared that knowledge with the children, they got knitted into Haworth too, until Virginia Woolf could write of the village, 'It expresses the Brontës; the Brontës express it; they fit like a snail to its shell.' May Sinclair said they 'drank and were saturated with Haworth . . . Haworth is saturated with them'.

As well as helping the Brontës put down roots, Tabby, along with Elizabeth, made the Parsonage a home. She often appears in Anne and Emily's brief, scrappy, misspelled diary papers. In Emily's 1834 paper, Tabby complains, 'Ya pitter pottering there instead of pilling a potate,' and ten years on, there she is again: 'Tabby has just been teasing me to turn as formerly to "pilloputate."' There might be only one way to peel a potato but there are many ways to spell it. When Charlotte later went to study in Brussels, she missed 'Tabby blowing the fire, in order to boil the potatoes into a sort of vegetable glue!'

Tabby permeates the novels too. She had no children, she wrote no books, and if she had not worked for the Brontës she might have lived her good, kind, generous life but ended up anonymous, storyless and unremembered. But she made her mark on Anne and her sisters, and she is vivid and present on the pages of their novels. Tabby is *Wuthering Heights*'s Nelly, and *Jane Eyre*'s Bessie, and, in *The Tenant of Wildfell Hall*, she is Rachel; a tougher, saltier, sharper character than the rest. She is honest and outspoken enough to warn Helen, 'if I was you, Miss Helen, I'd look *very* well before I leaped. I do believe a young lady can't be too careful who she marries.' She cares enough about Helen to cry about her misfortune, and also to be honest with her; she's the only one brave enough to tell her that Huntingdon is being unfaithful. Twice. She is very shrewd, a woman who, 'having sojourned for half a century in this land of sin and sorrow, has learned to be suspicious herself'. Huntingdon knows she sees him straight, and he is vile to her, but she puts up with it so she can help Helen. When Helen shuts her out, trying to cope on her own, Rachel urges her to 'give way to it, and cry right hard!' And although she is 'sober' and 'cautious', she is also brave and loyal enough to flee with Helen. She even chips in with her savings to help pay for their new life. In her fifties – the age Tabby was when she came to the Parsonage – Rachel insists, 'I'm not so old but what I can stand hard fare and hard work, if it's only to help and comfort them as I've loved like my own barns: for all I'm too old to bide the thoughts o' leaving 'em in trouble and danger, and going amongst strangers myself.' It could be Tabby speaking. In real life, Tabby's loyalty was returned; when in 1836 she slipped on ice and broke her leg badly, Elizabeth tried to send her away to recuperate, but Anne and her sisters insisted on nursing her themselves, going on hunger strike until their aunt capitulated.

Tabby's biggest gift to Anne was to show her the moors. Anne had always been taken out in the afternoons for an 'airing' (Patrick's word), usually by the servants Tabby replaced, Nancy and Sarah Garrs. But Nancy and Sarah weren't local. They didn't really *know* the landscape. As five-year-old Anne went through the grief of losing her two sisters, Tabby helped her make the moors her playground and her sanctuary. Tabby was, said Nussey, 'very active', and 'kept to her duty of walking out with the "childer"'. Inspired by Tabby, Anne would find solace in nature again and again.

Tabby arrived just after Anne had seen a very different side to the moors. Anne was four when she was caught up in the Crow Hill Bog Burst. On 2 September 1824, she went out as usual with the Garrs sisters, Branwell and Emily (who wasn't yet at school). They were supposed to stay on the Dimples, the gentle slope behind the Parsonage, but they didn't stop there. Anne didn't stick to the paths; in one poem, 'Z's Dream', she writes about the joys of tramping over 'forbidden ground' with 'rebel feet'. That September day, they roamed out on the moor itself. At about six o'clock, Patrick wondered where they'd got to, looked out of his window and was alarmed to find,

> The heavens over the moors were blackening fast. I heard muttering of distant thunder, and saw the frequent flashing of the lightning. Though, ten minutes before, there was scarcely a breath of air stirring, the gale freshened rapidly, and carried along with it clouds of dust and stubble; and, by this time, some large drops of rain clearly announced an approaching heavy shower. [Then came] a deep, distant explosion, something resembling, yet something differing from thunder.

The window shuddered. The bedroom shook.

The moor had exploded. Usually, the top layer of the peat blanket, the layer in which plants are decomposing to *become* peat, soaks up rain like a sponge, and anything it can't absorb runs off into streams. But after a hot, dry summer, the moor had dried out, shrunk and cracked. Now, sudden heavy rain poured into the cracks, seeping down into the thicker, deeper layers of peat. When the water hit the shale beneath, it had nowhere to go. And suddenly, as if the shale were turning in its sleep, shrugging off its covers of peat, the whole moor started to move. Liquefied peat surged out; a seven-foot-high torrent of sludge uprooted trees, toppled stone bridges and flooded fields, making, as the *Leeds Mercury*'s awestruck reporter wrote, 'a violence and noise of which it is difficult to form an adequate conception'. The torrent was nearly as black as ink, and it moved ominously slowly; one eyewitness calculated that 'a man had time to count his sins thrice over while the monster crept stealthily toward him'.

Several children were nearly swept away. Anne might have been one of them. Or perhaps she was further off, caught in the rainstorm rather than the bog burst itself, unsure what the explosions she could hear might be. Nancy and Sarah managed to find a porch for them all to shelter in. The children were huddled there, under Sarah's cloak, when Patrick found them. They were safe but only just. The near miss terrified him. 'We have just seen something of the mighty power of God,' he admonished his congregation. 'He has unsheathed his sword, and brandished it over our heads.' It could have been worse; 'He might have shaken and sunk all Haworth, as those parts of the uninhabited moors on which the bolts of His vengeance have fallen. Be thankful that you are spared.' Patrick sounds like Joseph in *Wuthering Heights*, swinging onto his knees in the middle of a storm to plead with God to spare the righteous and smite the ungodly, and warning Cathy, who has thrown off her shawl and bonnet to enjoy a good drenching, 'This visitation worn't for nowt . . . look aht, Miss – yuh muh be t'next.' When Patrick writes about the tourists who came to see the damaged earth 'in all the giddy frivolity of thoughtless youth . . . as if they dreamed not either of heaven or hell, death or judgment', you can almost see his lip curl.

None of this could have been reassuring to Anne. It doesn't make me feel particularly sanguine either as I head out for a walk on the moors with local historian Steven Wood. After staying up late the night before to read about the bog burst, I've woken up groggy, to find thick mist swathing everything, as if the small stone weavers' cottage I am staying in while researching at the Parsonage archive has been wrapped in cotton wool. Waterproofs on, I walk to Steven's house, crossing the roads gingerly; *Haworth welcomes safe and careful drivers* say the signs, but they don't seem to have attracted many – everyone roars over the blind summits at a terrifying lick.

I've asked Steven to take me for a walk because it seems the best way of getting close to the walks Anne took with Tabby. A tall, bearded ex-microbiologist in a high-performance outdoor jacket, Steven seems an unlikely substitute for a rosy-cheeked, floury-handed Victorian housekeeper, but he knows more than anyone about Haworth and the moors. He is interested in everything about Haworth *except* the Brontës; he wants to find out other stories about the place he lives in. Armed with a map app (called Maverick, of course), we set off.

Out on the moor, there's enough dense, swallowing mist to film a Kate Bush video. My late-night reading makes me slightly too aware of the skies (are they darkening?), of unfamiliar sounds (is that unholy thunder?), and unhelpfully worried about the state of the catotelm (the scientific name for that deep layer of peat). The heather is turning brown, and I don't pay its roots too close attention; I know my Sylvia Plath, and I don't want the roots inviting me to whiten my bones among them. (And they *do* look a lot like bones; Plath was right.)

Rain can come suddenly here. Rain *made* the moors. Fens are wet because of underground water, but moors are wet because rain pours down into them from the skies. With almost no trees, it sometimes feels all horizon; one big cloud about to empty out on you. Steven suggests I read Frank Thompson's eccentric 1978 volume called *The Perfect Companion: The First Authentic Guidebook to Bronteland* [sic] *in the History of the Yorkshire Dales*, where Thompson writes darkly, 'Be prepared for mists and dangerous boggy undergrowth and remember also that the weather can change so drastically that it has to be seen and endured to be believed.' He warns of pea-soup fogs that have killed many a man, some of whose bodies, he warns, *have never been found*. He states (with no evidence!) that Emily loved a 'wild boy of Oxenhope' and Patrick beat his wife. But he is not entirely wrong about the 'treacherous' moors. Because of the damp and the lack of oxygen, bodies buried on moorland can be dug up, thousands of years later, uncorrupted, with even their eyelashes still on. In *Wuthering Heights* the churchyard's 'peaty moisture is said to answer all the purposes of embalming on the few corpses deposited there'. Knowing this makes the bit in *Wuthering Heights* where Heathcliff digs up Cathy's body and embraces her corpse slightly less repulsive. But only slightly.

Even when it's not actually raining, the moors feel wet, water-logged, scarily unsolid. Steven tells me that in Yorkshire they used to say the earth could 'sway like a rantipole' – a see-saw – and the first moments of the bog burst must have been just like that. Steven warns me to watch my step; it's easy to trip and fall and find yourself up to your knees in water. And at one point he does fall, into vile-smelling water – and stoically continues our walk in wet socks.

As the sun starts burning away the mist, the colours become more vivid, more saturated. Steven tells me what Tabby would have been able to tell Anne: the bog burst wasn't supernatural or even extraordinary. Bog bursts just happened sometimes. In nearby Pendle, when the bog burst, people would say, 'Pendle's brussen hisself,' and there is even a valley there called Burst Clough. Tabby knew that soon the rifts in the earth would heal. Steven has walked every inch of the area, and even flown over it in a light aircraft, and there is scant trace of the bog burst now. As Anne lost her sisters, it might have been reassuring to know that just like the moors healed, so would she.

Patrick couldn't have given Anne this reassurance; he had never seen a bog burst before. He wasn't from Yorkshire and he didn't know the moors. Anne's aunt wasn't from Yorkshire either. She missed Cornwall, and found Haworth so cold that she barely left the Parsonage. But it was Patrick who really felt foreign. He had come a long way from the mud cabin in County

Down in Ireland where he had grown up in a large and very poor family. He never lost his accent and he was never allowed to forget he was an immigrant – and his children were constantly reminded of it too. He might be a clergyman, he might be educated, he might be a published author, but he was still Irish and the Irish were always being characterised as childish, lazy, primitive, dirty and alcoholic – in 1850, the novelist Charles Kingsley would write back disgustedly from Ireland about seeing 'human chimpanzees'. Anne was at school when Patrick was shouted down at the 1837 Haworth election hustings and twenty-year-old Branwell tried to intervene. The village made an effigy of Branwell, with a potato in one hand and a herring in the other, and carried it through Main Street before burning it. Branwell watched the grim procession go past from inside one of the village shops. The potato was particularly cruel; blights were already starting to affect Ireland's food supply. When, in 1845, the Great Famine hit, Anne only had to open the papers to find hysteria about Irish refugees. Anne knew that she was from the same place as the people pictured arriving in Liverpool; stick-thin and desperate, dressed in rags, with shocks of unkempt hair. When Branwell started drinking, Anne would hear that he was reverting to type. After Patrick was prescribed eye drops that smelled of alcohol, the gossip was so vicious that he had to carry a doctor's letter everywhere he went, to prove the haters wrong. Anne had her father's strong Irish brogue, too, until she lost her accent at school. So even though she was born in Yorkshire, she felt foreign; she felt like Agnes, arriving at her second job, like a 'thistle seed borne on the wind to some strange nook of uncongenial soil, where it must lie long enough before it can take root and germinate, extracting nourishment from what appears alien to its nature, if indeed it ever can'. Anne knew how hard it was to try to take root in an alien place.

My parents are from the Middle East, so they couldn't teach me which trees were good to climb and which were not, which berries I could pick and which were poison. Walking with Steven, I feel the way I always feel when I leave London – deracinated, ignorant, tongue-tied. It's all very well Anne saying, as she does in 'The Bluebell', 'There is a silent eloquence / In every wild bluebell', but what if you can't understand what the bluebells are saying? When I look up criticism on the poem I find scholars mired in debates about whether Anne meant a bluebell or a harebell, whether the Victorians used one word for both flowers, and whether the poem was original or inspired by one of Emily's. As if they couldn't both have seen a bluebell. Or harebell. This doesn't help. I thought I could at least correctly identify bluebells, but now I doubt myself, and feel even more disconnected, because I can't picture what Anne is writing about.

Stopping to scribble down the names of birds and trees and flowers, I remind myself that Anne didn't know these words either, not until Tabby taught them to her. She learned them on her walks, and I am learning them on mine. I learn that the little lilac flowers are the rarer bell heather, not the common ling; that hair moss and star moss look like their names – green tresses and verdant constellations – as does cotton grass, with its fluffy white heads. Tabby might have taught Anne to love the vivid sphagnum mosses in fluorescent red, pink, orange and green, or the spiky bog asphodel with its flowers the colour of sulphur. She might have helped her recognise the singing of the curlew, and the lapwing, and the lark. Tabby might have carried Anne over the becks when she was small, then showed her how to jump them or to step from stone to stone. When Anne was really little, Tabby might have shown her how to squeeze through the creep-holes made for sheep in drystone walls, and taught her to avoid the sunken patches full of rushes, and not to put her hands into the bee boles, the cavities in stone walls where beekeepers kept bees out of the wind, and not to be frightened if she flushed a grouse and it burst, angry and cackling, out of the heather. Steven tells me that they still burn the moors here (they call it 'swithening'), in patches for the grouse, and some days, Anne might have found it hard to tell whether it was smoke or mist swirling across the landscape – in 'Self-Communion', she wrote, carefully distinguishing one from the other,

> The mist is resting on the hill;
> The smoke is hanging in the air;
> The very clouds are standing still.

According to Nussey, as children, Anne and her siblings 'did not live "in" their house except for its uses of eating, drinking and resting. They lived in the free expanse of hill moorland, its purple heather, its dells and glens and brooks.' In the summer, Tabby might have shown Anne where to pick the best bilber-ries. I wonder if she baked them into the cakes Charlotte mentioned in her 'History of the Year' for 1829 where Anne, aged nine, is 'kneeling on a chair, looking at some cakes which Tabby has been baking for us'. In *Good Things in England*, the cookbook Florence White wrote in 1932, collecting recipes from home cooks up and down the country, because she believed English food was unjustly neglected, I find, alongside the stews and hotpots and instructions for how to cook swan, a recipe for Haworth Bilberry Pie. White is convinced the Brontës ate it, and maybe Tabby made it for them. Yes, it's a pie, not a cake, but it sounds delicious; bilberries are mixed with cooked apples, wrapped in shortcrust pastry and glazed with egg white and sugar. White says the pies should be served with 'cream if obtainable'. I imagine Anne and Tabby coming home from the moors on hot summer days, aprons full of blue-black berries, mouths stained purple with the juice. And I hope cream *was* obtainable.

According to Gaskell, Tabby made the moors rich with songs and stories too. Gaskell was rather judgemental about the fact that when Tabby told the children stories of 'bygone days of the countryside, old ways of living, former inhabitants, decayed gentry . . . family tragedies, and dark superstitious dooms', she did so 'without the least consciousness that there might ever be anything requiring to be softened down' and gave 'at full length the bare and simple details'. For a family of fledgling writers, she was a gift.

Tabby might have sung Anne the song Nelly sings to Hareton in *Wuthering Heights* which begins, 'It was far in the night, and the bairnies grat, / The mither beneath the mools heard that.' The 'mither beneath the mools' is the mother beneath the mould, or soil, an image that must have been both scary and reassuring to a girl whose mother really was beneath the mools. Gaskell said Tabby claimed fairies had lived on the moors in her childhood, but the mills and factories drove them away – maybe she still put out bread and cheese for them on Christmas Eve, like Joseph does in *Wuthering Heights*. Maybe Tabby told Anne about the treasure supposed to have been buried at the suggestively named Silver Hill, and that the Alcomden Stones were once a Druid temple. The stones look like an altar – probably made by ice, not Druids, but Tabby loved a good story. Perhaps she told Anne about 'moss-troopers', brigands who once haunted the wild, lawless moors, moving at speed in the dead of night, avoiding obvious routes and also avoiding the strange, disorienting paths that you find all over the moors; narrow paths that strike out confidently and then just peter out. They are the remains of turbary roads, cut from the farms and villages to get to where the peat was, so people could cut it for their hearths. Anne liked knowing the paths and the hiding places. In 1845, when she was twenty-five, she wrote two poems, both called 'Song', about a soldier who has won a war and now lives in a nice warm palace but misses living on the cold, wild moors. He proudly remembers, 'We know where deepest lies the snow, / And where the frost-winds keenest blow' and sighs, 'O for the wandering Outlaw's life again!'

Because Anne writes about 'the pathless moor' we go off-piste, Steven striding ahead, talking nineteen to the dozen about the intricacies of establishing manorial boundaries. The ground is springy. We are bouncing over at least six foot of peat, maybe twelve. It's like walking on a mattress. A bumpy mattress because it's all tussocks – tufts or clumps of matted grass, sedge and moss. Tussocks are also called hassocks, the thick firm cushions which people kneel on in church, and according to the *Oxford English Dictionary*, the very first hassocks were hacked out of moorland or bogs and shaped and trimmed and 'dressed' in fabric. Anne could have picked her way among the tussocks on the moors, or jumped from one to the next like stepping stones, and she might even have seen the turf hassocks at church. Maybe she felt it made sense to carve a hassock out of the landscape because some of her most ecstatic nature poems are lit up by the conviction that nature is God's work. In her poem 'In Memory of a Happy Day in February', an early taste of spring makes her cheer, 'I felt that God was mine.' As she joyously claims God, she's a long way from Patrick thinking the moors were erupting to warn people about hell. She repeats this claim in a passage in *The Tenant of Wildfell Hall*. Helen has just discovered her husband in the shrubbery with another woman. She sinks to the ground, feeling faint and shocked. She wants to relieve her 'burning, bursting heart' by prayer but she can't. Not until

> a gust of wind swept over me, which, while it scattered the dead leaves, like blighted hopes, around, cooled my forehead, and seemed a little to revive my sinking frame. Then, while I lifted up my soul in speechless, earnest supplication, some heavenly influence seemed to strengthen me within: I breathed more freely; my vision cleared; I saw distinctly the pure moon shining on, and the light clouds skimming the clear, dark sky; and then I saw the eternal stars twinkling down upon me; I knew their God was mine.

I can't believe Helen would have felt so comforted if she had discovered her husband's perfidy indoors.

Steven laments the way the moors are almost always described as bleak and empty. Charlotte said strangers could find 'no interest' in the moors, and invited Gaskell to visit 'in the spirit which might sustain you in case you were setting out on a brief trip to the backwoods of America. Leaving behind your husband, children, and civilisation, you must come out to barbarism, loneliness, and liberty.' If this was a joke, Gaskell missed it. She begins her *Life* by setting the scene with the 'wild, bleak moors', enumerating their 'solitude', 'loneliness' and 'feeling . . . of being pent-up by some monotonous and illimitable barrier'. She doesn't mention the mills, the factories, the quarries, or Haworth's bustling Main Street, or the small dairy farms all the way up the valley, some spilling out on the moorlands, where they kept sheep from a hardy breed called the Lonk. (They have quite a following. According to *Lancashire Life*, 'If you think Herdwicks are hard then you haven't met a Lonk,' while the Lonk Sheep Breeders' Association says, 'The Lonk sheep breed is over 200 years old and for a man who has pride in his stock they are very good looking free ranging sheep of the mountain class.') Gaskell doesn't comment on the Lonk. She certainly doesn't give the impression that in Anne's day, as Steven says, the moors weren't unpopulated, 'they were heaving!'

The main reason the moors look emptier now is water. In 1902, the Keighley Corporation bought up Stanbury Moor as gathering grounds for its reservoirs, then bought up all the farms. It wasn't quite the Highland Clearances but it did empty the moor. Farms were demolished, leaving piles of rubble, or they were wiped out so completely that you can only find them now by poring over old maps, or by spotting the sycamore trees; each farm had a sycamore, for shelter, and for kindling. Another reason the moors are lonely now is because Brontë fans wanted them to look like Charlotte and Gaskell said they looked. There are hardly any telegraph poles. A proposal to build wind farms was blocked by campaigners including Cliff Richard, star of the musical *Heathcliff*, which was notoriously promoted with its own bad reviews ('Withering rather than wuthering'). Now the moors really do look like the stark set of a 1973 play by Richard Crane called *Thunder*, which I find later in the Parsonage library: just a pulpit silhouetted against a cyclorama, used to project images of blizzards and thunderstorms, as if Crane has clarified the Brontës' psychodrama right down to the essentials – God and the moors, both louring with threat. No wonder his chorus of villagers say, 'By gum, it's bleak!'

As we continue our walk, I realise that if the bog burst today, Steven and I would have real trouble finding shelter. Our only option would probably be Top Withins. The ruined farm was preserved because it just *might* have inspired *Wuthering Heights*. It is not a sympathetic preservation; the old stones were repointed with stark, pale new cement, and the tops of the walls were cemented over. But by then the windows had already fallen in, and the chimney, roof and some of the walls, so instead of preserving the house, the Keighley Corporation and, later, Yorkshire Water, preserved its wreckage. Top Withins is all the more uncanny for having been arrested in the process of being ruined. There are Brontë fans wandering around, and couples holding hands, and I feel a bit guilty about stomping about with Steven and de-romanticising it stone by stone. Especially since I have made many wistful, dreamy trips up here myself.

Anne knew the moors weren't a 'waste', weren't empty. Tabby filled every inch of them for her. She taught Anne to pay close attention. It made her nature poems profound and enriching. It made her an acute observer of people, too, noticing details that gave her characters zest and nuance. And paying attention gave her pleasure. Nussey marvelled that when she went on a walk with Anne and Emily, 'Every moss, every flower, every tint and form, were noted and enjoyed.' Identifying trees and flowers could be a dry pursuit but Anne and Emily didn't just note them, they enjoyed them. In *Agnes Grey*, Anne writes, with a glint in her eye, about Agnes coping with boring walks with her selfish pupils and 'a couple of military fops', by hanging back to 'botanise and entomologise'. Not only does this strategy 'melt away' Agnes's 'spirit of misanthropy', it also attracts lovely (*lovely*) Weston, who sees her admiring some primroses she can't reach, rushes to pick them for her, and is soon walking with her, talking about much more than flowers. If Agnes wasn't so nice I'd suspect her of cunningly planning the whole thing. She presses the petals of one of the primroses between the leaves of her Bible and decides that she will keep them forever.

But botanising and entomologising wasn't just a way of attracting men. In Anne's 1845 poem 'Views of Life', she turns it into a whole philosophy. In her first draft she urged readers to 'notice every lovely thing', but later she changed the line to 'smile on every lovely thing'. It isn't enough to notice lovely things, you have to try to take pleasure in them even when you don't feel like it – maybe especially when you don't feel like it. Anne asked, 'Because the road is rough and long, / Shall we despise the skylark's song?' Of *course* not. Through Tabby, Anne learned to listen for the skylark's song even when nothing was going right in her life; to listen for it, and to love it.

Stomping on and up, Steven and I get to Ponden Kirk, the rocky outcrop Emily called Penistone Crag. Standing out on the high flat top, looking out over the vast sweep of moorland, it's easy to see why people thought it was a place of worship. It's so steep that in *Wuthering Heights*, Nelly (quoting Tabby, probably) says she's seen snow in the hollows there even in radiant high summer. Superstition clings to the kirk as tenaciously as snow. According to local lore, if a couple manage to crawl together through the hole under the crag, it counts as a marriage. So maybe when Hareton takes the younger Catherine for a walk and 'He opened the mysteries of the Fairy Cave' for her, Emily meant that they crawled through the hole and sealed their union with a kiss, or more. And maybe when she wrote the ending of *Wuthering Heights*, with Heathcliff and Cathy wandering the moors as ghosts, she was thinking of the darker version of the legend which said if a couple crawled through the hole and then failed to get formally married, they were doomed to die and to haunt the crag. Now I can actually see the hole, I'm not sure how two people would get through it together. It is not large. In his 1899 book *By Moor and Fell*, moor-mad novelist Halliwell Sutcliffe says just one person has to go through: 'if a maid can struggle through the narrowish opening in the rocks,' he says, 'she will be married before the year is out; if not, she is like to go unwedded all her days.' Even so, it's a spell that favours the svelte, and Whiteley Turner, a moustachioed one-armed travelling salesman who wrote *A Spring-Time Saunter*, the jolliest walking guide to the moors, in 1913, warns: 'we acutely realise bulky figures may stick fast midway'.

I peer down uncertainly. I'm less worried about getting stuck than about scrambling down off the crag in the first place. It is very steep. There isn't a path, only what Steven calls 'a path with the eyes of faith'. So not *actually* a path. And I don't think I have the requisite faith. Still, I hack down a little way.

I've just started seeing someone, another writer. We are in the very early stages. I don't know where it's going. I don't know if I want us to be married in a year. It seems a bit soon. It seems a bit final. I don't know if I want to be married at all. Thompson says in his *Perfect Companion* that if I crawl through the Penistone Crag hole, get married, and it doesn't work out, all I have to do is come back and crawl through the opposite way and I'll be widowed within a year. This is not a soothing idea. In fact, it seems a bit drastic. I pause, halfway down the outcrop, Steven waiting patiently on the top. *What would Anne do?* She wouldn't clamber and crawl for any man. She certainly wouldn't base her life on the caprices and uncertainties of magical beings. Leaving the cave to the fairies, I go back up and carry on walking along the ridge.

But now I'm missing the man I'm not yet calling a boyfriend, which reminds me of *The Tenant of Wildfell Hall*, where, early on in their relationship, Helen misses Huntingdon so much that all the fun goes out of her walks. The super-romantic woods, where ash trees swaying in the breeze make 'low music' backed by a 'dreamy hum of insects', trees 'kiss' the lake, or stretch their wide arms around it, just make her feel more alone:

'the greater the happiness that nature sets before me, the more I lament that he is not here to taste it'.

Like Helen, Anne seems to have enjoyed walking in company. As Steven and I loop back over the valley of Ponden Clough, I think about how Anne must have seemed odd to her sisters, who preferred romantic solitude. Anne didn't want to wander lonely as a cloud. Neither, in fact, did William Wordsworth. When he saw his famous daffodils, he was with his sister Dorothy. She took notes on their walk, and he used them to write his poem. He also edited her out. His daffodils are a 'crowd', all dancing the same way, and they make him feel less lonely. In Dorothy's diary, the daffodils are individuals: 'Some rested their heads upon these stones as on a pillow for weariness and the rest tossed and reeled and danced, and seemed as if they verily laughed with the wind.' She records snippets of their conversation, the weather, where they changed out of their wet clothes, and what they had for dinner (ham and potatoes, warm rum and water). Her daffodils are part of the warp and weft of life.

I've always felt sorry for Dorothy being cut out of the picture just so Wordsworth could commune with nature. I wish Dorothy and Anne had met. They almost could have done. There are not many degrees of separation between them: Branwell met Coleridge's son, Grasmere wasn't *very* far from Haworth, and Dorothy spent most of her childhood in Halifax which was even nearer. Dorothy's journals were published too late for Anne to read, but she could have encountered her in Wordsworth's poem 'Tintern Abbey', where he praises the 'shooting lights' in Dorothy's 'wild eyes', or in 'Home at Grasmere', where he talks about their perfect companionship, about how 'Where'er my footsteps turned, / Her voice was like a hidden Bird that sang'. Anne might also have read Thomas De Quincey's profile of Dorothy in *Tait's Edinburgh Magazine* in 1839, where he said, 'Miss Wordsworth was always ready to walk out – wet or dry, storms or sunshine, night or day.' He admired her 'gipsy tan' as much as her 'impassioned intellect', and called her 'the very wildest (in the sense of the most natural) person I have ever known'. Not everyone approved of Dorothy tramping about the countryside. One relative was so censorious that she was driven to defend herself, saying, 'So far from considering this as a matter of condemnation, I rather thought it would have given my friends pleasure to hear that I had courage to make use of the strength with which nature had endowed me.' So it must have been thrilling when De Quincey praised her bravery in print. Both Dorothy and Anne had stamina, too; Anne, who was supposed to be delicate, often walked twenty miles in a day. Like her sisters, she almost certainly wore heavy boots, which the village called eccentric. But if you are going to walk twenty miles, you can't be faffing around with dainty ladies' slippers.

As we come back through the village of Stanbury, Steven and I have racked up far fewer miles than Anne. In Haworth, he loads me up with useful reading and I head for the cottage, to make notes, and lentil soup, to try to get the wood-burner going (I will fail), and to reread Anne's poems, which make more sense now I know what and where she is talking about.

I know I'll miss this landscape when I go home to London. Anne missed it too, writing in 'Home' that she couldn't quite bring herself to enjoy the 'softly smiling skies' at Thorp Green, where she was a governess.

But give me back my barren hills
Where colder breezes rise:

Where scarce the scattered, stunted trees
Can yield an answering swell,
But where a wilderness of heath
Returns the sound as well.

Writing about the same landscape in *Agnes Grey*, Agnes calls it 'depressingly flat to one born and nurtured among the rugged hills'.

In Anne's second novel she exploits the full dramatic potential of the moors. The 'wilderness of heath' is like King Lear's blasted heath, an elemental landscape where the outcast Helen, who has lost all her illusions, starts to remake her life. Anne even gave the village near Wildfell Hall the very local name of Linden-car. 'Car' is a Yorkshire word that comes from the Old Nurse *kjar*, meaning bog.

Although Anne missed Haworth when she left it, she did find another landscape to love. The Robinsons, her employers, took her to Scarborough several times, and she fell in love with the sea. She couldn't get enough of it. In 'Lines Composed in a Wood on a Windy Day', which she wrote a few weeks before she turned twenty-three, the sound of the wind sends her into an ecstasy where, she writes, 'My soul is awakened, my spirit is soaring, / And carried aloft on the wings of the breeze'. She sees the withered grass shining in the sun, the bare trees tossing their branches, the dead leaves dancing in the wind, and the white clouds scudding across the blue sky, but it's not enough. She wants to follow the wind to the coast so she can

> . . . see how the ocean is lashing
> The foam of its billows to whirlwinds of spray,
> I wish I could see how its proud waves are dashing,
> And hear the wild roar of their thunder today!

At first, this makes my inner *Wuthering Heights* addict revolt. I don't want Anne to fall for new landscapes. I want her to be 'a native and nursling of the moors', as Charlotte called Emily – and Anne actually *was* nursed at Haworth, so she has more claim to the title. I want Anne to be obsessive about the moors, like Emily, who pined when she was away from them, and like Cathy and Heathcliff who roamed the moors as children and haunted them as ghosts. It seems fickle of Anne to suddenly decide she likes the sea too. But then I wonder if, when she first saw the sea, she recognised something.

When the young heroine of Frances Hodgson Burnett's *The Secret Garden* crosses the seas from India to Yorkshire, she glimpses the moors and asks, 'It's not the sea, is it?' There is a swathe of moorland on the north side of the Worth Valley, which Anne would surely have known, actually called The Sea. There is a connection. After Anne's death, Charlotte wrote about how she missed her when she went for walks, and how 'The distant prospects were Anne's delight and when I look round she is in the blue tints, the pale mists, the waves and shadows of the horizon'. This *sounds* like the sea, and maybe Charlotte meant it to. The sea was the vista their mother had grown up with and it exerted its pull. For much of Anne's life, she couldn't *get* to the moors. She had to go away to school, or she had to work far from home. She could fetishise the moors and fall apart when she was away from them, or she could see if she could find other landscapes to enjoy. She chose to fall in love with the sea.

Anne couldn't always be so pragmatic. She couldn't always make herself love nature, or even life. Her very first surviving poem, 'Verses by Lady Geralda', which she wrote at sixteen, is about feeling estranged from the natural world. Lady Geralda used to love the wind's wild music and its 'stormy breath' – such an intimate, visceral image, that breath – but now the wind just 'howls along the barren ground / With melancholy moan'. She doesn't know why the sun, skies, flowers and birds seem 'so sadly changed', and she worries over it and despairs about it, until she realises that nothing has happened to nature, but instead 'my heart is changed alone: / Nature is constant still.' It's a painful discovery because it means she can't blame nature. She has changed, and if she is going to get herself back, she'll have to change again. But it's comforting too because she knows that while her heart might go through any number of revolutions, nature will stay the same.

Nature is constant, too, in Anne's 1838 poem, 'The North Wind', about another unhappy woman. The poem's heroine is from the north, imprisoned in the south. She has sunk into insensibility. And then the north wind comes to comfort her, actually thunders into her prison cell to jolt her back to life. The wind promises that although she has lost her joy, 'The sweet world is not changed'. Nature is constant still. This doesn't exactly cheer her up but it does revive her deadened feelings. She asks the wind to 'Blow on', to wake her up, to remind her who she is, because now she's feeling 'hot tears', but anything is better than 'that dull gnawing tearless time / The stupor of despair'. She is 'confined and hopeless' but she begs the wind for solace:

> O speak of liberty,
> O tell me of my mountain home,
> And I will welcome thee.

I love that 'welcome' at the end; it's so hopeful. She's in a cell. Someone else has control over the key and the door. She can't let anyone in or out. But the wind can get in, whatever her jailers do or say. And she opens her arms to it. It is a tiny piece of home in this horrible, faraway place. It will make her feel less foreign, less estranged, less disconnected. It will remind her where she comes from, and who she is.

Eight years later, Anne took this idea further still, in 'Weep Not Too Much, My Darling', another poem about another imprisoned character, a man this time, who begs his lover to 'Say that the charms of Nature / Are lovely still to thee'. Stuck in his cell, the moonbeams he can see are 'crossed, deformed, and sullied' by the bars, but she can see the whole of the moon, and he wants her to tell him about it. Anne wrote poems that were themselves a kind of solace, because if you feel barred from nature (and the bars don't have to be literal) then reading about it can make you feel connected again, especially if what you are reading is a precise, exact evocation that is also suffused with ecstatic lyricism. Even when Anne's life was hard, even when she was far from home, she tried to smile on every lovely thing, to say the charms of nature were lovely still to her, just like Tabby taught her to.

Tabby stayed at the Parsonage for thirty-one years. She stayed even after she got too old and doddery to do much work, supervising the other servant and running the kitchen imperiously, and with humour. She saw Maria, Elizabeth, Branwell, Emily and Anne die, but when Charlotte fell ill, she gave up. It was as if she crumpled. She died six weeks before Charlotte, at eighty-four. She is buried, with her brother and sister, just over the wall from the Parsonage garden.

4

EMILY

or how to imagine yourself into another life

Although for a long time *Wuthering Heights* was my favourite
book, I can believe it was not the easiest thing in the world to
be Emily Brontë's sister. Emily was famously difficult and so
private that trying to write about her makes me feel a bit like
Lockwood, who only wants a friendly cup of tea with Heathcliff,
and keeps getting rudely shut out, reduced to whining, 'I don't
care, I will get in!' and, when he does, can't work out who
anyone is, or whether a pile of fluffy things are kittens or dead
rabbits. Emily being Emily – mordant and perverse – they are
dead rabbits. Emily wasn't biddable or nice. The word for her
is the word the younger Catherine teaches Hareton to pronounce
correctly, ordering him to 'Recollect, or I'll pull your hair!'
Emily was *contrary*.

   She is still impossible to pin down. Charlotte couldn't describe
her without getting tangled up in how she was 'Stronger than
a man, simpler than a child'. There are so many theories about
Emily. She was a sphinx. Her work came from nothing, from
the moors, from God. She was an atheist, a mystic, she thought
she was God. She was anorexic. She hated life and willed her
own death. She loved life and couldn't bear to leave it. She

loved men, she loved women, she only loved herself. Branwell wrote a story about her as 'a gurt bellaring bull' who has a tantrum and is straitjacketed and put to bed. Charlotte said she was stubborn and harsh. I quail at the weight of all this disputatious scholarship. Sitting in the Parsonage library, I feel as if I can hear the biographers all yelling at each other from the battered volumes, a clamour rising and rising, threatening to topple the tall glass-fronted bookshelves and crush anyone foolish enough to try to sift through it all.

I like the idea of Emily resisting her biographers as steadily as she resisted convention. But when I read about *why* she was supposed to be so unconventional, her deviations from the norm seem so minor. So what if she liked whistling, and floppy skirts and leg-of-mutton sleeves that were easy to move in? Were her long strides really so unladylike that she had to be nicknamed The Major? Under pressure to stop whistling, dress fashionably and walk small, no wonder she tried to ignore reality. Her name has almost become synonymous with wild, unfettered imagination, and when I first read *Wuthering Heights*, as an awkward, stuck teenager, it made me feel free.

So at first I am surprised to find that Emily and Anne were so close, 'like twins', said Nussey. Because wasn't Anne the rational one? Wasn't Anne the one who said she 'would rather whisper a few wholesome truths . . . than much soft nonsense'? And yet, as a child, Anne was Emily's best friend and conspirator.

When Anne was six, and Emily was eight, Patrick came back from a trip with presents for all the children. It was almost a year after their sister Elizabeth had died, and maybe Patrick was trying to draw a line under the past. He brought ninepins for Charlotte, a toy village for Emily and a dancing doll for Anne, but it was the toy soldiers he gave Branwell that entranced the children. When Charlotte saw them, she said,

> I snatched up one and exclaimed, 'This is the Duke of Wellington! It shall be mine!' When I said this, Emily likewise took one and said it should be hers. When Anne came down she took one also. Mine was the prettiest of the whole and perfect in every part. Emily's was a grave-looking fellow. We called him Gravey. Anne's was a queer little thing, very much like herself. He was called Waiting Boy. Branwell chose Bonaparte.

Compared to the champions who slugged it out at Waterloo, Anne and Emily's soldiers sound dull. But according to Branwell's account, Anne's hero wasn't queer little Waiting Boy, but Ross, named after the Arctic explorer John Ross. And Emily's hero was Ross's nemesis, William Parry. Ross's daring expeditions to find the fabled Northwest Passage, an ice-free sea route through the Arctic, had gripped the nation. In *Blackwood's Magazine* the children could read blow-by-blow accounts of ships trapped in ice, starving explorers eating their boots, frost-bite and polar bears, fearless rescues and lonely deaths. There were technical drawings of the explorers' kit, including, on later expeditions, a 'coat-boat', an inflatable dinghy which could transform into a cloak, its sail becoming an umbrella. Even now, this sounds like science fiction. Anne must have seen the famous 1818 picture of Ross, stalwart in blue, crossing a snowscape as white and glossy as meringue, to meet some jolly, fur-bundled Inuit. Ross was like the narrator of Mary Shelley's *Frankenstein*, published that same year, who dreamed of bringing 'inestimable benefit to all mankind'. Shelley's Arctic explorer gets stuck in the ice and meets a man (half dead, on a sledge, on an ice floe) who says he's created a monster. Ross found something scarcely less surprising; a mountain range blocking his path. He decided there was no Northwest Passage and set off for home.

But Parry, his second in command, disagreed, and the Admiralty liked an optimist. So Parry got his own ship, and Ross had to scrabble for funds to keep exploring. It was just like Anne to pick an underdog as her hero. Throughout the 1820s, while the real Ross and Parry were making rival voyages, Anne and Emily's small, wooden avatars were squaring off across the nursery floor. Anne didn't know that Ross's mountains would turn out to be a mirage, that his rival wouldn't find the Northwest Passage either, that it wouldn't be found until 1903. Anne only knew she wanted to imagine herself into another world.

The children called the soldiers the Young Men, always capitalised. Branwell gave them a backstory about making an 'astonishing voyage' to Africa where, to their horror, they spot a pair of giant footprints. Suddenly, they see 'black and tempestuous clouds which hurried to and fro as in some great and awful convulsions'. It could almost be the bog burst. They are terrified to see 'an immense and terrible monster' whose 'head which touched the clouds, was encircled with a red and fiery halo, his nostrils flashed flames and smoke, and he was enveloped in a dim, misty and indefinable robe'. This is nine-year-old Branwell in his 'dim, misty and indefinable' nightgown, his 'red and fiery' hair sticking up from sleep, as he explains in a helpful footnote. He's with 'three beings of much the same height as himself wrapped in clouds' – Charlotte, Emily and Anne, in *their* nightgowns. They are the 'genii', the Young Men's 'guardian demons'. Branwell adds sweetly that at first he only let his sisters borrow the soldiers, but then he let them have them to keep.

The Young Men took a while to become proper characters. At first, they were wooden metaphorically as well as literally. They even had names like Captain Tree, Stumps, General Leaf, Sergeant Bud and Corporal Branch. Branwell drew them in crayon looking half wooden, half human, half stiff, half in motion, as if they were only just stretching their creaking limbs and blinking open their painted eyes to read one of the tiny books the children had started making for them, in microscopic writing that looked like newsprint, on scraps of paper, envelopes, sugar bags, parcel wrappings and wallpaper, stitched together. In Deborah Lutz's illuminating book on the Brontës' stuff, *The Brontë Cabinet*, she wonders if the children made the books tiny so they could feel like giants when they held them. When I hold one, it fits neatly into the palm of my hand.

As they wrote and dreamed, their imaginary world took shape. They called it Angria. They drew maps, wrote constitutions, planned military campaigns, plotted coups and rehearsed passionate affairs. In what Branwell called a *'furor scribendi'*, and Charlotte called 'scribblemania', they grabbed stories from Tabby's gossip, Patrick's parish scandals and Elizabeth's memories of Penzance, from books they loved like Aesop's *Fables*, the *Arabian Nights* and Bewick's *History of British Birds*, and made them their own. They acted everything out, knowing that improvising is just writing on your feet, and writing is just improvising sitting down. They tried out different roles, different choices, different lives. One day, pretending to be Prince Charles escaping the Roundheads, Emily stepped out of Patrick's window onto a cherry tree, and broke a branch. (But some stories say it wasn't her at all, but the servant Sarah Garrs.) Anne and her siblings escaped themselves, as Cathy wished she could in *Wuthering Heights*, when she tells Nelly 'I *am* Heathcliff!', demanding, 'surely you and everybody have a notion that there is or should be an existence of yours beyond you. What were the use of my creation, if I were entirely contained here?'

Anne wasn't contained. She looked like she was sewing quietly but really she was waging war in Angria. She signed her stories and poems with the names of her characters, haphazardly spelled. Anne had a captive audience for her stories, willing actors for her plays. The children didn't write chronologically; instead, one story sparked another, and like soap-opera writers, when things got dull they invented long-lost characters to wake things up. Charlotte made Branwell's characters fall in love, and he sent hers to war. When he got too bloodthirsty, his sisters turned up, as genii, to 'make alive' the dead. In real life too many people had died on them; in Angria, death was not final. Nothing was final. No story was true, no writer had authority. They wrote rival versions of the same events, prequels and sequels, and they ventriloquised men of letters to satirise and slander each other. They were noisy and competitive and they didn't play nicely. Two lots of toy soldiers were 'maimed lost burnt or destroyed', and once they played so loudly that they scared Tabby and she ran to her nephew's house, saying 'yon childer's all gooin mad, and aw daren't stop 'ith hause only longer wi' 'em'. This was what Charlotte meant when she said *Wuthering Heights* was hewn in a 'wild workshop'.

Charlotte and Branwell took the lead at first, but Anne and Emily soon got fed up with being bossed about by the other two. While Charlotte and Branwell wrote about hot, exotic, faraway countries, Anne and Emily set their stories on the cold, wet moors. And Charlotte didn't like it. In 1830, when she was fourteen, she wrote a story about her noble hero Charles Wellesley visiting twelve-year-old Emily's domain, Parry's Land. Wellesley sneers, 'No proud castle or splendid palace towers insultingly over the cottages around.' But Emily and Anne were more interested in writing about the insulted people – the vulnerable, the outsiders, the oppressed – than about the aristocrats who tried to tower over them. Wellesley disdains the factories, and the country bumpkins who speak 'in a scarcely intelligible jargon', half childish prattle, half impenetrable Yorkshire dialect, and eat food Anne and Emily liked – 'roast-beef, Yorkshire pudding, mashed potatoes, apple pie and preserved cucumbers'. He is offended when his hosts offer him a napkin so he won't stain his clothes, feels 'a strong inclination to set the house on fire' and beats a small boy with a poker. The plucky child roars loudly, and is rescued. Sadistic Wellesley's keenest disappointment is that there are no 'tall, strong muscular men going about seeking whom they may devour'. In some ways, Charlotte never stopped writing about (or lusting after) 'tall, strong muscular men going about seeking whom they may devour'.

Maybe 'A Day at Parry's Place' was what made Anne and Emily break away from Angria a year later. At eleven and thirteen, they didn't have to put up with Charlotte's unsympathetic criticism. And anyway, she was away at school. Patrick had found a new (much better) establishment in Mirfield called Roe Head, and the plan was that Charlotte would get an education which she could pass on to her sisters. For now, Patrick was teaching Anne and Emily along with Branwell, so they were learning Latin, Greek and ancient history – none of which appeared on the usual curriculum for girls, which consisted of sewing (plain and fine), music, drawing, English, maths, history, geography and French. At Haworth, as well as studying with Patrick and Branwell, Anne and Emily were learning to draw from an artist in nearby Keighley, while a church organist taught them to play the piano. They could have gone on writing Angria with Branwell but he seemed to have reached a vainglorious dead end; he'd just written an 'Ode to the Chief Genius Bany', i.e. himself.

So they dreamed up a new world, and called it Gondal. In the archive in Haworth, I look at the index to one of the children's favourite books, Reverend J. Goldsmith's *Grammar of General Geography*, to see how Anne exuberantly vandalised it, pencilling in new place names: Gondal, then 'Gaaldine a large island newly discovered'. She knew, from Ross's misadventures, that the globe still had dark corners, and atlases were still being written, so why shouldn't Gondal be out there somewhere, waiting to be found, and why shouldn't the people of Gondal be discovering new islands too?

Gondal gave life zest. Anne and Emily's first joint diary paper, from 1834, starts breathlessly in the kitchen where they are peeling apples for an apple pudding, while Tabby interrupts because she wants them, of course, to peel potatoes instead. Emily goes on:

> Aunt has come into the kitchen just now and said, 'Where are your feet Anne?' Anne answered 'On the floor, Aunt.' Papa opened the parlour door and gave Branwell a letter . . . The Gondals are discovering the interior of Gaaldine. Sally Mosley is washing in the back kitchen.

Gondal and Gaaldine are tumbled in with Branwell's letter and Sally Mosley's washing, apples and potatoes, chores and lessons, and the grown-ups' incomprehensible questions (*Where are your feet?*), but while the girls are in the kitchen (untidy like the diary note, which is blotted, semi-legible, erratically punctuated and endearingly full of misspellings), in their heads, they are explorers, hacking through the undergrowth in search of thrills or treasure.

As well as breaking free of Charlotte and Branwell, Anne was escaping Angria's retrograde values. If you don't like the rules of the world you live in, sometimes you have to break them, and fantasy fiction – alternative universes, utopias and dystopias, science fiction, steampunk, paranormal stories, sword and sorcery epics and the rest – breaks the rules of everyday life. It can be freeing. It can make you feel nothing is sacred, anything can happen, everything can change. In Gondal, Anne was finding the radical imagination that would fire her novels.

She was saying stories didn't only happen in sultry, distant locations; they could happen in cold, familiar places too. Gondal was all 'mists and moorlands drear, / And sleet and frozen gloom'. Setting Gondal stories on the moors meant that Anne and Emily could *write* there too. In their 1837 joint diary paper Emily draws them – Anne in billowing sleeves, Emily with her back to us – writing at the dining table. Anne asks, 'Well, do you intend to write in the evening?' Emily replies, 'Well what think you?' and they agree 'to go out first to make sure if we get into a humour . . .' Meanwhile, at school, Charlotte was training herself to write with her eyes shut, gazing only into her own imagination.

Anne's head might have been in the clouds but her feet were firmly on damp peat. In Angria, wars meant parades and glory; in Gondal, they brought disillusionment and death. There were no genii to 'make alive' or conjure up a happy ending. Anne and Emily's characters have free will, make mistakes, face the consequences, die. They aren't wooden; they feel real. This was another break from Charlotte, who was flirting with postmodernism: in one Angrian story, Wellesley panics that he is 'a non-existent shadow – that I neither spoke, ate, imagined, or lived of myself, but I was the mere idea of some other creature's brain'. It's true that Charlotte has made him up, but in admitting this, she makes Wellesley unreal and insubstantial. It's clever, but it isn't emotionally satisfying.

Anne realised that at some point you have to stop living in someone else's stories and write your own. She was sick of the way Angrian women were all 'blighted lilies' who lost their minds over men and swooned and moped and faded. Was this all women could do? If she wanted something different, did she have to co-opt male power like Charlotte, creating heroes who strutted about, conquering land, conquering women, beating children, and having overblown Byronic crises? Instead, Anne and Emily decided to write heroines. Like Augusta Geraldine Almeda – AGA for short – who was a mash-up of Mary Queen of Scots and the future Queen Victoria.

Both Anne and Emily were fascinated by Victoria, who was almost exactly between their ages. Their 1837 diary paper records that Charlotte is sewing in one room, their aunt is sewing in another, Branwell is reading to Charlotte, and 'Papa gone out, Tabby in the kitchen – the Emperors and Empresses of Gondal and Gaaldine preparing . . . for the coronation which will be on the 12th July. Queen Victoria ascended the throne this month.' It's a jolt to go from the humdrum household routine to Gondalian royalty and then to a real queen and a real coronation. Ironically, while the Brontës were weaving stories about someone very like Victoria, the princess was longing for a life like theirs. Victoria was lonely, brought up strictly and separated from other children. At seven, the desolate princess and her governess would squeeze into a miniature phaeton, pulled by a pair of tiny Shetland ponies, and a footman would drive them round and round the empty grounds. Victoria's mother tied holly under Victoria's chin to make her keep her head up straight, controlled her access to books and newspapers, and read all her journals and letters. Victoria's first command as queen was to be left alone for an hour. She would go on to choose a husband because she fancied him, to stay on the throne for six decades, to have nine children, and to survive eight assassination attempts. She refused to carry the bulletproof parasol she was issued, with its chain-mail lining. She surrounded herself, in her long widowhood, with handsome young men, including a bluff Balmoral ghillie and an Indian servant who taught her to say 'hold me tight' in Hindustani. And she wrote. Sixty million words in all, sometimes two thousand words a night in her diaries, about everything from her pleasure at her husband putting on her stockings for her, to the state of her prime minister's teeth. She also wrote fiction. The heroine of *The Adventures of Alice Laselles*, a book Victoria wrote when she was ten (but which was only published in 2015), goes away to school, vanquishes injustice and, very poignantly, makes friends.

Victoria would have been enraptured and maybe a bit shocked by Anne and Emily's stunning, ruthless queen who loves, uses and leaves men to die of broken hearts, or get killed by her other admirers, or go to prison, or commit suicide (there are lots of them, so they need various grisly ends). When her past catches up with her, AGA is murdered on the moors.

At least I think that's what happens. Reams and reams of Angrian writing survives – the writing is tiny but at least it is *there* – but all that is left of Gondal are the poems. So trying to work out the story of Gondal is like trying to reconstruct a musical from just its songs. The dramatic peaks and troughs are there, the moments where the characters let rip and speak from their hearts, but without the prose it's hard to trace an arc between these moments of high drama or to work out who any of the characters are. Not that this has stopped Brontë scholars from trying. Fannie Ratchford, a librarian at the University of Texas, first came across scraps of Gondal in the 1920s, along with a warning that 'The whole is a mystery' and she should 'Pry no further'. But like a fairy-tale heroine opening a forbidden door, Ratchford couldn't help herself. She spent years poring over the tiny books, finding slivers of stories in other libraries and private collections, piecing the fragments together until she had pushed and shoved and finagled all of Emily's poems into one thrilling story she called *Gondal's Queen*. Yes, just Emily's. She ignored Anne. Sigh. So did the next scholar to wade into Gondal, the magnificently named William Doremus Paden, who decided to approach the task with cold precision. His story doesn't work either, maybe because Anne and Emily didn't write coldly and precisely, but in bursts, over decades, jubilantly contradicting each other, turning each other's stories inside out.

In her overheated 1936 biography *The Life and Eager Death of Emily Brontë*, Victoria Moore says Anne 'played the Gondal game passably, and applauded sweetly when Emily invented situations'. I mistrust this, not least because Moore is notorious for misreading the title of a poem by Emily called 'Love's Farewell' as 'Louis Parensell' and deciding it was the name of Emily's secret lover. Insisting 'We are not prudes any more', Moore speculates that Emily also loved women, and hints at her incestuous love for Anne. Moore even takes Emily writing in her diary paper, 'Anne and I have not tidied ourselves', as titillating evidence that 'Emily and Anne sometimes went around *déshabillé*'.

But maybe Emily didn't have any lovers. At least that's what I think after reading a whimsical, waspish novel written by Rachel Ferguson in 1931. *The Brontës Went to Woolworths* is about three sisters who live in an imaginary world, just like the Brontës, and are shocked out of it when they have a seance and summon up Charlotte and Emily. (Not Anne. Of course not Anne.) The Brontë ghosts are dowdy and unpleasant but they do stage an important intervention: they make the sisters realise that fantasy is preventing them living their lives. One sister has even refused a marriage proposal because she loves Sherlock Holmes too much to have room in her heart for a real man. And perhaps Emily, too, was so interested in her technicolour dreamworld that the real world seemed grey.

At school, Charlotte told one of her new friends, the forthright Mary Taylor, a bit about their 'making out' (their writing) and Taylor was amazed and a bit repelled. 'You are just like growing potatoes in a cellar!' she said. An 1896 *Spectator* review of Clement Shorter's book *Charlotte Brontë and her Circle* explained this 'country-bred' metaphor, describing the way potatoes will grow 'great green shoots thirty or forty feet long straggling out towards' the sun, just like the Brontës' 'experience grew, like the potato, to unhealthy proportions in a single direction'. It was true that, sustained by Angria and Gondal, Anne and her siblings were turning inwards. At a birthday party they went to, they didn't know how to play hunt the slipper, and here we go round the gooseberry bush. They were losing the knack of living in the real world, of getting on with real people.

*

Charlotte did make two friends at Roe Head. While Taylor was from a radical, nonconformist family, and would become so incensed by the lack of opportunities for women in England that in 1845, aged twenty-eight, she would emigrate to New Zealand, Ellen Nussey was more conventional. The petted youngest child of ten, Nussey grew up in a house so nice that Branwell called it 'paradise'. Nussey never worked for a living, never married, and never lived outside her family. Her friendship with Charlotte survived many ups and downs, including Charlotte keeping her literary career a secret, refusing to marry Nussey's brother, and having the effrontery to marry someone else.

Nussey saw herself as Charlotte's number-one friend, particularly because Charlotte wrote her such flirty, tender letters. Vita Sackville-West pronounced them 'love letters pure and simple'. It's easy to see why. Charlotte told Nussey, 'If we had but a cottage and a competency of our own I do think we might live and love on till Death.' When Nussey hid some presents in her bag, Charlotte chided her, 'You ought first to be tenderly kissed and then afterwards as tenderly whipped.' Charlotte stroked Nussey's head and said, 'If I had but been a man, thou wouldst have been the very ticket for me as a wife.'

Reading a (much tamer) letter over his new wife's shoulder in 1854, Charlotte's husband Arthur Bell Nicholls called the correspondence 'dangerous as Lucifer matches'. He issued an ultimatum: Nussey must either burn the letters after reading, or he would censor them. Nussey agonised over how to reply. She came up with a formula as sneaky as a lawyer's. 'My dear Mr Nicholls,' she began. 'As you seem to hold in great horror the *ardentia verba* of feminine epistles, I pledge myself to the destruction of Charlotte's epistles, henceforth, if you pledge *yourself* to *no* censorship in the matter communicated.' The commas around 'henceforth' are key: Nicholls thought Nussey was promising to destroy *all* her letters from Charlotte. But Nussey thought she was only promising to destroy any *future* letters, and *then* only if Nicholls didn't censor them. When Charlotte said Nicholls was now happy for them to write 'dangerous stuff', Nussey wilfully misinterpreted it, noting, 'Mr N continued his censorship so the pledge was void.' She didn't destroy a word.

After Charlotte's death, Nussey wanted to be the keeper of the Brontë flame. But Nicholls kept tamping her down, and as Charlotte's widower, he owned the copyright to the letters. Taylor didn't want Nussey courting publicity either. Taylor disliked the *Life*. When she read a review which summed up Charlotte's life as one of 'poverty and self-suppression', she wrote acidly that none of the critics 'seems to think it a strange or wrong state of things that a woman of first-rate talents, industry, and integrity should live all her life in a walking nightmare of "poverty and self-suppression"'. Nussey didn't think it was 'strange or wrong' either. Like Gaskell, she was keen to promote Charlotte as 'a Christian heroine, who bore her cross with the firmness of a martyr-saint'.

In a pencil sketch of Nussey as a young girl, she looks doughy and half finished, with a shy smile and soft waves of hair, but in later pictures, she looks sad, her mouth set. It's hard not to feel sorry for her. Her friendship with Charlotte was the most interesting thing about her. As she clung to it, she fell out with Taylor. She also got scammed.

In 1889, the wily journalist Shorter flattered Nussey into selling some of her treasured letters to his friend Thomas J. Wise. Wise was a serious book dealer and bibliographer, but also a notorious forger. He promised to save the Brontëana, preventing it from being 'scattered to the winds and lost to the world', but instead, he sold it off piecemeal, split manuscripts, and misattributed poems. And now a lot of it *is* lost to the world – another reason it's so hard to establish anything firm about the Brontës, ever.

When Nussey realised what they were up to, she accused Wise and Shorter of 'greed and grab', and they said she was hallucinating. Nicholls was devastated when he lent them a lock of Charlotte's hair and it was returned 'sadly reduced in size . . . a few hairs in stead of a long thick tress'. After that, he started burning papers, including, maybe, some of Anne's. But although Wise was nefarious, I have to be grateful to him because he was the first to publish Anne's poem 'Self-Communion'.

When Charlotte returned to Haworth in June 1832, after a year and a half at Roe Head, she plunged back into Angria. She was sixteen, and although Patrick thought she was now ready to take over the education of fourteen-year-old Emily and twelve-year-old Anne, he was worried about all the time she spent hunched over her desk writing tiny books. (Now the books were tiny not just so their toy soldiers could read them, but so the grown-ups couldn't.) Fearing for Charlotte's eyesight, Patrick gave her a notebook in Christmas 1833, with the direction, 'All that is written in this book must be in a good plain <u>and legible hand</u>.'

She dutifully wrote a few poems on historical themes in the book, but they lack the fire of the real writing she was doing, in Angria.

Since I can't go to Gondal, I do the next best thing and visit Ponden Hall, a manor house which both Anne and Emily fictionalised furiously. Once the home of the Heaton family, Ponden Hall is three miles across the moors from the Parsonage. The Brontës had the run of the Heatons' library, and Anne might have sheltered in the house's porch during the bog burst. Ponden Hall has been claimed as the real Wuthering Heights. The year carved above the door is 1801, the same year as *Wuthering Heights* begins. But what makes my heart beat faster is that some of Ponden Hall dates back to the 1500s, just like Wildfell Hall. Clutching my copy of Anne's novel, I confirm it definitely *is* a 'superannuated mansion of the Elizabethan era', built of 'dark grey stone' with 'thick stone mullion windows'.

The novelist and critic Stevie Davies thinks both Wildfell Hall and Wuthering Heights are descended from 'a common Ur-hall in Gondal'. Perhaps this is it. Perhaps Anne and Emily would walk over the moors to use the library at Ponden Hall, pretending they were going to some great Gondal hall, sometimes as princesses who would be feted and feasted, sometimes as outlaws who would have to break and enter.

Steve Brown and Julie Akhurst, who own the house, let me in. They are running Ponden Hall as a bed and breakfast, and restoring it room by room. As I sit in the great hall with its dark oak beams, huge flagstones and smoke-blackened fireplace, I think of Lockwood sitting with Heathcliff in 'the radiance of an immense fire, compounded of coal, peat, and wood'. And I think of Gilbert visiting Helen at Wildfell Hall, and, looking around, I'm ticking it all off in my head. Yes, this is a 'tolerably spacious and lofty room'; yes, it is 'but obscurely lighted by the old-fashioned windows'; yes, the chimney piece does seem to be carved of 'grim black oak'.

I imagine Anne sitting where I'm sitting, drinking tea with the five Heaton brothers. 'Heaton' sounds a lot like all the 'H' names in both *The Tenant of Wildfell Hall* and *Wuthering Heights*: Heathcliff, Hindley, Hareton, Huntingdon, Hargrave and Hattersley. The Heatons owned quarries and coal mines, cotton and corn mills, and they had lived in the house for three hundred years. Gauche Robert Heaton apparently had a crush on Emily. Once, when they were having tea, a dog gave birth to a litter of puppies at her feet, and he was mortified, but she didn't care. He planted a pear tree for her in the garden. Its remains are still there, but the Heatons aren't any more. In 1898 Robert died, the last of their line, and Ponden Hall soon went out of the family altogether.

Perhaps as Anne made small talk at Ponden Hall, she let herself imagine the house falling into ruin, becoming like Lord Byron's house. All the Brontës were obsessed by the poet, who had inherited Newstead Abbey as an obstreperous ten-year-old. Byron loved the way one wing was open to the wind and weather, and cows roamed the cloisters:

Through thy battlements, Newstead, the hollow winds
whistle:
Thou, the hall of my Fathers, art gone to decay;
In thy once smiling garden, the hemlock and thistle
Have choak'd up the rose, which late bloom'd in the way.

Maybe Anne imagined fire creeping up the walls, the great fireplace crumbling, windows falling in, until the hall was a 'stern and gloomy' mess. Then she'd push the hall to the top of the hill so it became 'the wildest and the loftiest eminence in our neighbourhood', 'too lonely, too unsheltered' to live in, but perfect for stories. Looking out of the window, she would imagine the garden reverting to wilderness, the topiary growing unkempt so that

> the old boxwood swan, that sat beside the scraper, had lost its neck and half its body: the castellated towers of laurel in the middle of the garden, the gigantic warrior that stood on one side of the gateway, and the lion that guarded the other, were sprouted into such fantastic shapes as resembled nothing either in heaven or earth, or in the waters under the earth; but . . . presented all of them a goblinish appearance, that harmonised well with the ghostly legions and dark traditions our old nurse had told us respecting the haunted hall and its departed occupants.

Ponden Hall is sadly low on topiary but it did once have a ghost, a rather cheerless ghost who only turned up when one of the Heatons was about to die, presumably to give them the bad news.

The hall is cosy now, but it's clearly taken a lot of hard work to make it so. Anne is clear about how cold and dreary Wildfell Hall is to live in. She won't quite let me be romantic. I resent her for it. Especially when we go upstairs, and I geek out over the bedrooms. The one on the east gable end of the house has a single-paned window that looks just like the window from *Wuthering Heights*. Steve and Julie have commissioned a carpenter to make a box bed, just like Cathy's, all dark panels and soft pillows and crisp sheets, and it's all I can do not to climb into it, shut the door, curl up and scratch my name in the wood, over and over. Because in my heart I don't want to grow up and give up romance. I want to be Cathy, in bed, plotting mischief with Heathcliff and scribbling in my books. Maybe I always will. Yet, when I gaze out of the window, I remember I *don't* want to be Cathy when she's a miserable ghost, begging to be let in, hoping for Heathcliff and getting Lockwood instead, who rubs her wrist to and fro on the broken window-pane until her blood soaks the bedclothes.

After twenty years, Cathy does get her heart's desire. Heathcliff dies and they're reunited and their love transcends law and society and pettiness and muddle. But somehow this doesn't exhilarate me like it used to. In *The Tenant of Wildfell Hall*, Helen tells Gilbert they can have a spiritual union, love after death, too. But as she says, 'We shall meet in heaven,' she looks so mad – 'her eyes glittered wildly, and her face was deadly pale' – that it's clear that Anne thinks it is a very bad idea. And Gilbert says it's 'little consolation to think I shall next behold you as a disembodied spirit, or an altered being, with a frame perfect and glorious, but not like this!' He agrees that they can't be together, because she's married to someone else, but even as he tries to leave, he can't help himself. 'I held her to my heart,' he says, 'and we seemed to grow together in a close embrace from which no physical or mental force could rend us.' As for Helen, while she tells him to go, at the same time, he says, 'she held me so fast that, without violence, I could not have obeyed her'. The hug says it all; spiritual love after death is nothing like being in each other's arms, striving and messy, real and alive.

As a teenager when I read Cathy calling her body 'this shattered prison' and longing 'to escape into that glorious world, and to be always there, not seeing it through tears, not yearning for it through the walls of an aching heart', I sympathised with her feeling that her body was a prison. I longed to get free of my newly complicated, newly clunky body too. But now I'm not so sure. Cathy only escapes her body by dying. Now, I shrink from the idea of Cathy and Heathcliff soaring free of the dungeon that is human life. I don't want freedom that only comes after death – and not even straight after death: Cathy has to wait for Heathcliff to die too, and in the meantime, she shivers and screams on the moors and bangs at the windows of her childhood home. After all this, her happy ending doesn't feel empowering, but escapist. It also feels like a throwback to Angria where death is not the end and romance continues beyond the grave. And doesn't Heathcliff sound like one of Angria's 'tall, strong muscular men going about seeking whom they may devour'? My boyfriend is five foot ten on a good day, and built like a pipe cleaner, but at least he's real.

I'm starting to question whether Emily was really more free than Anne. I've been feeling sad that when Anne grew up, she left behind Gondal's wide-open spaces and emancipated heroines for domestic interiors and heroines trapped by jobs (Agnes), men (Helen) and repression (both). I believed Charlotte when she said, in a preface to Emily's poems she wrote after her sister's death, 'Liberty was the breath of Emily's nostrils; without it, she perished.' But was Emily really so committed to liberty? Charlotte was trying to explain why Emily only managed three months at Roe Head in 1835. Charlotte had come back from the school and she had been teaching her sisters at home for three years. But then Roe Head's headmistress, Margaret Wooler, made her an offer the Brontës couldn't afford to refuse: Wooler wanted Charlotte to come back to the school as a teacher, and while the pay would be negligible, she would throw in an education for Emily. So at seventeen, Emily set off. But, said Charlotte, 'her health was quickly broken: her white face, attenuated form, and failing strength threatened rapid decline'. Certain that 'she would die if she did not go home', Charlotte sent Emily back to Haworth. For good.

It set a pattern. Emily always found it hard to leave home. She couldn't stick at the only job she ever got, as a teacher in Halifax. When, in 1841, aged twenty-three, she went to Brussels with Charlotte to study French, she was miserable. Eventually she happily settled into doing the housekeeping, becoming, said Charlotte, 'something of a recluse'. Gaskell said while Anne was *shy*, Emily was *reserved*; Anne fought her shyness to speak out, but Emily exerted an iron control over her own voice. She had, said Nussey, 'a strength of self-containment seen in no other – She was in the strictest sense a law unto herself, and a heroine in keeping to her law.' None of this feels, to me, like Emily was breathing liberty; in fact, Emily's life, bound to her own hearth, feels very *un*free.

In 'The Caged Bird', a poem Emily wrote in 1841, she identifies with a hawk she rescued from an abandoned nest on the moors who is 'like myself lone, wholly lone' and longs for 'Earth's breezy hills and heaven's blue sea', and for 'liberty'. She wants to free him, but ends with a dodge:

> But let me think that if today
> It pines in cold captivity,
> Tomorrow both shall soar away,
> Eternally, entirely free.

It might sound liberating but they *won't* soar away tomorrow. Emily can't free the hawk because she's tamed him and he wouldn't survive in the wild. Empathising with the hawk's unhappiness doesn't help the hawk, and it doesn't help her either, because she feels flightless and trapped, and wishes the hawk could soar so she could feel some kind of release. Two days after writing this stanza Emily was still worrying about liberty and wrote her famous poem about her 'chainless soul'. But even that contains a prayer to 'Leave the heart that now I bear / And give me liberty'. Her soul isn't chainless; her heart is weighing her down. And the chains aren't real like the hawk's cage; they are inside her. She has made them herself.

Anne wrote a poem that is almost a companion piece to 'The Caged Bird'. 'The Captive Dove' is also about a bird who moans because it can't fly. But Anne says the dove's sadness comes not from captivity but from solitude; 'The heart that nature formed to love / Must pine neglected and alone.' Emily disagreed. She *prized* solitude. To discourage conversation, she'd prop up a book on the kitchen table to read while she kneaded bread, or she'd bang away at the piano, or she'd snub anyone who tried to talk to her. At nineteen, she wrote, 'I'm happiest when most away / I can bear my soul from its home of clay.' She didn't just want to run away from people, but to shed her flesh to become 'only spirit wandering wide'. This untitled poem is euphoric but unnervingly incorporeal. While I always loved the way, in another of Emily's odes to liberty, the wind sends 'Man's spirit away from its drear dungeon soaring, / Bursting the fetters and breaking the bars', now I wonder if it's enough for just the spirit to be free. It might not be enough to achieve mental freedom on your own, locked in your cage. You might, at the very least, have to find someone to talk to, like Anne's dove.

Or you might have to smash your way out, like Helen does in *The Tenant of Wildfell Hall*. Helen chases freedom from the beginning of her story, where she chafes against the 'constraint and formality' of life with her uncle and aunt. Her aunt advises her to 'Keep a guard over your eyes and ears' and to think of her heart as a 'citadel' she has to defend from men who want to 'besiege' it, but Helen wants to open up to love. She falls for Huntingdon because he frees her from another suitor, the aptly named (dull) Boarham. Helen can't wait to share Huntingdon's 'graceful ease and freedom'. But soon he becomes her 'reigning tyrant', and his bad behaviour pushes her into a role she never wanted as his 'angel monitress'. As an endearment, this is ugly, but it gets worse; he calls her his 'pretty tyrant', then his 'little exorbitant tyrant'. Having dreamed of enjoying his society 'without restraint', she now has to restrain herself, and feels, she says, that 'my thoughts and feelings are gloomily cloistered within my own mind'. Huntingdon says she's 'made his fireside as comfortless as a convent cell' and he's not wrong; she's forgotten how to have fun, and they're both in the cell together. Then he *actually* imprisons her. He seizes the keys to her desk, cabinet and drawers, and confiscates her cash and her jewellery. She realises she is literally 'a slave, a prisoner'. There's no point, now, looking for mental freedom. She has to physically get free. She has to leave him. She has to run away to Wildfell Hall where despite 'the bleak wind moaning round me and howling through the ruinous old chambers' she makes a corner of the house 'snug' and 'cheerful', makes art, brings up her son and finds new love.

In *Wuthering Heights*, Emily wrote about a heroine who got trapped in a miserable marriage too, but Cathy only ends up that way because she thinks that marrying Heathcliff will be degrading, because he isn't a gentleman. Far from being free, she's internalised the chains society uses to bind her – the snobbery, the status anxiety – and that's why she is unhappy. And although this is a novel where women *can* leave their husbands (Isabella manages to leave Heathcliff), Cathy doesn't go. She stays inside her cage and, like the hawk, Emily doesn't free her. Maybe she thought freeing her spirit was enough.

Anne wanted to free Helen for real, from a plight she made as realistic as she could because she didn't want her novel to be dismissed. She might have learned that lesson from reading *Maria, or the Wrongs of Woman*. Mary Wollstonecraft's 1798 novel is also about a woman trapped in a bad marriage. Wollstonecraft wrote it after her polemic *A Vindication of the Rights of Woman*, and it tackles many of the same themes. Her heroine marries a cruel libertine who takes away their daughter and has her locked up in a mental asylum, a 'gloomy receptacle of disjointed souls'. In this unlikely place, Maria's consciousness is raised. She starts asking, 'Was not the world a vast prison and women born slaves?' She realises 'marriage had bastilled me for life' and that like the prisoners of 1789, she needs a revolution to set her free. The law won't help because the laws back up men.

When Wollstonecraft died of puerperal fever after giving birth to Mary Shelley, she left behind more than one ending to *Maria*. In my favourite, Maria befriends a female warder, a working-class woman who has been abused, beaten, raped and prostituted by men. They get free and form a new, renegade family unit, bringing up Maria's daughter together. It's intoxicating. But it's also implausible. The whole novel is so far-fetched that it allows readers to think that what happens to Maria could never happen in real life, to finish the book with their opinions and prejudices intact.

Anne doesn't let her reader off the hook. In *The Tenant of Wildfell Hall*, Huntingdon doesn't need to lock up his wife because he has absolute power over her already. Wollstonecraft's heroine is imprisoned by her husband; Anne's heroine finds out that since the law gives men power over their wives, marriage is *itself* a prison, where she is nearly driven mad. When Huntingdon takes the keys, he is only showing Helen the power he's always had. The novel's relentless realism means that no one can read it and say it could never happen.

For some readers, *The Tenant of Wildfell Hall* is so realistic that it can show them exactly what to do. A few weeks after my visit to Ponden Hall, an activist I know, who campaigns against violence against women and girls, sends me an article from the *Sydney Morning Herald*. It's by a Christian woman whose husband dragged her around by her hair, punched her and tried to brainwash her by highlighting passages of the Bible about how wives should submit to their husbands. He censored her reading, too, but he couldn't see the harm in *The Tenant of Wildfell Hall*. It was just a Victorian novel; how dangerous could it be? As his wife read it, she felt like she was reading her own story. She thought that if a clergyman's daughter could write a novel where a woman left a bad man like that, why should she stay with one 150 years later? It gave her the strength to get away from the abuse, to walk out of the story written for her and write her own. *The Tenant of Wildfell Hall* feels liberating because for some readers it actually is.

And for all its commitment to cold, hard truth, *The Tenant of Wildfell Hall* puts a high value on imagination. Huntingdon's flaw is that he has no empathy. 'Just imagine yourself in my place,' Helen says to him, warning him that if he isn't nicer to her, she'll stop loving him. His feeble response is, 'It is a woman's nature to be constant – to love one and one only, blindly, tenderly, and for ever – bless them, dear creatures!' His assumptions are as tired as his language. Unable to imagine anyone changing, he can't change himself. So he is doomed to drink himself to death, while Helen is able to imagine her way into a new life. For Anne, imagination was a route to change in the real world.

But Emily didn't feel the same way, and as they got older, a rift opened up between them. Anne wrote in 'Self-Communion' that once they had been 'trees that at the root were one' but now they were 'sundered'. Emily clung to imagination as an evasion of real life, a refusal. At twenty-six, in her poem 'To Imagination', she rejected 'the world without' as 'hopeless', and pledged allegiance to 'the world within'. Anne often thought the world was a mess but she always had hope, always thought change was possible. She didn't want to live in Emily's supernatural 'world within', warmed by the heat of 'suns that know no winter days' – and she didn't want to live in Gondal either. A few months after this poem was written, Anne and Emily went on holiday together to York, and they clashed. Anne wanted to see the sights but Emily just wanted to play Gondal. In Anne's 1841 diary paper, she asked, 'How will it be when we open this paper? I wonder whether the Gondalians will still be flourishing.' When the day came to open the paper, as usual, four years later, in 1845, the sisters gave different answers. Emily's was a triumphant yes: 'The Gondals still flourish bright as ever.' But Anne wrote wearily, 'The Gondals are at present in a sad state . . . The Gondals in general are not in first rate playing condition – will they improve?' For her, they never did. She outgrew them.

There's an echo of Anne's journey in Antonia Forest's 1961 novel *Peter's Room*, which is practically Gondal fan fiction. Five snowed-in children play at Gondal until things go wrong, and in the wake of a gun appearing and a window shattering, one child says, 'I think the whole thing's quite mad. And I think those Brontës . . . must have been absolutely mental, still doing it when they were thirty, nearly!' Anne felt the same way. She saw Emily retreat further and further into fantasy until she gave up on reality. In one of Emily's last poems, which she wrote in 1846 and revised in the last year of her life, she asks,

> Why ask to know the date – the clime?
> More than mere words they cannot be;
> Men knelt to God and worshipped crime,
> And crushed the helpless . . .

Emily doesn't bother specifying where and when she is writing about because she thinks people are cruel and hypocritical everywhere and always. It's unsettlingly nihilistic.

Emily had always seen life as a power struggle. Nussey remembered how, on the moors one day, 'Emily, half reclining on a slab of stone, played like a young child with the tadpoles in the water, making them swim about, and then fell to moralising on the strong and the weak, the brave and the cowardly, as she chased them with her hand.' In an 1839 Gondal poem she asked herself, 'Do I despise the timid deer / Because his limbs are fleet with fear?' She decides she does not, but it's clear that while she doesn't *hate* the deer, she is aligning herself with the hunter.

Emily comes over as physically tough in another story, told by John Greenwood, the Haworth stationer who sold them the paper they wrote their novels on. He described how she saw her mastiff, Keeper, fighting another dog and

> rushed at once into the kitchen, took the pepper box, and away into the lane where she found the two savage brutes

each holding the other by the throat in deadly grip, while several other animals, who thought themselves men, were standing looking on like cowards as they were, afraid to touch them – there they stood gaping, watching this fragile creature spring upon the beasts – seizing Keeper round the neck with one arm, while with the other hand she dredges their noses with pepper, and separating them by force of her great will, driving Keeper, that great powerful dog, before her into the house, never once noticing the men, so called, standing there thunderstruck at the deed.

This story rings true, as does Gaskell's story about Emily being bitten by a rabid dog and, again, running into the kitchen, this time grabbing a hot iron off the stove and putting it to her arm to cauterise the wound.

But I don't believe the sadistic tale, discredited by most recent biographers, about Emily 'punishing' Keeper by punching him in the face. This story has been told again and again to back up theories about Emily's 'animalistic' nature, as Stassa Edwards put it in a recent piece for the online magazine *The Toast*, which prompted comments that Emily was a 'savage dog abuser', a 'scumbag', 'contemptible' and other less quotable epithets. In *Wuthering Heights*, the dogs have names like Thrasher, Wolf and Growler. Heathcliff hangs a dog, Hareton hangs a litter of puppies; Edgar and Isabella quarrel so violently over a dog that they nearly pull it apart, while their guard dog, Skulker, viciously clamps his jaws around Cathy's ankle, and has to be throttled by a servant to let go. The puppy Skulker later fathers is called Throttler.

Maybe these scenes of violence between animals and men made Gaskell believe that Emily would beat her dog. From Gaskell on, Anne and Emily are often contrasted, with Anne described as sweetly, meekly hyper-feminine, while Emily is characterised as brutishly male. (Is this what Victoria Moore meant when she wrote gnomically, 'Anne has become male with Emily's own maleness'? Who knows.) Constantin Heger, who was Emily's teacher in Brussels, said bluntly, 'she should have been a man'. Specifically he thought Emily should have been 'a great navigator', because of her logic, reason and tenacity. And in another of Greenwood's anecdotes, he doesn't know whether to praise Emily's womanly virtues or to admire her ability to shoot a gun. According to him, Patrick would call her for shooting practice and 'Let her be ever so busy in her domestic duties, whether in the kitchen baking bread, at which she had such a dainty hand, or at her ironing or studies, "wrapt in a world of her own creating"', she would drop it all and 'tripping like a fairy down to the bottom of the garden' she would take a shot, 'return to him the pistol, saying, "load again papa" and away she would go to the kitchen, roll another shelf-ful of teacakes, then wiping her hands, she would return again to the garden'. It's unintentionally ludicrous, and this tractable girl does not sound much like the woman who wrote 'I'll walk where my own nature would be leading / It vexes me to choose another guide'. Charlotte found Emily less amenable, griping to her editor, W. S. Williams, that she took some handling: 'It is best usually to leave her to form her own judgment, and especially not to advocate the side you wish her to favour; if you do, she is sure to lean in the opposite direction, and ten to one will argue herself into non-compliance.' When Emily was in Brussels and the other students teased her about her clothes, she retorted, 'I wish to be as God made me.'

But in other stories, Emily is gentle, especially to animals. It's been bothering me that Heathcliff hangs Isabella's spaniel, Fanny, especially because Anne had a spaniel too, with a similar name. Flossy was an eager-eyed, silky-haired black-and-white spaniel, who liked her comfort and, Anne said affectionately, 'relished a sheep hunt'. I don't like the idea of Emily killing her off in fiction. But when I go back to *Wuthering Heights* again, I find that Emily doesn't let Fanny die. Nelly releases her from Heathcliff's noose, and when Isabella reclaims her, Fanny 'yelp[s] wild with joy at recovering her mistress'. This sounds more like the Emily who Nussey remembered 'kneeling on the hearth, reading a book, with her arm round Keeper', and who, along with Anne, gave the dogs their leftover porridge every morning. It also sounds more like the woman who, writing her diary paper alone in 1841, ended by 'sending from far an exhortation of courage! to exiled and harassed Anne wishing she was here.'

After Robert Heaton's death, the library at Ponden Hall was auctioned off in Keighley. The books that didn't sell were torn up and used to wrap vegetables. A Shakespeare First Folio just disappeared. During my visit, I ran my hands along the bookshelves in the library, feeling woebegone. Julie Akhurst emails me a list of the books the library once contained, listed by subject, from Agriculture to Science, all gone now. There is one called *Fun for Every Day in the Year*, and without it, how do I know what fun I should be having today? What knowledge was lost when *Simple Minstrelsy* and *Gypsum as a Manure* were sold? I wonder how many of these books Anne read, how many shaped her, and where they are now.

Then I hear mutterings about a First Folio that turned up in Yorkshire in the 1930s. It was given to the Craven Museum in Skipton by Ann Wilkinson, whose brother was a mill owner and the tobacco baron behind the outrageously named blend Skipton Shag. No one knows where she got it. Could it have come from Ponden Hall?

I go to see for myself. Craven Museum is a riot of curios – a hippo's skull, all yellow snarling teeth, jostles for space with an Iron Age quern, vicious cockfighting spurs and a St Luke's Gospel, made for soldiers in the First World War, with 'PLEASE CARRY THIS IN YOUR POCKET AND READ IT EVERY DAY' on the front. Next to it is the piece of shrapnel the book stopped. Private H. Fell was serving in Salonika with the 7th South Wales Borderers when a shell exploded. The gospel saved his life. I think about him as I find the First Folio. The curators have given it the star treatment, in a purpose-built room, with an audio-visual display voiced fruitily by Sir Patrick Stewart. I get excited when I read that it is incomplete. The opening pages are missing – the very pages where a Heaton might have pasted in a Ponden Hall bookplate! Maybe Anne encountered Shakespeare through these pages, and maybe there is more than one way a book can save a life.

Ponden Hall's lost books make me wonder again about what became of the lost Gondal prose. Perhaps Charlotte burned it. She came to fear 'the fiery imagination that at times eats me up'. She started calling Angria her 'opium', a 'web' she'd got stuck in, a 'burning clime where we have sojourned too long'. In 1839, she wrote a formal 'Farewell to Angria'. She assumed her sisters did the same with Gondal, and that the only person still playing in their childhood worlds was their unredeemed fantasist of a brother. So she might have felt betrayed, if, after she lost her sisters (Emily in 1848, and Anne just five months later in 1849), she found a pile of Gondal manuscripts. She has foxed scholars with the way she introduced the posthumous edition of her sisters' poetry, saying,

> It would not have been difficult to compile a volume out of the papers left by my sisters, had I, in making the selection, dismissed from my consideration the scruples and wishes of those whose written thoughts these papers held. But this was impossible . . . I have, then, culled from the mass only a little poem here and there.

What does Charlotte mean by 'culled'? Does she mean she *destroyed* 'only a little poem here and there'? Or does she mean she has only *selected* a few poems to publish? If so, what happened to the rest? Does 'the mass' mean just the Gondal poems, or also the prose? And is she right about Anne and Emily's 'scruples and wishes' or is this a smokescreen to cover the fact that she's been destroying their work? Charlotte was right to worry about what people would think of the Angria and Gondal writing. Gaskell, the first person outside the family to read any of it, called it 'creative power carried to the verge of insanity'. When Charlotte said, of Emily, 'Having formed these beings, she did not know what she had done', she made Emily sound like an innocent in the grip of an immoral creativity that took her by force and had its way with her. Maybe she just wanted to reassert some control.

But I don't think Charlotte destroyed the Gondal prose. I think Emily burned her own prose to protect her privacy, and I think Anne burned hers, and I don't know why until I find myself at an exhibition at Tate Modern in London. I read that Agnes Martin, the twentieth-century queen of geometric abstraction, often destroyed paintings that didn't pass muster. She shredded the canvases with a box cutter, or threw them off the mesa in New Mexico, where she lived. When she was dying, at ninety-two, she asked her dealer to destroy two paintings for her. He thought they were perfect and magnificent but he did it because he trusted Martin. Maybe I should trust Anne more too. Maybe she knew what she didn't need to hang on to, and put everything she didn't want preserved in the fire. And maybe, watching the flames, she felt free. Because it can be liberating to break the ties that bind you to the past.

5

CHARLOTTE
or how (not) to be a sister

I am weighing a brooch of Charlotte's in my hand. I've asked the Parsonage to bring it out of their archive so I can have a good look. It's ornate, heavy and Victorian, a brooch to wear on your chest like a battleship wears a figurehead on its prow, to make you feel safe, and to ward off evil forces – possibly by being so very ugly. The brooch is all curlicues, except for the oval at its centre, which is made of Anne's hair, plaited, glassed over, and edged with copper, which has stained some of the hair green. The rest could be dirty blonde or light reddish brown and to my frustration I can't quite tell. I had hoped to adjudicate between Nussey, who said Anne's hair was 'a very pretty light brown', and Juliet Barker, who looked at other locks of Anne's hair and said Nussey had remembered it wrong, and Anne's hair was darker. One reviewer of Barker's biography described his 'slight depression' at this minor controversy, and I know what he means, but I also hate that I can't say for sure if she was a blonde or a brunette. Surely, with around fifty locks of Brontë hair in various archives around the world, many of them Anne's, it should be possible to decide once and for all. Anne's hair has even been put under a microscope by archaeological scientists, who established that she probably had a balanced diet, but didn't say anything about the (to me) more crucial issue. I realise with embarrassment that I want Anne to be a brunette because I am one, and then I wonder if Helen's dark hair in *The Tenant of Wildfell Hall* makes it more or less likely. I wonder when the hair in the brooch was cut. It was probably soon after Anne died, and then it might have been posted to a hairworker to make mourning jewellery, which was the only kind of jewellery you could wear after losing someone. The hair would be boiled, to clean it, and then weights would have been attached to the strands, and it would be woven into shape. Or, Charlotte might have bought a mass-produced brooch and done the boiling and weighting and weaving herself, because hair jewellers were forever mixing up hair, or replacing tricky hair with hair that was easier to handle, or even with horse hair. When I think that this hair might not even be Anne's, *I* feel slightly depressed.

It almost feels too intimate to be holding this brooch, imagining Charlotte pinning it on and remembering taking a pair of scissors to her dead sister's hair. Did she wear it always? Did she clutch it at tough times like Helen in *The Tenant of Wildfell Hall*, who only takes one valuable thing with her when she leaves her husband, a gold watch with a hair chain (Anne doesn't say whose hair), which she nervously entwines in her fingers for protection, for comfort, for luck? I put down the brooch. It is too heavy with grief. Part of what I've always loved about the Brontës is that they were sisters. As a girl, I wished I had a sister, to share clothes with, to sing into hairbrushes with, to talk boys with. My little brother was no help with my crushes or my wardrobe crises. I read the Brontës as a story of sisterly solidarity. Gaskell, who also longed for sisters, did the same. She wrote that 'the affection among all three was stronger than either death or life' and even described 'the one heart of the three sisters', which makes them sound less lovingly connected than alarmingly conjoined. Gaskell found writing the *Life* such an immersion in sisterly love that it spurred her into reconnecting with the stepsister she had been estranged from for twenty-five years.

Everything I have requested from the archive for the day is in a large box. I slip the brooch back into its packet and pull out one of Charlotte's tiny books. It's her first surviving work, just 64mm by 42mm. She made it for Anne in January 1828, the month Anne turned eight, sewing the cover together out of scraps of grey and blue spotted and flowered wallpaper. 'There was once a little girl,' it begins, 'and her name was Ane.' Apart from a dark moment where Anne's mother gets seasick and Anne has to look after her, the story is tender and joyous. Anne goes on adventures to the castle and the sea, and Charlotte illustrates it all, in minute drawings: a castle with a jaunty pennant, a jolly rowing boat and sailing ship. I want to try to understand how Anne and Charlotte's relationship changed, what happened between the book and the brooch.

Six years later, when Anne was fourteen, Charlotte (who was eighteen, and old enough to be nicer) wrote a cruel little story in the voice of one Wiggins. He's a caricature of Branwell, so some people think Branwell said the things he said. But it was Charlotte who wrote the story where Wiggins sounds off about his sisters. He calls Charlotte 'a broad dumpy thing', and Emily 'lean and scant, with a face about the size of a penny'. And when he comes to the youngest, he says, 'Anne is nothing, absolutely nothing.' He doesn't just dismiss her looks; he dismisses her entirely. 'What! Is she an idiot?' he is asked. 'Next door to it,' says Wiggins. How did Anne feel when she read this? And did she worry about it when, a year later, she was sent off to study at Roe Head, where Charlotte would be one of her teachers?

It was October 1835. Back in June, Patrick had told a friend that he wanted to keep 'dear little Anne' at home another year, but Charlotte was only teaching at Roe Head because it would allow her to educate one of her sisters, and as Emily couldn't cope, Anne had to go in her place. Anne must have been anxious. Maria and Elizabeth had gone to school and had returned to die. Emily had just come back from school a shadow of her former self. Maybe Anne felt, as May Sinclair ominously put it, like 'the last victim'. But Anne also knew she had to get an education; she would have to earn a living one day. And maybe she hoped Charlotte would show her the ropes.

But Charlotte was finding being the big sister a heavy responsibility. After all, she'd started in the middle, with Maria taking the role of second mother to the little ones, while Elizabeth was slated to be the family housekeeper. Now Charlotte had to look after her younger siblings. She'd already had to teach her younger sisters at home, and then taken a job with little pay so that she could get an education for Emily. Three months into that education, she'd had Emily sent home. And now she would have to look after Anne. But

Charlotte was slower to help her youngest sister, and their time together at Roe Head set up a pattern of guilt and self-justification that continued their whole lives, and into Anne's afterlife too. For Anne, Roe Head was a crash course in the dark side of sisterhood.

It's striking that while the Brontës are so famous for being sisters, few of their heroines have sisters; neither Jane Eyre nor Caroline Helstone, Shirley Keeldar nor Lucy Snowe. Certainly not Cathy Earnshaw. As for Anne's heroines, Helen has a brother. But Agnes has a sister, and their relationship reveals a lot about how Anne felt about Charlotte.

Mary is five years older than Agnes (Charlotte was four years older than Anne). Like the Brontës, the Greys have lost siblings and Mary and Agnes are the only two who have 'survived the perils of infancy'. Agnes chafes at being 'always regarded as *the* child, and the pet of the family', sheltered and protected till she's 'too helpless and dependent – too unfit for buffeting with the cares and turmoils of life'. Trying to help with the housework, she is told to play with her kitten, for 'it was time enough for me to sit bending over my work, like a grave matron, when my favourite little pussy was become a steady old cat'. When she says she'd like to be a governess, her parents laugh, but it's her sister who is most scornful. 'What can you be dreaming of?' she scoffs. 'Only think, what would you do in a house full of strangers, without me or mamma to speak and act for you . . . You would not even know what clothes to put on.' The more I read Charlotte on Anne, the more I can see where this bossy voice comes from.

As Anne arrived at Roe Head, I wonder if Charlotte hoped that her little sister would be like Mary Rivers in *Jane Eyre*, who proves 'a docile, intelligent, assiduous pupil'. Mary is apparently based on Anne and she is 'reserved . . . gentle . . . distant', while Diana (who most scholars believe was based on Emily) is tall, strong-willed, 'handsome', 'vigorous', with 'animal spirits'. But really they are a dull pair, clever, pious and 'so similar' that Jane can barely tell them apart. They operate as a unit, like Gaskell's heart-sharers, never really thinking for themselves. They are, maybe, the sisters Charlotte wished she had; like the sisters in Christina Rossetti's 1859 poem 'Goblin Market' who are 'Like two pigeons in one nest', 'Like two blossoms on one stem.'

Charlotte was more honest in *Shirley*. Rose and Jessy Yorke are complicated and real. She writes about how

Rose was quite accustomed to be admonished by that small hand. Her will daily bent itself to that of the impetuous little Jessy. She was guided, overruled by Jessy in a thousand things. On all occasions of show and pleasure Jessy took the lead, and Rose fell quietly into the background; whereas, when the disagreeables of life – its work and privations – were in question, Rose instinctively took upon her, in addition to her own share, what she could of her sister's. Jessy had already settled it in her mind that she, when she was old enough, was to be married; Rose, she decided, must be an old maid, to live with her, look after her children, keep her house. This state of things is not uncommon between two sisters, where one is plain and the other pretty.

Did Charlotte, who drew and painted Anne over and over again when they were children, feel anxious that she might be doomed to keep house for her pretty sister? In *Shirley*, Charlotte steps out of the narrative to fling us forward several years, to describe Jessy dying 'tranquil and happy in Rose's guardian arms', and Rose emigrating, just like Mary Taylor did. Rose wants to 'see the outside of our own round planet', and tells Caroline flatly, 'I am resolved that my life shall be a life. Not a black trance like the toad's, buried in marble; nor a long, slow death like yours.' Did Charlotte feel that in order to free Rose from the pressure to be good, she had to kill off her sister Jessy?

I'm thinking about this as I arrive at Roe Head School. It is in Mirfield, only fourteen miles from Haworth, but even now it feels further. There is no direct route, and you have to scoot around Bradford to get there. The steep hills are nearly the death of my boyfriend's twenty-year-old Citroën, and after we get back to Haworth, we have to find a garage to replace a section of the ruptured exhaust.

Out on the busy main road, I recognise the school from two nearly identical drawings Charlotte and Anne made; drawing the building must have been on the curriculum. Set up high, it's a three-storey grey-stone house, with bow windows looking out over Dewsbury and the Calder Valley. A plaque says all three sisters went there, and I'm pathetically glad to find Anne hasn't been excluded. Anne later became passionate about education, so I think she'd love the fact that Roe Head is a school again now; a thriving special needs school with the mantra 'quality of life, for life', rated outstanding by Ofsted for their work with children with multiple disabilities, and admired for their creative approach to helping children communicate – another thing Anne might have appreciated, especially if she did already have asthma, or perhaps a different trouble with speaking. Later, when Anne got her first job as a governess, Charlotte wrote to Nussey that 'it is only the talking part that I fear. But I do seriously apprehend that [her employer] will sometimes conclude that she has a natural impediment in her speech.' Maybe Anne stuttered. In 1848, she apologised for writing Nussey 'a shabby little note' because, she said, 'you must know there is a lamentable deficiency in my organ of language which makes me almost as bad a hand at writing as talking unless I have something particular to say'. Perhaps Anne could talk but didn't – unless she had something to say. All her letters to Nussey were short. In 1847 she only semi-apologised for writing on 'such a tiny sheet of paper . . . having none more suitable at hand; but perhaps it will contain as much as you need wish to read or I to write, for I find I have nothing more to say'. Anne was always concise. And very shy. Certainly, she had trouble speaking her mind while at Roe Head.

It was a school run by sisters. The headmistress, Margaret Wooler, was the oldest, in her forties, dressed like an abbess; super-dignified and imposing, in embroidered white dresses with her long hair plaited in a coronet. She would become Charlotte's friend, and Anne's too. She would be one of the few mourners at Anne's funeral, and she would give Charlotte away at her wedding. She pops up in *Jane Eyre* as Miss Temple, who feeds Jane seed cake and trusts her, and later gives her a job. Wooler was a good and pragmatic teacher. When the girls convinced themselves that a lady ghost walked the unused third floor, her silk dress rustling as she trailed the floorboards, Wooler cured their fears by sending them upstairs after dark. 'No ghost made herself visible even to the frightened imaginations of the foolish and the timid,' said Nussey, and so 'the whitened face of apprehension soon disappeared, nerves were braced, and a general laugh soon set us all right again'. When, on a school trip, the horse bolted, Wooler got the girls to pull the cart home themselves. She made sure they ate well, walked a lot, and played games on the lawns. She encouraged them to be curious too, telling stories about her experiences during the Luddite riots. Anne could see for herself how fast the world was changing. It was her first glimpse of the Industrial Revolution. There were mills and steelworks near the school and coal wagons rumbled past on the way to Huddersfield. There was also poverty and unrest.

Wooler and the four younger sisters who worked at the school were a model of a grown-up sisterly relationship for Anne and Charlotte; later, they would dream of setting up their own school together, or maybe even taking over the Woolers'. Charlotte once gushed to Miss Wooler about 'the value of sisters' affection to each other; there is nothing like it in the world, I believe, when they are nearly equal in age and similar in education, tastes and sentiments'. But in the same letter, she complained, 'I cannot persuade my sisters to regard the affair [of selling some railway shares] precisely from my point of view,' and said Emily was 'not quite so tractable and open to conviction as I could wish'. She reminded herself, 'I must remember that perfection is not the lot of humanity,' which sounds a little snide; do her sisters have to do what she wants to be perfect?

She added tetchily that 'those we love . . . vex us occasionally by what appear to us unreasonable and headstrong notions'.

The Woolers taught Italian, French and German, as well as the accomplishments (music and drawing), and English, maths, history and geography. The curriculum was based on Hester Chapone's 1773 *Letters on the Improvement of the Mind*. This peculiar book is framed as a series of letters Chapone wrote to her teenage niece, lecturing her on everything from how to study history (by reading Homer, Plutarch and 'do not forget my darling Shakespeare') to how to make and keep friends. Chapone had long had a reputation for being dull: in Richard Sheridan's 1775 play *The Rivals*, the flighty heroine Lydia Languish hears her principled aunt coming and orders her maid to 'hide these books. Quick, quick! – Fling *Peregrine Pickle* under the toilet – throw *Roderick Random* into the closet – put *The Innocent Adultery* into *The Whole Duty of Man* – thrust *Lord Aimworth* under the sofa – cram *Ovid* behind the bolster – there – put *The Man of Feeling* into your pocket' and, finally, with all the naughty books squirrelled away, sighs 'now lay *Mrs. Chapone* in sight'.

But Chapone also talks a lot of sense. Anne might have agreed that 'Virtue and happiness are not attained by chance . . . they must be sought with ardour'. And, never vain, she might have thought Chapone was right to rail against women who 'strive against nature to alter ourselves by ridiculous contortions of body, or by feigned sentiments and unnatural manners'. Chapone confirmed Anne's belief that she should 'honestly search into all the dark recesses of the heart'. Refreshingly, Chapone also advised her niece, 'do not be afraid of a single life', especially if the alternative is marrying for money, which she calls 'detestable prostitution'.

I doubt Charlotte enjoyed teaching from Chapone. Charlotte's whole oeuvre can be read as a rebuttal of Chapone's statement that 'It is plain, from experience, that the most passionate people can command themselves'. Passion is the word most overused about the Brontës. Recently a row divided the Brontë Society, and passions ran so high at one meeting that the society's president, writer Bonnie Greer, used her Jimmy Choo shoe as a makeshift gavel to keep order. Every single journalist who reported this said the passion was appropriate. I am not sure Anne would agree. At Roe Head, Anne kept her head down, worked hard, and won a good conduct prize. But Charlotte was wrung out by passion – and just as desperately by trying to control herself. Unable to get free and write, all she could do was hate. She hated teaching, which she called 'wretched bondage', and her pupils, who were 'dolts' and 'fat-headed oafs'. She wrote darkly, 'If those girls knew how I loathed their company they would not seek mine as they do.' Later, she poured her rage into *The Professor*. Her anti-hero William Crimsworth is unlikeable in many ways – he is snide, secretive, cold, disingenuous, snobby, priapic, petty – but it's his misogyny that really sticks in the craw. His pupils are all flirts and fools, entitled pretty girls. In *Agnes Grey*, Agnes doesn't get on with her pupil Rosalie, but she does try to help her make better decisions about who to marry, and how she might be happier. And in real life, Anne would stay in touch with her pupils, the Robinson sisters, and became their trusted confidante. Charlotte was amazed at the quantity of letters they wrote to Anne, and by how respectfully and affectionately they treated her. She couldn't fathom why a teacher would befriend her pupils. For Charlotte, pupils just got in the way.

And Anne was one of them. Maybe that's why Charlotte barely talked to her at Roe Head. Instead, she poured out her troubles in a barrage of letters to Nussey, wrote a bitter, despairing diary, and made up wild stories. Receiving a letter from Branwell, she said, 'I lived on its contents for days.' She felt more connected to him, back at the Parsonage, than to Anne, who was sharing a building with her – and maybe also a room, maybe even a bed. Perhaps Charlotte was trying to be professional, and not to treat her sister as a favourite. Perhaps she was frustrated that her salary didn't even cover the basics; they both still relied on cast-off clothes from their godmothers, and Charlotte had to ask her friends to pay postage on her letters. Charlotte resented sacrificing herself for Anne, but it was a sacrifice Anne had never asked for.

Roe Head could have been a chance for Charlotte and Anne to become friends. But instead, they were moving further apart. They weren't even sharing their writing. In her fevered diary Charlotte describes how once, when she was supervising her class, she dreamed up a new Angrian heroine, and felt that she was 'as clearly before me as Anne's quiet image, sitting at her lessons on the opposite side of the table'. To Charlotte, Anne seems unreal, just an 'image', compared to the intensely vivid woman inside her head.

In the same journal, Charlotte blurted out, 'I am just going to write because I cannot help it.' I've seen this line used as an inspirational quote on countless writing blogs, but when

Charlotte wrote it, she wasn't inspired; she was losing her grip, spellbound by her hero, the Duke of Zamorna, a 'spurred and fur-wrapped demi-god' who was *not* nice to women. One night she imagined him so vividly that she felt 'I was quite gone. I had really utterly forgot where I was . . . I felt myself breathing quick and short as I beheld the Duke lifting up his sable crest, which undulated.' Her erotic reverie was broken by a pupil asking what she was thinking about. But sometimes Charlotte found herself in a dream she couldn't wake from. Like when she conjured up a story about 'the tall man washing his bloody hands in a basin and the dark beauty standing by' – in Angria, all the men are tall and all the women are beautiful. She saw them 'with irksome and alarming distinctness'. She fell into a trance, and when some girls came in to get their curl-papers, they wondered if she was unconscious or asleep. It terrified her. 'I wanted to speak, to rise – it was impossible – I felt that this was a frightful predicament – that it would not do. The weight pressed me as if some huge enemy had flung itself across me. A horrid apprehension quickened every pulse I had.' She forced herself up, declaring, 'I have had enough of morbidly vivid realisations.' Charlotte was scared of what she called, in a letter to Nussey, 'the fiery imagination that at times eats me up and makes me feel society as it *is*, wretchedly insipid'. But she didn't stop, couldn't stop.

She wrote to the poet Robert Southey for advice. His reply has become infamous. He was unlucky enough to tell a woman who would become a more popular and enduring writer than him that 'Literature cannot be the business of a woman's life'. But he also said some useful things. He was right and astute to warn Charlotte that 'The day dreams in which you habitually indulge are likely to induce a distempered state of mind; and, in proportion as all the ordinary uses of the world seem to you flat and unprofitable, you will be unfitted for them without becoming fitted for anything else'. I don't want to be *too* nice to Southey. After all, he was a man who got his daughters to fill an entire room with 1,400 books they bound, by hand, in printed cotton cut from their old dresses. But it's too easy to cast him as a nineteenth-century Michael Winner saying *calm down, dear*, and to forget that his advice made Charlotte give up Angria, which was a good deci-sion not just for her writing but for her life.

Charlotte's two letters to Southey are fascinating because they are so straightforward. She told Southey she wanted fame, talked frankly about her guilt about writing and her fear that she was writing 'senseless trash', and admitted 'sometimes when I'm teaching or sewing I would rather be reading or writing; but I try to deny myself'. The words jump out: *I try to deny myself.* It's as if, as Lucasta Miller says, Charlotte isn't just trying to put down her pen but to stamp out her identity. She would go on to put denial at the centre of her writing. If courage is Anne's theme, Charlotte's is denial.

Anne did make friends with one girl at Roe Head but, devastat-ingly, Ann Cook died a year after leaving the school. Charlotte wrote, slightly stunned, and with some melodrama:

> Wherever I seek for her now in this world, she cannot be found no more than a flower or a leaf which withered twenty years ago. A bereavement of this kind gives one a

glimpse of the feeling those must have who have seen all drop round them, friend after friend, and are left to end their pilgrimage alone. But tears are fruitless, and I try not to repine.

While actually teaching Ann Cook, Charlotte had been less kind; she describes sitting with 'A Cook one side of me, E Lister on the other and Miss Wooler in the background. Stupidity the atmosphere, school-books the employment, asses the society'.

Despite making a friend, Anne was horribly homesick at Roe Head. She missed Emily. In her poem 'Alexandria and Zenobia', two characters with 'Hearts that have grown together' are devas-tated at being separated. Anne was almost certainly unable to afford postage, so all she could do was miss her sister on the page. 'Alexandria and Zenobia' was a Gondal poem. And another reason Anne and Charlotte were divided at Roe Head was because while Charlotte was in Angria, Anne was in Gondal; they were living in different worlds.

In *Agnes Grey*, when Agnes's sister sinks 'into a state of dejection' over the family's changed fortunes, Agnes wants to help her, but she can't because, she says, 'I was so fearful of being charged with childish frivolity, or stupid insensibility, that I carefully kept most of my bright ideas and cheering notions to myself.' Mary can't let go of her view of Agnes as childish, frivolous, stupid or insensible, the *little* sister, and it silences Agnes, makes her unable to reach out. At Roe Head, the more unhappy Anne became, the less she felt able to talk about it. A few months after writing 'Alexandria and Zenobia', she wrote another poem, 'A Voice from the Dungeon', about a woman who feels that she is 'buried' and 'done with life', all 'pining

woe and dull despair . . . solitude and gloom', with 'No hope,
no pleasure', not even intellectual satisfaction: 'I am grown
weary of my mind'. She can't sleep because she has bad dreams,
and when she has a good dream, about being reunited with her
son and her lover, it quickly turns to horror because she finds,

> . . . I could not speak;
> I uttered one long piercing shriek.
>
> Alas! Alas! That cursed scream
> Aroused me from my heavenly dream;
> I looked around in wild despair,
> I called them, but they were not there . . .

It's a roaring howl of homesickness, loneliness and the terror
of having no one to tell. Today Anne's misery, helplessness,
hopelessness and her inability to enjoy life, to make decisions
or to do anything to make herself feel better, would probably
be diagnosed as depression.

Anne had spells of listlessness and despair throughout her
life, and in *Agnes Grey*, she wrote about a similar dark time
where Agnes, like Anne at Roe Head, is away from home,
with people who don't care about her, and learns to be 'a
close and resolute dissembler'. Instead of confiding in real
people around her, or even in letters, she pours out her heart
to God, writing that 'My prayers, my tears, my wishes, fears,
and lamentations, were witnessed by myself and heaven alone'.
She also finds another confidante who, like God, won't
talk back or betray her: the page. As Agnes describes how she

finds comfort in writing, she sets out a working theory of confessional poetry:

> When we are harassed by sorrows or anxieties, or long oppressed by any powerful feelings which we must keep to ourselves, for which we can obtain and seek no sympathy from any living creature, and which yet we cannot, or will not wholly crush, we often naturally seek relief in poetry – and often find it, too.

Writing enables her 'to unburden the oppressed and swollen heart', making poems she calls

> relics of past sufferings and experience, like pillars of witness set up in travelling through the vale of life, to mark particular occurrences. The footsteps are obliterated now; the face of the country may be changed; but the pillar is still there.

Reading Anne's poems can feel like being let in on secrets. She takes the reader into her most intimate thoughts and feelings. She makes us the priest in the confessional. She speaks honestly and shamelessly about what people usually keep hidden.

At Roe Head, Charlotte was turning inwards too. She was plagued by the nihilistic fear that she wasn't real; she felt like she was in 'a continual waking Nightmare', no better than 'a stalking ghost'. It wasn't just the teaching. She was also worrying about her 'evil wandering thoughts' and her 'corrupt heart', and turning Nussey, who wore her piety on her sleeve, into a saint whose virtue made her feel bad. 'I am not good enough for you, and you must be kept from the contamination,' she said. She felt 'smitten at times to the heart with the conviction that your Ghastly Calvinistic doctrines are true' – that she wasn't one of the elect, and was headed for hell. She knows these doctrines are ghastly (so ghastly she's capitalised the word) but she can't help getting drawn in. 'I abhor myself,' she writes, 'I despise myself – if the Doctrine of Calvin be true I am already an outcast.' She didn't even notice when Anne fell ill.

It's impossible to say exactly what Anne's illness was. In Edward Chitham's 1991 biography, he suggests that it was 'a psychic crisis during which Anne subconsciously understood her feminine role as producer of children, and was both attracted and paralysed by it'. His evidence is that Anne's Gondal heroine in 'A Voice from the Dungeon' has a son, a 'darling boy', and that Anne made, he says, 'several' drawings of babies' heads in 1837. Actually, she made three. She also drew an oak, an elm and some wooded landscapes, but no one has suggested she was having a psychic crisis about trees. I find it a little upsetting to see a sixteen-year-old's near-fatal illness reduced to girlish hysteria. Because whatever Anne had, it nearly killed her. The Reverend James La Trobe, who visited her while she was ill, said she had severe gastric fever and 'her life hung on a slender thread'.

La Trobe wasn't a Church of England clergyman but a Moravian, a dissenter. It was bold of Anne to ask for him. She must have wanted help from someone who wouldn't patronise her or fob her off. She thought she was dying, she thought she might be going to hell, and she wanted to face her fears and find out the truth. La Trobe said she soon got over her shyness and that as they talked frankly, 'her heart opened to the sweet views of salvation, pardon and peace'. Maybe Anne asked for a Moravian because she was feeling the same Calvinist terrors as Charlotte and she knew the Moravians believed what she would come to believe herself, that anyone could be saved. Maybe Anne knew that on his deathbed Samuel Johnson had asked for a Moravian minister (La Trobe's uncle, in fact) to talk salvation. Maybe she'd just heard La Trobe was a good person to talk to. He was. And he listened to her, which no one else was doing.

When Charlotte belatedly realised how ill Anne was, she lashed out at Wooler, accusing her of what she felt guilty of herself: neglecting Anne. She took Anne home, and that was it for Anne's education. It was cut short, after two years and three months. What happened between the sisters at Roe Head repeated itself again and again over the years. Anne, like Agnes, grew 'accustomed . . . to keeping silence . . . to wearing a placid smiling countenance when my heart was bitter within me'. When she was miserable, she knew, again like Agnes, that she 'must restrain and swallow back my feelings . . . go down with a calm face, and smile, and laugh, and talk nonsense – yes, and eat too, if possible'. Meanwhile, barred from Anne's real feelings, Charlotte misunderstood, patronised and underestimated her; for Charlotte, Anne was always a 'Poor child!' She tried to protect Anne but she never really trusted her. 'I hope she speaks absolute truth,' she commented doubtfully on a letter Anne wrote to her in 1841.

*

From Charlotte, Anne learned to guard her privacy, because if she did speak, she would be misinterpreted. She learned to protect her own writing. She learned to be competitive; the Brontës' entire oeuvre wouldn't exist if it weren't for their sibling rivalry, and Anne's and Charlotte's novels speak to each other and rewrite each other most fiercely. Anne learned to look for allies outside her family. She learned that other women wouldn't necessarily be her cheerleaders. But she also became *too* private. She kept everything to herself and this had a huge impact on what happened to her work after she died. If Anne had predicted that her legacy would be so trampled and confused, she would surely have done more to protect it. She might have begun by making sure her work didn't end up in Charlotte's hands.

When Charlotte sorted through Anne's papers after her death, she was surprised by the unpublished poems. 'I own to me they seem sad,' she wrote to her publishers, who were bringing out a posthumous edition of Anne's and Emily's work, 'as if her whole innocent life had been passed under the martyrdom of an unconfessed physical pain.' The word 'unconfessed' is telling; she wants to be Anne's confessor, her confidante, but instead she has to turn detective, finding 'mournful evidence' about her true feelings. When Charlotte says Anne was 'reserved even with her nearest of kin' she sounds gutted. She's been shut out. Charlotte was wrestling with these feelings, as well as her grief, when she had to decide what to do with the work Anne left behind. *Agnes Grey* had done respectably, but *The Tenant of Wildfell Hall* had been a hit. Its first edition had sold out in six weeks, and the second edition was selling well at the time of Anne's death. Further editions would surely have followed. The bad reviews hadn't hurt sales at all; in fact, they might even have helped.

But Charlotte felt bruised by her own bad reviews, and furious about her sisters'. When the critics called the sisters 'unwomanly', for Charlotte it was Southey all over again. So she fell back on her old strategy of denial. *The Tenant of Wildfell Hall* had come in for most of the flak. With its scenes of men behaving badly, and its heroine leaving her husband, it seemed the most 'unwomanly' of all. So Charlotte denied it. First, she flatly refused to sanction any further editions. '*Wildfell Hall* it hardly appears to me desirable to preserve,' she told the publishers. 'The choice of subject in that work is a mistake; it was too little consonant with the character, tastes and ideas, of the gentle, retiring, inexperienced writer.' She restated her opinion, more vehemently, in the 'Biographical Notice of Ellis and Acton Bell' she wrote to introduce her sisters' work. (Ellis was Emily's pseudonym, while Acton was Anne's.) 'The choice of subject was an entire mistake,' she said. 'Nothing less congruous with the writer's nature could be conceived.' The book might be coarse, but Anne wasn't; she was 'pure', and had simply made a mistake. Charlotte wanted 'to wipe the dust off [her sisters'] gravestones, and leave their dear names free from soil'. But in trying to save Anne from censure, she made her sound both boring and untalented, calling her 'sensitive, reserved, and dejected', 'well-meant', 'melancholy', 'sad', a woman who bore unhappiness with 'mild, steady patience' throughout her 'brief, blameless' life. She damned Anne's work with faint praise saying she wanted the power, the fire, the originality of her sister [Emily], but was well endowed with quiet virtues of her own. Long-suffering, self-denying, reflective, and intelligent, a constitutional reserve and taciturnity placed and kept her in the shade, and covered her mind, and especially her feelings, with a sort of nun-like veil, which was rarely lifted.

This assessment stuck. Because of Charlotte, Anne is seen as the third Beatle. Emily is the wayward genius Lennon, Charlotte is McCartney, talented but controlling, and everyone forgets George Harrison wrote 'Here Comes the Sun'. But at least that song still has pride of place on *Abbey Road*. For many years, Anne's best novel was nearly impossible to get hold of, 'little known' as Gaskell wrote in 1857, and anyone who wondered why could read Charlotte's harsh verdict. Charlotte, more than anyone, is responsible for Anne being seen as 'the other Brontë'.

In 1854, a publishing house called Thomas Hodgson brought out a fly-by-night edition of Anne's second novel. They wanted it to be cheap, to squeeze into one volume, so they cut it to fit. After Charlotte died in 1855, her publishers wanted to bring out their own edition of *The Tenant of Wildfell Hall*. Not knowing any different, they used Hodgson's hacked-about text.

Over a century later, it is the one usually reprinted. There are better versions, such as the 1996 one edited by Stevie Davies or the 2017 Vintage Classics edition. But the mutilated editions are still every-where. My own copy of the novel is a mutilated edition. It takes a while to find one that isn't. I get slightly obsessive about checking, and find butchered texts in bookshops, in libraries and on friends' bookshelves, all bought in good faith, because unless you knew they weren't right, you couldn't tell.

Is this just nit-picking, though? How bad can the edit be? I put the texts side by side and go through them, page by page, to find out. It is laborious work and it's also *infuriating*. (Not least because most of the italics have been removed from the mutilated text, robbing much of the dialogue of intensity and, in some cases, sense.) As I compare and contrast, I get more and more upset that Anne's best novel is still barely available in its intended form, and convinced that this helps explain why her work has been undervalued. In these chopped-up texts, the start of the novel makes no sense because the opening of Gilbert's letter is missing. So we have no idea who Gilbert is or why he is telling the story. He seems anonymous and unmoored. The physical details are missing: that Gilbert is writing to Halford on 'a soaking, rainy day' when 'the family are absent on a visit' and he is alone, 'looking over certain musty old letters and papers, and musing over past times'. The lovely detail about his 'well-roasted feet', which immediately makes me warm to this comfort-loving character, is gone. But most importantly, cutting the start of the letter robs Gilbert of his reason for writing: he wants to nurture his friendship with Halford, and has taken up his pen not 'to apologise for past offences, but, if possible, to atone for them' (a motivation which gathers meaning as the book goes on). Gilbert promises 'frankness and confidence' and a 'full and faithful account', setting up the novel's concern with truth.

The editors of the mutilated edition even cut the fact that Gilbert is writing from his library, which makes us wonder, when we find out he is a farmer, how his circumstances have changed. Anne created suspense, and manipulated narrative time with as much skill and panache as Emily, but you wouldn't know it, reading this text. You wouldn't even know that Gilbert was writing a letter, because this isn't revealed until nearly the end of the first chapter, and then it comes as a jolt. And without knowing that Halford has shared some confidences, and Gilbert is telling his story in return, it's nonsensical for Gilbert to call the letter 'the first instalment of my debt'. The edits aren't even *consistent*.

There are other odd anomalies; when Gilbert promises to share Helen's diary in the next chapter 'and call it,—', we never know what he calls it, because all the chapter titles have been cut. It seems a shame not to know that Gilbert is titling the start of the diary 'The Warnings of Experience', and to muddle this major turn in the novel as it shifts from Gilbert's story of falling for Helen and wondering what her secret is, to the revelation of that secret in her diary.

Many of the cuts make Anne seem meeker and less contentious than she really was. When one of Huntingdon's friends asks, miserably, 'Gentlemen, where is this all to end?' the prurient editors cut the sinister response, 'In hell fire.' When Helen sees her husband flirting with another woman, they cut her threatening (if only in her diary) to 'retaliate', working out who she'd flirt with, and tartly commenting that her husband would hate it because 'he knows he is my sun, but when he chooses to withhold his light, he would have my sky to be all darkness; he cannot bear that I should have a moon to mitigate the deprivation'. This makes Helen meeker too, and possibly this is why her barbed assessment of her husband's friend Hargrave is also cut, along with her resolve 'to cherish' this view of him until she is sure she doesn't have to distrust the friendship he is pushing on her. So Helen seems more naive and more hapless – and less interesting – than Anne wrote her. Helen's decision to hide her troubles from her aunt is cut too, so she can come across as very stubborn for trying to cope with the fallout of the marriage alone; in the original, this is part of a chilling conspiracy of silence between women. And a great deal of the force of the novel is blunted by the excision of the two pages where Helen realises that her husband has almost certainly had an illegitimate child with his mistress.

I don't know why they cut a passage where Helen's heart aches for this woman's husband, and, recalling Cowper's lost sailor, compares him to a 'shipwrecked mariner cleaving to a raft, blinded, deafened, bewildered, he feels the waves sweep over him, and sees no prospect of escape; and yet he knows he has no hope but this, and still, while life and sense remain, concentrates all his energies to keep it'. And some of the cuts seem completely random and wilful, like the removal of Huntingdon's sulky 'Humph!' when Helen is more interested in her book than in him. Do the editors think it is rude? No; they've left in other 'humphs'. Just not this one. However, 'beastly' is beyond the pale, as is 'blast', and Huntingdon's response to Helen asking him to let her leave the marriage – 'No, by Jove, I won't!' – is trimmed to just 'No', taking much of the heat out of the scene.

And right at the end, when Gilbert tells us 'how happily my Helen and I have lived and loved together' it is trimmed to 'lived together' – G. D. Hargreaves, who first went through the two editions side by side in the 1970s, as angrily as I am going through them now, thought it was cut for propriety's sake. Which makes me rage. These people are *married*!

Much more damagingly, Anne's chapter about Helen becoming a mother is slashed to five lines of Helen thanking God for giving her a child. Which is all very nice, but in the original Anne went on to show that Helen was clinging to her faith and hope against all odds. 'But where hope rises, fear *must* lurk behind,' she continues, saying every time she holds her baby, she is terrified he'll be taken from her. She tries to convince herself that if he dies, he'll go to heaven, but this is no consolation. She also fears that he will live to curse his own existence, to become as bad a man as his father. And Huntingdon is getting worse. At first he was glad about the 'acquisition' of a son (such a cold, mercantile word), but now he has become impatient with the baby's 'helplessness' and 'stupidity', and jealous that Helen is giving their son so much attention. He will 'positively hate that little wretch' if she carries on, he says. He can't 'waste my thoughts and feelings on a little worthless idiot like that'. He calls the baby a 'senseless, thankless, oyster' and a 'little selfish, senseless sensualist', not realising he is describing himself. This is fine, savage writing. Anne is showing a marriage falling apart, a boy with no male role model, and a man who behaves badly because he has never grown up himself.

Anne is calling on men to take responsibility for their children, to enjoy being fathers, to recognise how hard and wonderful motherhood is and to value it and share it. Cutting all this, and leaving just her gratitude, makes her sound like a pious, blissed-out yummy mummy. Finally, the preface is gone so these editions lack Anne's own words, in her own voice, on how she felt about the novel. Stevie Davies rightly calls the mutilated editions 'worthless to the modern editor'.

The more I learn about how Charlotte treated Anne and her work, the sadder I feel. I was so invested in the idea of the three sisters working together, sharing pages, helping each other to get published, supporting each other. I hate knowing that in truth, their story is partly about sibling rivalry, betrayals, recriminations and turf wars. It's tempting to interpret the whole of the Brontës' afterlives – all the biographies, all the scholarship, all the fan fiction – as part of the same story, with readers and critics getting drawn in, taking sides, defining themselves by which Brontë they feel most sympathy for.

So many writers have echoed Charlotte's snide put-down of Anne as 'nothing, absolutely nothing'. Like Margaret Oliphant, who wrote in 1897 that Anne had 'no right to be considered at all as a writer but for her association with these imperative spirits'. Or the journalist Percy C. Standing who visited Anne's grave that same year and took it upon himself to give her the epitaph of 'the least industrious of the Brontë sisters'. How many novels had Standing written by the time he was twenty-nine? How 'industrious' does a woman have to be, if writing two novels and a raft of poetry, much of it while holding down a full-time job before there were maximum weekly working hours, is not enough? Did Standing realise that Emily only wrote one novel? A year later, in the preface to a new edition of the sisters' novels, Mary Ward wrote: 'It is not as the writer of *The Tenant of Wildfell Hall*, but as the sister of Charlotte and Emily Brontë, that Anne Brontë escapes oblivion.'

In John Malham-Dembleby's woeful 1911 book *The Key to the Brontë Works*, Anne's entry in the index begins 'as understudy to Charlotte'. Malham-Dembleby has his cake and eats it, saying Charlotte helped write *The Tenant of Wildfell Hall*, but also that it is rubbish. May Sinclair's overwrought biography *The Three Brontës* came out the following year and rings with the tiresome refrain 'poor Anne'. Sinclair does at least recognise *The Tenant of Wildfell Hall*'s power, but she thinks *Wuthering Heights*'s 'lightning should have scorched and consumed *Agnes Grey*'. By 1929 Anne had still not been the subject of a dedicated biography, so W. T. Hale stepped into the breach with a short monograph. Unfortunately, his conclusion was both absurd and depressing: 'The Gods were not kind to her: no men except her father's curates ever had a chance to look at her. But the gods must have loved her, after all, for they did not prolong her agony. They let her die young.' Anne wouldn't get a decent, dedicated biography until Winifred Gérin wrote hers in 1959.

I get angrier as I read the stage versions of Anne's life. It's somehow worse when the criticism comes in the form of words put into Anne's own mouth. So in Dan Totheroh's 1931 play *Moor Born*, Anne dismisses her poems as 'just little things'. Three years later, in John Davison's *The Brontës of Haworth Parsonage*, Charlotte writes a book first (which is *not* what happened), and Anne gasps in amazement and (*unforgivably*) asks Charlotte where she gets her ideas. Davison doesn't give Anne many lines and stipulates those she has must be spoken 'timidly' or 'fearfully' – and what he makes her say is so inane that it's a relief when he cuts her off with her own tubercular cough. The stage directions are just as upsetting in Clemence Dane's 1932 play *Wild Decembers*, where Anne is 'tiny' and 'gentle', speaks 'quietly', where even her coughs are 'piteous', and she is described as a mouse at the door of its hole, not daring to venture out. By the 1940s, the Brontës were making their screen debuts. The cheesiest film ever made about them is *Devotion*, in which Charlotte and her hot Belgian professor visit an amusement park, go through a Tunnel of Mystery and emerge looking dazed and post-coital. I plough through its (awful) novelisation and find the noveliser (the *noveliser*!) opining that '*Agnes Grey* . . . lacked the deep fire and tragedy of the others'. There are some places I wish my quest for Anne had never led me.

By 1948, in Martyn Richards's play *Branwell*, Anne is 'small, gentle, and pretty without character', always doing the ironing and tying Branwell's cravat. I don't know how the actor managed to keep a straight face when Emily told her to keep trying and maybe she'd manage to write a book, not a work of genius, but something people would enjoy. And then she had to go ahead and *thank* her. This Anne is surrendered and pathetic. But at least she is there. In their cult 1990s Brontë spoof *Withering Looks*, the two-woman theatre company Lip Service explain that Anne is not there because she has popped out for a cup of sugar. In her 1992 book *The Essence of the Brontës*, Muriel Spark finds Anne is *not* essential, and regrets that she once praised Anne whom she now regards as 'the literary equivalent of a decent water-colourist, as so many maidens were in those days'. From a fellow novelist, this seems a little ungenerous.

As I sit in the cold Parsonage library, reading in mounting fury, the staff tell me no visitors ever ask about Anne except, sometimes, vague questions such as 'What was the name of the "other" sister?' or 'What did Anne write?' But it's rare for a day to go by without someone asking where Heathcliff is buried. Anne is less solid, less known, than even her sister's *fictional* characters. She has become a byword for underachievement, neglect and exclusion. Back in London, an actor friend says at a party, 'I'm not doing too well at the moment, but at least I'm not Anne Brontë.' I watch an episode of the animated sitcom *Family Guy*; Charlotte and Emily talk (in RP) about their literary prowess, and when Anne interrupts (in a cockney accent) to say she's started her period, Charlotte congratulates her on finally having achieved something. All this makes me feel the same sense of burning injustice about Charlotte's unsisterliness as I did when I was a child complaining to my parents, as children do, that they were *so unfair*. If it makes me this angry, then would Anne have borne it with 'mild, steady patience'? I hope not.

The other myths Charlotte created after her sisters' deaths, when she was grieving and hounded by her critics, have mostly been dismantled. A seismic shift came in 1913 when Charlotte's letters to Monsieur Heger were published, transforming her in the public eye from suffering saint to saucy minx. After that, for a while, Emily was the top Brontë and Charlotte's reputation plummeted. In her riveting metabiography *The Brontë Myth*, Lucasta Miller calls this the 'Charlotte-as-bitch' phase. It climaxed in 1999 with a novel by true-crime writer James Tully called *The Crimes of Charlotte Brontë*, which I find uncanny. Tully has read all the same books as me and has a lot of fun drawing wildly different conclusions. In his murder mystery, Charlotte's path to marriage is paved with corpses. The man she marries, her father's curate Arthur Bell Nicholls, begins by poisoning Branwell. Then he starts an affair with Emily, who gets pregnant and confesses all to Anne but she's too dismal to do anything but tell Charlotte . . . who is jealous because she fancies Nicholls too! Despite the implausible murders and the bizarre portrayal of fuddy-duddy Nicholls as a stud, Tully captures something truthful about Charlotte and Anne. His Charlotte complains that the dying Anne (who she has helped poison!) gives herself the airs of a saint, and she resents nursing her when she could be enjoying her fame in London. Tully also makes much of the fact that Charlotte didn't manage to write anything nice on Anne's gravestone.

I emerge from the library feeling slightly grubby. And also guilty. I call my brother up and demand we go out for curry. I should be glad to have him. I *am* glad to have him. He's steady and patient and generous and kind. He's not poisoning me. He's not preventing me being published. He's not mistrusting or patronising me or ignoring me or going behind my back. Yes, we still bicker like we are eight and six and in the back seat of our parents' car, but we're not competitive with each other, we're not jealous. I think we thrive on our differences. I'm glad he's not a sister. Maybe sharing clothes might have shaded into stealing clothes and returning them (if at all) stained or stretched beyond repair. And maybe sharing ideas would have been equally traumatic. I'm glad my brother's not a writer. He's not scrambling for the same material, squabbling over my interpretation of events, ripping off my ideas, rewriting me, censoring me, burning my manuscripts. If Branwell hadn't gone off the rails, Anne might have had the bond with him that I have with my brother. Instead, jostling for space with Charlotte generated a friction that might have been good for Anne's writing but was bad for her life, and even worse for her afterlife.

Charlotte gave Anne an odd, troubled memorial in *Shirley*. She had written two-thirds of the novel before her sisters fell ill, and had planned to kill off Caroline Helstone. But when she returned to the book after Anne's death, she couldn't face it. Caroline was based on Anne, at least on the meek, dull Anne of Charlotte's 'Biographical Notice', while unconventional, macho, nature-loving Shirley Keeldar was Emily. The trouble was that while Charlotte's other heroines struggle to reconcile passion and denial, in *Shirley* Charlotte tried to simplify things, giving all the passion to Shirley, and all the denial to Caroline. It drained the life out of both. Shirley barrels along, doing what she wants until she is stopped by marriage. Caroline simply endures. She doesn't express her feelings so they fester inside her. She does spark into life when she argues about religion – as Anne did – but most of the time she seems headed for death (just as Charlotte thought Anne was), and a maudlin death at that, a death that only matters because it makes other characters sad and provides them with an opportunity for personal growth.

In the wake of Anne's death, Charlotte decided to do something different. She waved her pen like a magic wand and made all Caroline's wishes come true, up to and including a reunion with her long-lost mother. She married her off to the man she loved, and having promised (or threatened) on the very first page, 'If you think . . . that anything like a romance is preparing for you, reader, you never were more mistaken,' she swerved and found a husband for Shirley too. With its double wedding, the chapter Charlotte called the 'Winding-Up' is like the end of a Shakespeare comedy, with all the loose ends tied up, all the loose cannons married off, and the same feeling of deep unease, because life can't be that easy, can it? Mess can't be cleared away, people can't marry the most plot-convenient people, blood can't be swept up as a new ruler sweeps in. Charlotte knew she was giving Caroline what *she* wanted her to have, and that Anne might not have wanted these things at all. She knew that while she was doing all this she was vilifying *The Tenant of Wildfell Hall* and denying it the oxygen of publicity. Her guilt churns through the novel.

Anne had indulged in some wish-fulfilment too, in *Agnes Grey*. By the end, Mary recognises her little sister's worth. While Agnes earns money as a governess, Mary does very well out of selling her drawings. By the time Mary announces her engagement to a local vicar, the sisters have stopped competing, and Agnes is uncomplicatedly happy about going home to help with the preparations and 'to make the best of her company while we have her'. Agnes is now able to see that Mary needs to be the older sister – she is 'twenty eight, and as sober as if she were fifty' while Agnes is more wide-eyed, and still likely to get endearingly flustered around the man she fancies. They have defined their own identities, and can respect each other's differences. In the conversations they have around their father's death, and their mother's plans, they sound, at last, like equals. And you get the sense that if they hit another rocky patch, they will survive it too. Because that's what siblings have to do. You can break up with a friend or just drift apart. But even if you are not speaking, even if one of you is dead, a sibling is always a sibling. You are joined at the root. Whatever happens, Agnes and Mary will always be the sisters who grew up sharing a room, a bookcase and a 'little bed', the sisters who both cried on the night before Agnes left for her first job, and didn't talk about it, but found themselves in bed, 'creeping more closely together from the consciousness that we were to part so soon'.

While in real life, Anne didn't get this kind of closeness with Charlotte and her experience of having her as a sister was bruising and complicated, since then she has thankfully been rescued by a different sisterhood. Feminists have claimed Anne as their own. One of the first was the critic Inga-Stina Ewbank whose 1966 book *Their Proper Sphere* considered Anne alongside her sisters, applauding her 'moral passion'. In 1968 Philippa Stone made Anne the heroine of her novel *The Captive Dove*. Critics like Elizabeth Langland, Juliet McMaster, Antonia Losano and Naomi Jacobs have shone a light on Anne. She is finding her moment. And Charlotte would be surprised if she knew that the sister she characterised as morbid and serious has been claimed by feminist comedians. In 2013, Bridget Christie's stand-up show, *A Bic for Her*, inspired by the marketing of pastel-coloured biros for women, imagined the Brontës struggling to write with black 'men's' pens, and Anne, furious at getting less attention than her sisters, skulking around the Parsonage and trying to put them off their writing by banging pans and breathing loudly. Christie's Anne is intimidating, not a wimp, and says she is writing *The Tenant of Wildfell Hall* just fine with her non-pastel pen because, she says, rather threateningly, she's always had man's hands. Also in 2013, the comedy series *Psychobitches* imagined the Brontës as puppets in bonnets, squabbling on a twenty-first-century therapist's couch. Sarah Solemani's coy, self-assured Anne shrugs off her sisters' taunts that she's like a wet weekend in Morecambe, soft as a mouldy teacake, and was beaten up by her own pupils. She doesn't care. After all, *her* book sold out in six weeks. Perhaps we're still reading and writing about the Brontës as though we are part of their family, still trying to settle their old scores, but at least now Anne sometimes gets to win.

6

AGNES
or how to work

'How delightful it would be to be a governess!' thinks Agnes
Grey at the start of Anne's first novel. 'To go out into the world;
to enter upon a new life; to act for myself; to exercise my
unused faculties; to try my unknown powers; to earn my own
maintenance . . . And then, how charming to be entrusted with
the care and education of children!' Are the exclamation marks
sincere? Is Anne being sarcastic? Everyone knows governesses were overlooked and crushed. But *Agnes Grey* is not satire.
Agnes promises that 'Shielded by my own obscurity, and the
lapse of years, and a few fictitious names, I do not fear to
venture; and will candidly lay before the public what I would
not disclose to the most intimate friend'. And Anne really was
honest in *Agnes Grey*. She committed to realism. You could film
the whole novel without once having recourse to a candelabra
or a smoke machine. Inga-Stina Ewbank thought she took it
too far, that 'In her anxiety to picture life that is drab, she
sometimes produces art that is dull'. But Anne was also criticised
for doing the opposite, and observed with irritation that '*Agnes
Grey* was accused of extravagant over-colouring in those very
parts that were carefully copied from life, with a most scrupulous
avoidance of all exaggeration'. She didn't need to exaggerate

because the truth was shocking enough. But her excitement about starting work isn't snark because Anne didn't know it would be grim to be a governess. One reason we know it now is because she wrote about it: when *Agnes Grey* was published in December 1847, it was the first novel to really lift the lid on the profession.

Even so, her optimism makes me sigh. I don't want Anne to be the good girl diligently slogging away. It seems more fun to be Charlotte and Branwell, raging and sneering at their bosses, or Emily, hating employment so much that she mostly avoided it. I don't want Anne to be excited about setting off for her first job in April 1839 when, at the time, all her siblings were at home and writing like the wind.

Charlotte had finally left Roe Head that Christmas, after three and a half years and more than one resignation threat. A few weeks later, Branwell had come home from Bradford, where he had tried and failed to establish himself as a portrait painter. It must have been a blow for Patrick who had scrimped and saved to pay for Branwell's art lessons and – possibly – to send his son to London to try to get into the Royal Academy in 1836. If Branwell did go, he probably suffered the fate of one of his Angrian heroes, Charles Wentworth, who visits a capital city and, felled by 'aimless depression', wanders around, unseeing, and listless, feels as if the cathedral dome will 'thunder down in ruins over his head', and is overwhelmed by 'flashes of feeling' and 'striking sparks from his mind'. These sound like symptoms of seizures. Branwell did have seizures – which he might have made worse by, like Wentworth, 'feeding his feelings with "little squibs of rum"' – but no one knows when they started. If his seizures began when he was a boy, perhaps that's why he was never sent to school, and perhaps later they made it hard for him to hold down a job. If Branwell travelled south, nothing came of it. Instead, while his sisters were at Roe Head, he turned one of the Parsonage bedrooms into a studio, and started painting local bigwigs, in between churning out Angrian fantasy, and bombarding the editor of *Blackwood's* magazine with peremptory, misspelled letters, one beginning 'SIR, READ WHAT I WRITE', another practically illegible because, he explained, he had injured his right hand while boxing and was writing with his left. Unsurprisingly he never got a reply. So when a friend of Patrick's offered to help him set up a studio in Bradford, it seemed like his best chance at a career. But after six months, he was back. He hadn't managed to establish himself, he was in debt, and he didn't know what to do next. And then Emily returned too, from her first – and only – job as a teacher at Law Hill school near Halifax, where she'd had to work seventeen-hour days, and had startled her pupils by telling them she preferred the school dog to any of them. She'd lasted six months.

Charlotte was offered a way out of the job market altogether, when Nussey's boring brother Henry proposed. She replied with the ultimate iteration of *it's not you, it's me*: 'I have no personal repugnance to the idea of a union with you,' she said, '– but I feel convinced that mine is not the sort of disposition calculated to form the happiness of a man like you.' Ironically this letter, in which Charlotte bravely turned down her chance for financial security, recently sold at Christie's for over fifty thousand dollars.

I start to feel differently about Agnes's (and Anne's) optimism. Anne must have had a lot of gumption to leave home in April 1839, at nineteen, to try to do what her older siblings were finding so impossible. All the things Agnes wishes for – to go out in the world, to enter upon a new life, to act for herself, to exercise her unused faculties, to try her unknown powers and to earn her own maintenance – are things I've wished for, over the years; things women have fought for the right to do, and are fighting for still.

When Anne left, maybe, like Agnes, she scandalised the servant (yet another character based on Tabby) by kissing the cat goodbye, and put her veil over her face once she was in the gig so she could cry in private. And maybe when she arrived at the Inghams' (the Bloomfields in the book), she found herself, like Agnes, 'stilling the rebellious flutter of my heart'. *Rebellious flutter* is interesting. This is going to be an adventure.

Charlotte, though, told Anne's departure as a tragedy: 'Poor child! She left us last Monday; no one went with her; it was her own wish that she might be allowed to go alone, as she thought she could manage better and summon more courage if thrown entirely upon her own resources.' I wonder if Charlotte was quoting Anne – *courage* was a word Anne used a lot – and I can't help feeling that Charlotte's real anxiety was for herself. Admitting she hadn't yet found a new job, she joked, 'I have lately discovered I have quite a talent for cleaning . . . so, if everything else fails, I can turn my hand to that . . . I won't be a cook; I hate cooking. I won't be a nurserymaid, nor a lady's-maid, far less a lady's companion, or a mantua-maker, or a straw-bonnet maker, or a taker-in of plain work. I won't be anything but a housemaid.' The banter rings a little hollow; Charlotte's sister (her poor, little, incapable sister) had beaten her to it.

Anne was the first to be a governess in a family home – Charlotte and Emily had both taught at schools – so she didn't know what to expect. The Inghams lived at Blake Hall, in Mirfield, not far from Roe Head, and Anne probably got the job through James La Trobe who had christened all five Ingham children. Anne taught seven-year-old Cunliffe and five-year-old Mary, and her salary was £25 a year, which Agnes sharply notes is not much for a wealthy man to pay the person teaching his children. I examine pictures of the Inghams. Joshua Ingham has fulsome sideburns and a supercilious air, while his wife Mary looks phlegmatic in high-maintenance, shiny sausage curls, a vast silk crinoline and a black lace mantilla. I can't imagine Anne liked Ingham's politics – he helped enforce the new Poor Law Act in Mirfield, draconian legislation which Patrick campaigned against. He was deeply puritanical, and didn't let his daughters go to shops, use mirrors or wear perfume. When he caught one girl looking at herself in a mirror, he had all her hair cut off to punish her vanity. His wife notoriously said Anne was a very unsuitable governess who tied the children to a table leg so she could get on with her writing. But Mary only came out with this story when the Brontës were famous so perhaps she told it to get a bit of their refracted glamour. She was wrong to imagine that Anne was doing much writing at Blake Hall. It was only at her second job that she began 'Passages in the Life of an Individual' which almost certainly became *Agnes Grey*.

But Mary Ingham did have good reason to be annoyed with her ex-governess because in the novel her family, thinly disguised, are unsparingly anatomised. Anne noticed everything: when the Inghams treated her shabbily, when they bickered about their children, when they squabbled over food. Blending into the background, into the darkest corner of a church, into an alcove at a party, she watched without being watched. She was a connoisseur of the tiny, telling detail. Like when Agnes mercilessly notices that her pupils' crude, misogynist uncle 'had found some means of compressing his waist into a remarkably small compass; and that, together with the unnatural stillness of his form, showed that the lofty-minded, manly Mr Robson, the scorner of the female sex, was not above the foppery of stays'.

Anne also wrote feelingly about the difficulties she faced. Charlotte said the Inghams were 'desperate little dunces', 'unruly, violent . . . modern children'. Trying to keep order, Anne found herself doing things she really didn't want to do. Agnes holds down one violent child, shakes another and pulls her hair. Sometimes, she has 'to run after my pupils to catch them, to carry or drag them to the table, and often forcibly to hold them there till the lesson was done'. The spoiled Mary Ann Bloomfield

preferred rolling on the floor to any other amusement: down she would drop like a leaden weight; and when I, with great difficulty, had succeeded in rooting her thence, I had still to hold her up with one arm, while with the other I held the book from which she was to read or spell her lesson. As the dead weight of the big girl of six became too heavy for one arm to bear, I transferred it to the other:

or, if both were weary of the burden, I carried her into a
corner; and told her she might come out when she should
find the use of her feet, and stand up: but she generally
preferred lying there like a log till dinner or tea time . . .
and would come crawling out, with a grin of triumph on
her round, red face.

Mary Ann's little sister Fanny spits in Agnes's face. But worst of
all is their brother Tom. When Agnes first arrives, Tom drags his
rocking horse to the centre of the room, makes his sister hold the
reins while he mounts it and makes Agnes watch 'how manfully
he use[s] his whip and spurs'. She hopes aloud he won't use them
on a real pony. 'Oh, yes I will!' he says, whipping harder. 'I'll cut
into him like smoke!' He hits his sister 'to keep her in order' and
hits and kicks Agnes, and he's strong, and it hurts.

In the nastiest scene in the book, Tom appears 'running in
high glee . . . with a brood of little callow nestlings in his
hands'. He likes torturing birds. 'Sometimes I give them to the
cat; sometimes I cut them in pieces with my penknife; but
the next, I mean to roast alive.' Soon he is 'laying the nest
on the ground, and standing over it with his legs wide apart,
his hands thrust into his breeches-pockets, his body bent
forward, and his face twisted into all manner of contortions in
the ecstasy of his delight'. Sickened by his gloating, Agnes tries
to persuade him not to torture the baby birds, but he won't
listen so she grabs a large stone and crushes them flat. It's a
mercy killing, and a brutal one. Agnes must have had to steel
herself to do it. Anne too. Because this actually happened. When
Gaskell asked Charlotte about it, Charlotte said 'that none but

those who had been in the position of a governess could ever realise the dark side of "respectable" human nature'.

Agnes realises Tom wants to 'persecute the lower creation' – not just birds and animals but girls and women. Mrs Bloomfield tells Agnes off for spoiling Tom's pleasure, and Agnes retorts, 'When Master Bloomfield's amusements consist in injuring sentient creatures, I think it is my duty to interfere.' Mrs Bloomfield thinks 'the creatures were all created for our convenience' and 'a child's amusement is scarcely to be weighed against the welfare of a soulless brute'. But Agnes doesn't back down. She says Tom shouldn't be encouraged to torture birds. He should learn mercy. It's the most she has said since she arrived. She's found her voice.

Anne had too. In connecting violence against women to violence against animals, Anne anticipated the work of activists like the unstoppable Irish campaigner Frances Power Cobbe, who in 1878 justified the shocking title of her essay 'Wife-Torture in England' by saying, 'the familiar term "wife-beating" conveys as remote a notion of the extremity of the cruelty indicated as when candid and ingenuous vivisectors talk of "scratching a newt's tail" when they refer to burning alive, or dissecting out the nerves of living dogs, or torturing ninety cats in the series of experiments'. Cobbe campaigned against both domestic violence and vivisection because she felt both were on a spectrum of male violence. If Anne had lived, maybe she would have joined her.

As it was, her incandescent anger at the Inghams is so palpable in *Agnes Grey* that some people think she haunts what remains of their house. Blake Hall was demolished in 1954 and its grand staircase, hand-carved from dark and fabulously burled yew, was sold.

The opera singer Gladys Topping bought it for her house in Quogue, Long Island. She claimed that one evening in 1962, while meditating, she heard footsteps on the stairs and emerged to find a young woman in a full skirt, shawl, hair in a bun, holding a candlestick: Anne Brontë, straight out of central casting.

In December 1839, after eight months, Anne got fired for not being tough enough with the children. It must have been galling to fail. When Agnes is fired, she starts job-hunting at once, to 'redeem my lost honour' and because she is 'not yet weary of adventure'. Anne did the same. While she had been away, Charlotte had taken a temporary post with a family called the Sidgwicks. From there, she wrote depressed letters to Nussey about 'the long history of a private governess's trials and crosses' – although she only worked there for two and a half months. Charlotte also refused a second marriage proposal, from another curate. Meanwhile, Tabby moved out to live with her sister, feeling she wasn't up to the housekeeping any more, so Emily took over, helped by their eleven-year-old servant Martha Brown. As for Branwell, he had been reading with Patrick, hoping to equip himself for teaching, and soon after Anne returned, he set off to be a tutor in the Lake District, stopping en route to drink until 'the room spun round and the candles danced', saying 'farewell of old friend whisky' before he knuckled down to work.

Anne was unemployed for four months. Perhaps, like Agnes, she resolved 'to take things coolly' next time; certainly, in her diary paper of 1841, she is pleased that she has 'a little more self-possession'. As Agnes goes from her first job to her second, the tone shifts from hot rage to icy, scalpel-sharp wit. Agnes isn't so ground down by what she is forced to do and witness; she is more able to laugh at the world and at herself. If Anne was already considering how she could write about her experience, she might have picked up a novel called *The Governess*, which had been published the year before. But she would not have recognised much of what was in it. Written by salonista Marguerite Gardiner, Countess of Blessington, *The Governess* is one of the 'silver fork novels', as the critic William Hazlitt derisively called them, all dandies and dilettantes, cads and coquettes, and lovingly detailed descriptions of achingly fashionable clothes. Blessington's heroine Clara Mordaunt is a dazzling beauty forced into governessing after her father's financial collapse and suicide. In a series of improbable adventures, she gets her fortune back and becomes a countess – just like her author! Blessington's own rags-to-riches life, surviving a poverty-stricken childhood and an abusive first marriage, before she could marry an earl, write books, and be painted, oozing out of a silk dress, in a picture which Byron said 'set all London raving', must have given her a more expansive idea of what constituted realism. But no one who had been a governess could believe that at the end of the novel Clara's ex-employers ever afterwards 'treated the governesses . . . with more humanity; giving as a reason, that there was no knowing whether they might not, at some future period, become heiresses, or countesses'.

Maybe this made Anne think she *could* make people treat their governesses with more humanity, not by suddenly turning the governesses into countesses, but by showing employers how they had been inhumane. Agnes says her 'design . . . [is] not to amuse, but to benefit those whom it might concern' and that 'if a parent has, therefrom, gained any useful hint, or an unfortunate governess received thereby the slightest benefit, I am well rewarded for my pains'. It did succeed with some readers. Lady Amberley, the suffragette and (incidentally) Bertrand Russell's mother, wrote in her diary in 1868, that she had 'read *Agnes Grey* . . . and should like to give it to every family with a governess and shall read it through again when I have a governess to remind me to be human'.

Being a governess, and sharing stories with her sisters and friends about their working lives, raised Anne's consciousness. She realised she had a story on her hands, a story no one was telling, an explosive story about what went on behind closed doors of houses up and down the country, a story that needed to be told. She wanted to write about employers like the Sidgwicks, who forced Charlotte to socialise, and then told her off for being shy. To be fair, Charlotte was probably not the *best* governess. She called her pupils 'little devils incarnate' and 'riotous, perverse, unmanageable cubs', and the Sidgwicks said she was always taking offence, or taking to her bed. But it is also true that one child threw a stone at her, and cut her forehead. And that when the same child later told Charlotte he loved her, Mrs Sidgwick jeered, 'Love the *governess*, my dear!'

Anne wanted to write about how governesses were loaded up with work that had nothing to do with teaching. Charlotte had 'to wipe the children's smutty noses or tie their shoes or fetch their pinafores or set them a chair', and was given 'oceans of needlework, yards of cambric to hem, muslin nightcaps to make, and, above all things, dolls to dress'. Agnes has to wash and dress six-year-old Mary Ann, 'no light matter' because 'her abundant hair was to be smeared with pomade, plaited in three long tails, and tied with bows of ribbon' and because 'at one time she would not be washed; at another she would not be dressed . . .; at another she would scream and run away'. At her second job, she has to do the boring bits of her pupil's embroidery.

It can't have escaped Anne that Branwell was having a much easier time of it. While Anne had to live in her employers' homes (sometimes even sharing a room with her pupils), Branwell was in lodgings. He had privacy and time to do some serious walking and writing, and perhaps to have the odd fling; Juliet Barker has argued persuasively that while he was in the Lakes, he had an illegitimate child with a farm labourer's daughter. Perhaps that's why he was fired in June 1840.

Anne had no time for flings. Agnes is drily funny about how she was expected to be constantly on call:

> I had, as it were, to keep my loins girded, my shoes on my feet, and my staff in my hand; for not to be imme-diately forthcoming when called for, was regarded as a grave and inexcusable offence: not only by my pupils and their mother, but by the very servant, who came in breath-less haste to call me, exclaiming, 'You're to go to the schoolroom *directly*, mum, the young ladies is WAITING!!' Climax of horror! actually waiting for their governess!!!

And she wasn't even paid well. Charlotte would take a job in March 1841 for just £20 a year, of which £4 was deducted for laundry. The anonymous author of the teasingly titled 1856 book

Hints to Governesses by One of Themselves claimed she was once offered just £6 a year. When Anne came to find her second job, she boldly decided not to go through a recommendation but to advertise, and to ask for double her previous salary. After all, thanks to Patrick, she could teach Latin and German as well as the accomplishments. On 8 May 1840, she set off for Thorp Green, near York, to work for the Robinsons, on £50 a year.

Thorp Green was seventy miles from home, 'a formidable distance', Agnes says, ten hours by gig, coach, coach again, railway and phaeton. Even now it takes a long time. When I go, Ann Dinsdale from the Parsonage meets me at York, having already taken a bus to Keighley and two trains. We take another train to Cattal and then a taxi for the last four miles. When I tell the driver why we're there he asks, 'Which Brontë? Emily or Charlotte?' He hasn't heard of Anne. 'If it was a million-pound question on *Who Wants to be a Millionaire?* – name her three novels – I couldn't do it.' I reassure him. She only wrote two.

In the August heat, as we walk along Anne's 'quiet green lanes, and smiling hedges', the wheat fields are gold, the hedgerows frill and foam with life, cow parsley froths along the verges, and field poppies catch the sun. It is softer and greener than Haworth, and not scoured by fierce winds – but Agnes finds it 'depressingly flat'. The Robinsons' house burned down in 1895, but it has been rebuilt as a school. It is hosting a summer camp, and as we wander around it, we hear singing, and cheering, and stamping feet. I tell Ann about my dreams about Anne, and we discuss whether we would like to be haunted by her or not.

At the Robinsons', Anne's pupils were older; the girls were twelve, thirteen and fourteen, and their brother was eight. In the novel, they are the Murrays, and Agnes mainly teaches sixteen-year-old Rosalie and fourteen-year-old Matilda. She insists that she is not exaggerating about their bad behaviour. 'Had I seen it depicted in a novel, I should have thought it unnatural,' she says, but 'I saw it with my own eyes, and suffered from it too'. Rosalie is a man-stealer. Matilda is a tomboy. Both are cruel.

At first I wasn't sure why Anne emphasised that unlike the nouveaux riches Bloomfields, the Murrays were 'genuine thoroughbred gentry', especially as in real life there wasn't much difference in class between her two employers. Agnes is sure the Murrays will treat her with more respect. She's something of a snob. But she changes. The Murrays turn out to be no better than the Bloomfields, Agnes learns that 'genuine thoroughbred gentry' treat their governesses as badly as anyone else – and Anne explodes the idea that class equals gentility. It was crucial to tackle this idea, because it was everywhere. It looms large in a review of *Jane Eyre* published in the *Quarterly Review* in 1848 which has become infamous. I look it up, wondering how terrible it can be.

It is worse than I could have imagined. The critic, Elizabeth Rigby, would become Lady Eastlake a year later and she writes very much from an employer's point of view. She insists that Charlotte is wrong about Rochester's friends. They can't be ladies, or they would never treat Jane so badly. They talk 'like parvenues', she says, and 'bully the servants in language no lady would dream of using'. For Rigby, the trouble is that governesses are supposed to be ladies who only have to work because of reduced circumstances. (They have to be ladies because otherwise how can they teach their pupils to be ladies?) But once a lady falls and becomes a governess, she isn't a lady any more. But she is also not a servant. 'I don't trust them governesses,' says a housekeeper in *Vanity Fair*. 'They give themselves the hairs and hupstarts of ladies, and their wages is no better than you nor me.' Rigby decides that, to avoid transgressing 'that invisible but rigid line which alone establishes the distance between herself and her employers', governesses must isolate themselves, refusing friendship with both their employers and the servants. By now I am quite irritated with Rigby, so I take a break and look her up. I find some calotypes of her taken by a pair of photographic pioneers in Edinburgh. She has chosen to do her hair in a style I can only describe as Princess Leia gone wrong. I am instantly pleased – even though I know I am being unkind.

Rigby comes unstuck when she tries to apply her theories to the latest report from a new charity called the Governesses' Benevolent Institution. Set up in 1843, the institution's aim was to advise governesses on investing their money wisely, and to give grants to the worst off. But they were so overwhelmed by requests for help that they realised they had to tell these women's stories and push for change. They produced a devastating series of reports. About women who started governessing at sixteen and were still going in their sixties, and still hadn't earned enough to save a penny. Women who lost their jobs when their pupils grew up, and found that, after a certain age, no one wanted to employ them. Women who supported their families for years, but found no one willing to return the favour. These worn-out women, often ill or disabled, ended up on the streets, in hospitals or in lunatic asylums. When Florence Nightingale took over the Institute for the Care of Sick Gentlewomen in 1853, she noticed that most of her patients were governesses, because, heartbreakingly, 'it is the cheapest lodging they can find'. Rigby's response to these stories was churlish and inadequate – and still all about class. She lamented the lot of 'these afflicted and destitute ladies, many of them with aristocratic names', but blamed 'fine-ladyism' for their troubles; she said they must have been employed by middle-class women who didn't know how to treat a governess. This kind of class bigotry meant critics just refused to believe Anne's portraits of the upper classes behaving badly. Reviewing *The Tenant of Wildfell Hall*, the *Literary World*'s critic thundered, 'can this sort of half-civilisation, half-brutification, be characteristic of English society . . .? Is it customary to find the combination of the boor and the bravo . . . in hereditary possession of long-descended estates . . .?' Well, yes, Anne said, it was.

Charlotte was most upset by Rigby's observation, 'We need the imprudencies, extravagancies, mistakes, or crimes of a certain number of fathers, to sow that seed from which we reap the harvest of governesses.' Patrick wasn't imprudent, extravagant or a criminal. He was just poor, and that was why his daughters had to teach. Charlotte got her revenge in *Shirley* when she lifted chunks from Rigby's review and put them, word for word, in the mouths of Mrs Pryor's cruel and objectionable old employers. It's very satisfying.

But a more effective argument against Rigby might have been just to send her a copy of *Agnes Grey*. Anne shows how even a governess who doesn't want to cross Rigby's 'invisible but rigid line' can still get caught in a quagmire of class uncertainty. Agnes complains that having to call her pupils Master and Miss undermines her authority, and about feeling 'like one deaf and dumb who could neither speak nor be spoken to'. Even going for a walk is a trial:

> As none of the . . . ladies and gentlemen ever noticed me, it was disagreeable to walk beside them, as if listening to what they said, or wishing to be thought one of them, while they talked over me, or across; and if their eyes, in speaking, chanced to fall on me, it seemed as if they looked on vacancy – as if they either did not see me, or were very desirous to make it appear so. It was disagreeable, too, to walk behind, and thus appear to acknowledge my own inferiority . . . Thus . . . I gave myself no little trouble in my endeavour (if I did keep up with them) to appear perfectly unconscious or regardless of their presence, as if I were wholly absorbed in my own reflections, or the contemplation of surrounding objects.

Anne found this humiliating and exhausting. But she also started to realise that her unease might be a gift to her as a writer.

Unease can be radical. It can be a hammer to crack society wide open and expose its taboos and mores. Anne realised that the problem was bad education. *Agnes Grey* is an antidote to the ubiquitous conduct books for girls; it shows how children go wrong. Tom Bloomfield will end up like his horrid uncle, a cruel fop – or like Huntingdon in *The Tenant of Wildfell Hall*. Rosalie Murray is taught to value wealth and status so she marries a rich man who will never make her happy, and looks set to pass on the misery to her own daughter. Anne shows how girls who are given nothing but polish, finish and dinner-party conversation are not prepared for life, taught to think for themselves, or warned about the perils of bad men. In real life, Anne tried to fight this, taking pride in teaching well, and teaching subjects girls didn't usually study.

At Thorp Green, with access to the Robinsons' books and the libraries of York and Scarborough, Anne also furthered her own education. Maybe that's where she discovered Mary Wollstonecraft's *A Vindication of the Rights of Woman*, with its demand for state-funded co-education. Certainly, Wollstonecraft's clarion call to 'Strengthen the female mind by enlarging it' reverberates through *Agnes Grey*. Wollstonecraft wrote *A Vindication* messily, indignantly, in six short weeks during the French Revolution when everything seemed up for grabs. She couldn't have imagined that, soon after she died, her ideals would be trodden in the dust, as governments everywhere clamped down on revolutionary ideas. Her sisters ended up living hand-to-mouth, going from one humiliating governess job to another, and as they got older and poorer, the idea of boys and girls being educated together, for free, must have seemed pure fantasy. Wollstonecraft's dream wouldn't come true until after the Second World War.

In the meantime, many governesses thought marriage might save them. Another novelist Anne probably discovered while at Thorp Green was Jane Austen. Charlotte famously hated Austen; 'the Passions are perfectly unknown to her', she said, and 'she rejects even a speaking acquaintance with that stormy Sisterhood'. But Anne's writing has often been compared to Austen's. They both value reason and wit, balance satire with empathy, they both try to make their heroines happy. And in *Agnes Grey*, Anne both echoes and questions *Emma*.

In Austen's novel, two governesses are saved by marriage. Jane Fairfax is saved before she even has to try the 'slavery' of governessing. But Miss Taylor has been Emma's governess for sixteen years before she gets caught in drizzle one day, a man fetches an umbrella and soon they are walking down the aisle. Anne might have questioned Austen's penchant for sending her heroines out into bad weather to find men – as Anne was forever getting bad colds, this might not have been her most effective strategy. I think she also felt there was more to Miss Taylor's story than Austen was telling. She remixed it in *Agnes Grey*, signalling what she was doing by giving Agnes's suitor the same name as Miss Taylor's; they are both called Mr Weston.

Miss Taylor's marriage is supposed to be true love, but is it really? Her pupil has outgrown her, and she must be wondering how long she will be kept on as a paid companion. Maybe she doesn't want to uproot herself after sixteen years in one place. Maybe she knows, anyway, governesses have a shelf life, and she'll find it hard to get another job. Maybe fear drives Miss Taylor into the drizzle, and maybe that's why she lets herself be rescued. Marriage is her exit strategy. Anne was careful not to make it Agnes's.

Agnes's Weston is a gentle, overworked curate. He has just lost his mother, his rented rooms don't feel like home and he has 'nowt to live on', but he still sends the poor widow Nancy Brown a sack of coals for her cold cottage. He is full of common sense, firm faith and unaffected sweetness. Oh, and he has a deep, clear voice, a lovely smile, and he preaches well. I have quite a soft spot for Weston myself. In a riff on Austen's umbrella scene, Anne describes Rosalie and Agnes leaving church in heavy rain. They have begun a silent battle for Weston's affections. Rosalie is a dog in the manger; she doesn't want Weston, but she doesn't want anyone else to have him either. As they leave church, she haughtily sets off for the carriage, under the footman's umbrella, leaving Agnes to get drenched . . . and then Weston appears with an umbrella! Agnes is so flummoxed that she says no thank you, she doesn't mind the rain. 'I always lacked common sense when taken by surprise,' comments the older Agnes, mouth twitching in amusement. Luckily, Weston walks Agnes to the carriage anyway, which puts 'an unamiable cloud upon [Rosalie's] pretty face' – as if she has made the rain herself, and hoped it would soak her rival.

There's no rain as Ann Dinsdale and I reach the church Anne was thinking of, in the village of Little Ouseburn. The sun is relentless, and it's a relief to step into the church's cool, dark interior. The Holy Trinity Church is small and solid. Most of it dates back to before the Normans, and some of it is built with stone salvaged from Roman ruins. Putting down my dusty rucksack, I sit at a pew, feeling safe and calm. This church is here to stay. It was Agnes's happy place, 'for at church I might look without fear of scorn or censure upon a form and face more pleasing to me than the most beautiful of God's creations; I might listen without disturbance to a voice more charming than the sweetest music to my ears; I might seem to hold communion with that soul'. She does worry that by gazing at Weston, she is 'mocking God with the service of a heart more bent upon the creature than the Creator', but she comforts herself by reasoning that 'it is not the man, it is his goodness that I love', and that 'We do well to worship God in His works'. I would like to show this passage to anyone who says Anne was tortured by self-denial. It's the best justification for lusting after a curate I've ever read. And while she sat in this pew, Anne might have been lusting after her own curate, a real one, back in Haworth.

William Weightman was twenty-six, a clever, charming, classics-loving brewer's son from Appleby. Anne had seen a lot of him in the four months she was unemployed. In fact, he went on a bit of a charm offensive, taking her and her sisters on such frivolous jaunts as a lecture in Keighley – at night! – and when he found out that none of them had ever had a valentine, he wrote them one each, posting them in secret from Bradford. They called him 'Celia Amelia' because he fancied a different girl each week, but was he interested in any of them? In January 1842, Charlotte told Nussey how Weightman 'sits opposite to Anne at church sighing softly and looking out of the corners of his eyes to win her attention – and Anne is so quiet, her look so downcast – they are a picture'. Charlotte seems to have been quite taken by him herself. She wrote about him incessantly, and painted his portrait – surely a ploy to gaze at him with impunity. She was always linking him with other women – a classic deflection technique – and when Nussey asked if she was falling for him, Charlotte protested too much: 'Let me have no more of your humbug about Cupid, etc . . . it is all groundless trash.' Perhaps Weightman spurned her because later she called him 'a thorough male-flirt'.

It's typical of reserved Anne that the first poem she (probably) wrote about Weightman isn't about being in love but about how to hide it. In 'Self-Congratulation', which she wrote in January 1840, she remembers sitting around a fire, 'conversing merrily'. When she hears a man approach, she forces herself not to tremble or blush, even though her spirit burns and her heart beats 'full and fast!' And she confesses to 'aching anguish' and 'bitter burning woe'. I think Anne liked and wanted Weightman, but she could also see he was an incorrigible charmer; and perhaps, before giving him her heart, she wanted to see if he'd grow up.

He didn't get the chance. In September 1842, he caught cholera while out visiting the sick and died, at just twenty-eight. A few weeks later Anne bravely wrote a poem that begins 'I will not mourn thee, lovely one', comparing the man she is (not) mourning to the morning sun because his life was 'full as bright' and calling him 'hopeful and beloved'. Maybe Weightman's hopefulness was what Anne liked most. And maybe her raw passion, as she describes the 'darling' with an 'angel smile' and even 'the pleasures' that are now buried in his tomb, explains why neither she nor Charlotte released the poem. Anne couldn't go home for Weightman's funeral, where Patrick said, through his tears, 'we were always like father and son', and was so upset that instead of giving his sermon without notes, as usual, he read it out. Weightman's memorial tablet still has pride of place at the church in Haworth, and it praises him for orthodox principles, active zeal, moral habits, learning, mildness and, endearingly, for affability.

Staring up at the pulpit in Little Ouseburn, I feel desperately sad for Anne. If only she had married a man who was *affable*! I am overwhelmed by how much death there is in Anne's story. She was twenty-two when Weightman died. He hadn't made it to his thirtieth birthday. Nor would she. Her mother hadn't made it to her fortieth.

I feel suddenly glad that I have just celebrated my fortieth in a room above a London pub, with salted caramel cake, and fizz, and dancing to A-ha in a sparkly dress, and people I love; glad I marked it and glad to be alive and hitting the (maybe) midpoint of my life, because not everyone gets this far.

What would have happened if Weightman had lived? Anne did want love, wishing, in 'Self-Communion' for

> One look that bids our fears depart,
> And well assures the trusting heart
> It beats not in the world alone –

But if she had become Mrs Weightman, she might not have become Acton Bell. And, having lost her love, she memorialised him on the pages of her novel, giving Weston his kindness, but making him sober and steady too.

Weston was also a perfectly plausible suitor for Agnes – exactly the kind of man Anne could have married, the kind of man Charlotte did marry. Anne works hard to make us believe that Weston is The One. He must be good because he cares so much about animals. When Agnes's pupil Matilda gleefully lets her dog savage a baby hare, Weston comforts Agnes with bluebells, which he's remembered she likes, and, she says, 'it was something to find my unimportant saying so well remembered: it was something that he had noticed so accurately the time I had ceased to be visible'. She finally feels *seen*. Weston also saves a cat, which is such a reliable writer's trick for making a character likeable that the screenwriting guru Blake Snyder wrote a whole book about it in 2005, called *Save the Cat! The Last Book on Screenwriting That You'll Ever Need* (it has two sequels). While villains might boil bunnies, heroes should save cats (like Sigourney Weaver in *Alien*) or pet dogs, or give bread to a starving child like *Disney*'s Aladdin. Weston, however, *does* save a cat, rescuing Nancy Brown's cat from the Murrays' gamekeeper. And Snyder is right; it does make me root for him. Even more when, at the end of the novel, he saves a dog.

Not just any dog. Snap is a puppy Matilda can't be bothered to look after, so Agnes steps in, and Snap becomes her 'companion, the only thing I had to love me', another fictional avatar of Flossy, the dog the Robinsons gave Anne. In the novel, the Murrays cruelly take Snap from Agnes and give him to a rat-catcher who is 'notorious for his brutal treatment of his canine slaves'. And then one morning, Agnes is walking alone on Scarborough Sands and there he is, 'frisking and wriggling' with joy. She kisses Snap again and again before noticing who's with him. Weston has rescued him. And now he wants to rescue her. Or does he? The thing is, by the end of *Agnes Grey*, Agnes doesn't need rescuing.

I only realise how innovative this is when I go back to *Jane Eyre*. It's strange reading Charlotte's novel after *Agnes Grey*. I can see how it must have surprised Anne when she read it as a work in progress. Given how much Charlotte hated governessing, Anne probably expected her to tackle the subject with ruthless realism. After all, she had already eviscerated her old school. But instead, Charlotte gave Jane a foxy boss, a kind housekeeper and just one charming pupil. And a romance. Governesses who fell for their employers took a huge risk. T. E. Lawrence's mother Sarah was a governess who got pregnant by her boss, an Irish baronet, in 1885. He ran away with her but had to cut ties with his old family (including, wrenchingly, his four daughters). He and Sarah couldn't marry, and despite using false names, they never quite escaped the stigma of illegitimacy. And this was almost a best-case scenario for a governess who had an affair with her boss. What was vanishingly unlikely was Jane's story of becoming Rochester's equal and wife and mistress of his house.

If Jane's story is the fairy tale, the nightmare appears in a book called *Miss Weeton: Journal of a Governess*. It was only published after a local historian made a startling find in a Wigan junk shop in 1925: a dusty book of letters and some fragments of memoir by a Lancashire woman called Nelly Weeton who tried to escape governessing by marrying, in 1814, when she was thirty-seven. But marriage did not save her. In bleak staccato she describes how she was

> Repeatedly turned out destitute; twice imprisoned . . . having myself been beaten almost to death; several times obliged to flee for my life . . . turned out only for complaining . . . I was threatened with being sent to a Lunatic Asylum, only for asking for food. Cloaths I could

not procure until I got them on credit. . .With my bruises thick upon me . . . was I imprisoned for two days . . . now expecting nightly or daily to be murdered – or, worse, sent to a Lunatic Asylum in my right mind; for so I was threatened . . . I expected to be . . . driven out destitute . . . so that I kept myself locked up day and night in my bedroom, going out only by stealth in the evening, to fetch provisions . . . On returning one night, I found my room on fire, and my bed burnt!

She left, but her husband took their child. There is little light in Weeton's story. The saddest thing is that she needn't have married at all and only did it because she was desperate to get out of governessing, after one job where her employer was a drunk, violent bully, and her first pupil fell into a fire and died, and another job where she felt 'totally excluded from all rational society'. When she agreed to get married, after knowing her husband for a shockingly short time, she had just saved enough money to be thinking seriously about starting her own dairy farm. I wish she had.

I also wish Agnes didn't give up work at the end of *Agnes Grey*. I like Weston. I really do. But I don't want Agnes to lose her independence, or her income. Even Jane resists Rochester when he orders her, on their engagement, to 'give up [her] governessing slavery at once'. But when they do marry, she stops teaching Adèle and sends her to school, even though she knows the horrors of schools. Adèle's first school is 'too strict . . . too severe' and makes her pale, thin and unhappy. How does Jane know the next school will be any better?

Charlotte's friend Mary Taylor gave her a hard time about her attitude to working women. She would give her an even harder time when she read *Shirley*, in which Caroline only wants to work because she feels so bored and aimless. When Shirley worries that work can 'make women masculine, coarse, unwomanly', Caroline's response is far from robust:

> And what does it signify whether unmarried and never-to-be-married women are unattractive and inelegant or not? . . . The utmost which ought to be required of old maids, in the way of appearance, is that they should not absolutely offend men's eyes.

Who cares if women *offend men's eyes*? Why doesn't Caroline defend work as a way for women to attain self-respect and earn money? Taylor hated the way Charlotte presented work as something women could 'indulge in – if they give up marriage and don't make themselves too disagreeable to the other sex'. She called Charlotte 'a coward and a traitor', and took up the pen herself, to write a book called *The First Duty of Women*, about how women should earn money. At seventy-three, she wrote her first novel, *Miss Miles*, which asks, 'Are righteous means of helping themselves never to be found for women?' In *her* novel, the idle rich fall apart when hard times hit Yorkshire, while working women thrive.

By the time Weston proposes, Agnes has become one of the resourceful, fulfilled working women Taylor rewards with happy endings in *Miss Miles*. Agnes has been dissatisfied and exploited, but she has turned her working life around. She has learned how to get work, how to hang on to it, how to get paid better for it, how to draw boundaries, how to retain her dignity and her self-esteem, how to manage difficult employers, how to find meaning in her work, and even pleasure – once she leaves the Murrays to work with her mother.

Alice Grey is an enterprising woman with a refreshing view of things. She doesn't worry about marrying off her daughters, saying breezily, 'it's no matter whether they get married or not: we can devise a thousand honest ways of making a livelihood'. When she is left a widow, she decides to go to work too. She doesn't have to. Her daughter Mary offers to take her in, and her long-lost father writes to say that if she'll admit she was wrong to disobey him by marrying a poor clergyman, he will 'make a lady' of her again, and remember Mary and Agnes in his will. It's a way out of poverty, and a guarantee of a future for her daughters. But Mrs Grey refuses.

Instead, she resolves to 'gather honey' for herself. It's a lovely phrase, making work sound both productive and sweet, and beehives are, of course, ruled by queens. Alice and Agnes set up a school, and Agnes finds there is 'a considerable difference between working with my mother in a school of our own, and working as a hireling among strangers, despised and trampled upon by old and young'. *A school of our own* has a pleasing Woolfian resonance for twenty-first-century feminists. It was also Anne's dream.

Anne and her sisters had first thought of following the example of the Woolers from Roe Head and setting up their own school in the summer of 1841. Maybe Anne thought about the school Mary Wollstonecraft had set up with her sisters, on feminist principles. Even Emily daydreamed about the three of them being 'merrily seated in our own sitting-room in some pleasant and flourishing seminary'. When their aunt offered them a loan of £100, and Margaret Wooler offered them her school, it seemed a genuine possibility. But Charlotte scuppered it. She had become consumed by a 'wish for wings'. She longed to travel. So she came up with a new plan: she and Emily would go to Brussels for six months, to improve their French. She told her aunt they would only need £50 to set up the school, and the other £50 would cover their trip. But secretly she rejected Wooler's offer, and told Emily that she planned to stay longer in Brussels. It is not clear how much finagling Charlotte did. But it seems unfair that she chose Emily to come with her, when Anne was better both at teaching and at leaving home. Charlotte said fuzzily, 'Anne might take her turn at some future period, if our school answered,' and admitted that 'Anne seems omitted in the present plan' (using the passive as if it is not her fault), 'but if all goes right I trust she will derive her full share of benefit from it in the end'. She added, vague and fervent, 'I exhort all to hope. I believe in my heart that this is acting for the best; my only fear is that others should doubt and be dismayed.' I am sure Anne *did* doubt it was for the best, and that she *was* dismayed. She even thought about resigning her job and taking over the Parsonage housekeeping, but the Robinsons pleaded with her to stay, so in the end Tabby returned to the Parsonage, and Anne stayed where she was.

The school never did get off the ground. Charlotte and Emily spent ten months in Brussels, and then Charlotte went back for another year, teaching, on a paltry salary of £16. When, finally, in the summer of 1844, she was ready to start the school, she ignored Anne's suggestion to put it in Scarborough, and instead planned to squeeze their pupils into the remote, cramped Parsonage. No wonder no one replied to the adverts she printed for 'The Misses' Brontë's Establishment for the Board and Education of a limited number of Young Ladies'. That autumn, they gave up the school idea for good.

Until Anne made it true on the page. Agnes's school *is* in Scarborough, in a large respectable house, on a broad white road, with a narrow slip of garden out front, and a flight of steps to a trim, brass-handled door. Agnes often takes the pupils for walks by the sea, her 'delight'. And although Agnes leaves to marry Weston, *Agnes Grey* does end with one working woman happy, independent, and resolutely at her post; Mrs Grey goes on gathering honey and the school lives on. Her story shows that you can marry happily, and things can still go wrong. Your husband can lose all your savings on an unwise investment. You can lose your husband. And instead of hoping to be rescued (because Mrs Grey's father offers her exactly that, a fantasy of rescue), you can rescue yourself. If you are brave enough and resourceful enough. Because in *Agnes Grey* work isn't just a distraction for bored women, it's the key to independence. And it's reassuring to know that if Agnes ever wants or needs to earn her own living again, she won't be daunted.

7

BRANWELL
or how bad love can destroy you

To learn about Anne's brother – and hoping to mix business with pleasure – I go to the Black Bull in Haworth. It was Branwell's favourite pub – and some say it still is. A ghostly figure in a top hat has been seen there, a shadow that keeps dashing out of sight. Regulars have smelled cigar smoke, heard glasses smash in the dark, and even felt a spirit walk right through them.

I know this because I have watched the 2005 episode of *Most Haunted* that investigated the Black Bull. Shock-haired medium Derek Acorah has barely arrived before he is huffing and puffing and clutching his chest, apparently because he has caught spectral tuberculosis. The programme makers stress that Acorah has no idea why they have come to this particular pub, and this is where I start to lose faith, because Haworth is not shy about its Brontë connections. Even if Acorah missed all the signs to the 'Brontë village', surely he must have spotted the Brontë Balti house, the Wuthering Heights pub, the Villette Coffee House, the Eyres and Graces shop, and the block of retirement flats named after Heathcliff. Even out on the moors there are weathered wooden signposts to the Brontë waterfall and to Top

Withins in both English and Japanese. Can Acorah really have no clue which famous tubercular ghosts might be haunting the Black Bull? Now he says he can see a small man with pointed features and red hair, who liked a drink. Asking the spirits for a name, he mutters that it sounds like *Bradwell*. *Bradwell*? *Bradwell*? And finally he's got it. *BranWELL*, he says, putting the stress in the wrong place. Presumably it's hard to get an exact pronunciation when a name is coming through from the Other Side. The programme speculates that Branwell haunts the pub because he was a broken man who could not let go . . . of Emily stealing 'his' novel, *Wuthering Heights*. Yawn!

This ancient theory started with Branwell's friend William Dearden. Branwell read him some pages of a work in progress, which later Dearden thought must have been part of *Wuthering Heights*. Anyway, Dearden said, no 'inexperienced girl' could have written 'revolting' Heathcliff. He even put his theory into a poem:

Let us hope
In charity, it never entered brain
Of woman to conceive and to produce
A character without a single trait
Of nature to redeem it, and without
A prototype in man or demon – such
Such as the foul Caliban of *Wuthering Heights*.

Soon all Branwell's friends were vehemently agreeing. The theory refused to die, even after Stella Gibbons satirised it in her 1932 novel *Cold Comfort Farm*, where the absurd Mr Mybug believes

Anne was a drunkard, and Branwell wrote twelve hours a day to keep her in gin. In 2014, the *Keighley News* reported that a Bradford writer named Chris Firth was trying to prove Branwell's authorship with help from the forensic linguistics and stylometry experts who showed that Robert Galbraith was really J. K. Rowling.

To me – and most biographers – it seems pretty clear that Branwell *didn't* write *Wuthering Heights*. But I do get a shiver down my spine when the *Most Haunted* ghost-hunters look at a print of one of Branwell's paintings. It is the famous one of the sisters – now in the National Portrait Gallery – where Branwell painted himself out, crudely covering himself with a pillar. But because Branwell was never very good at mixing paints – and because all oil paint becomes transparent with age – his face has started emerging. I don't think it looks like a paranormal white haze, but it does feel eerie; because Branwell started out as the star of the family, the cherished boy, the genius, and became the ghost at his sisters' feast.

Tonight, the Black Bull is packed; the sound system blares cheesy noughties dance mixes, and the covers band who will play later are gaffer-taping their cables to the swirly carpet. Everyone is eating roasts and everything is super-bright except for the replica of Branwell's chair, which sits, lonely, on a dark landing halfway up the stairs, roped off so that even if you wanted to have a drink with him, you couldn't. I do the next best thing, and take a whisky (Branwell's top tipple) to a corner, with my copy of Daphne du Maurier's terrific revisionist biography *The Infernal World of Branwell Brontë*. His anxious face stares up at me from the cover; nervy eyes, red hair curling forward, glasses sliding down his, yes, pointy nose.

I feel bad about the whisky, because didn't Anne *hate* alcohol? But not that bad. In fact, in the warm fug of the Black Bull, I feel huffy with Anne, and affectionate towards Branwell, who knew how to have a good time, who was marinating himself in liquor even while he was secretary to Haworth's Temperance Society. I imagine him taking minutes with a mischievous glint in his eye, then adjourning to the Black Bull to let off steam. His friend, the railway engineer Francis Grundy, called him 'Poor, brilliant, gay, moody, moping, wildly excitable, miserable Brontë'. Du Maurier's Branwell is a dreamer, an adventurer, whose party trick was writing with two hands at once, who loved steam trains and kept 'fugitive scraps' of writing in his hat. Like du Maurier, I've long had a soft spot for Branwell. I've been seduced by his danger, his impishness, by the sadness that weighed him down. I've been fascinated by the way he inspired the heroes of his sisters' novels; and, to be honest, I've been more than a bit interested in those heroes.

I grew up longing for Heathcliff. It was only when I returned to *Wuthering Heights* as a grown-up that I realised I didn't want a man who would con Hindley out of his property and drive him into an early grave, trick Isabella into marrying him and then beat her (and hang her dog), deny Hareton an education, and terrorise his ill and weak son, use him as bait to kidnap the younger Catherine and finally let him die of neglect. As, with some pain, I tore Heathcliff out of my heart, I turned to Rochester. But he is not much better. He locks up his wife in the care of unimaginative, booze-ridden Grace Poole. He could have sent her to one of the new asylums pioneering care without the use of restraints. Instead, Bertha is imprisoned in the house she was supposed to be the mistress of, and Rochester goes on a sex tour of Europe, sleeping with women he callously categorises by nationality and rank – 'English ladies, French comtesses, Italian signoras, and German Grafinnen'. Rochester flirts mercilessly with Jane while pursuing Blanche Ingram, and only after she goes cold on him does he propose to Jane. He's swindling Jane into bigamy so he's lucky she agrees to a tiny wedding, and doesn't have any relatives or friends to dig into his past. He lies about the laughter in the attic, the fire and the woman who comes into Jane's room at night and rips her veil in two. He bullies Jane about her clothes. Even after he is forced to reveal his secret, he is too self-obsessed to think of anyone but himself. When Jane refuses to run away with him, he seizes her, grips her painfully, shakes her and threatens to crush her. Neither Heathcliff nor Rochester are exactly love's young dream. Or at least they shouldn't be. As early as 1863, Caroline Norton, always ahead of her time, was raging that 'Ever since Jane Eyre loved Mr Rochester, a race of novel-heroes have sprung up whose chief merit seems to be that . . . they could "knock down a Mammoth or a Megatherium". Brutal and selfish in their ways, and rather repulsive in person, they are, nevertheless, represented as perfectly adorable.' But she was a lone voice. By 1939 it was not at all weird for the film of *Wuthering Heights* to be trailed as 'THE GREATEST LOVE STORY OF OUR TIME . . . OR ANY TIME!'

Why did Charlotte and Emily do it? Why did they make these horrible men 'perfectly adorable'? And why didn't Anne? I think Charlotte got it half right when she said Anne 'had, in the course of her life, been called on to contemplate, near at hand, and for a long time, the terrible effects of talents misused and faculties abused' and that 'what she saw sank very deeply into her mind; it did her harm'. Anne had a front-row seat for the crisis of Branwell's life. She saw it up close, and couldn't prevent it. Charlotte was right that it upset her sister deeply. It also inspired her best writing.

It all started when Anne found Branwell a job. It can't have been easy to persuade the Robinsons to let her feckless brother tutor their son. It was January 1843, and Anne had been working for them for two and a half years. They trusted her. She knew that while Branwell had the brains to teach, he didn't have the tact or sticking power, patience, resilience and grit. But she hoped he would rise to the occasion. Branwell needed the money (he would get £80 to Anne's £50). He had just tried and failed yet another career, on the railways, where he earned a dizzying £130 a year, but managed to waste much of it on 'malignant yet cold debauchery' and got fired in April 1842 for keeping bad accounts and (possibly) embezzlement. But he had been writing. He made his print debut (five years before his sisters made theirs), in June 1841, publishing a poem in the *Halifax Guardian*. Now he was writing hard and getting his work out in the world. Maybe at Thorp Green, away from his drinking pals, he would get the time and space he needed to make real headway.

Anne was writing too. She'd begun 'Passages in the Life of an Individual', which would become *Agnes Grey*. But she was bored and lonely. Although she liked her pupils, she found Mrs Robinson vapid, and hated watching her push her daughters into marriage. She felt starved of intelligent conversation; stifled, like Agnes, by feeling that 'Never a new idea or stirring thought came to me from without; and such as rose within me were, for the most part, miserably crushed at once, or doomed to sicken or fade away, because they could not see the light'. She wanted Branwell's company. Especially as they were both in mourning.

Just a few weeks after losing the lovely curate William Weightman, their aunt Elizabeth died in October 1842. The cause of death is listed, unceremoniously, as 'exhaustion from constipation'. Branwell sobbed right through Weightman's funeral – they had been genuine friends – and wrote from Elizabeth's deathbed that he was 'witnessing such agonising suffering as I would not wish my worst enemy to endure'. Anne didn't make it to Haworth in time to see her aunt before she died, but she did go to the funeral in November. Now she could wear mourning clothes, now she could grieve openly, now she could look on the outside how she felt on the inside. When she went back to Thorp Green in January 1843, Anne took Branwell with her.

It was Branwell's chance to finally come good. But he ruined everything by falling in love with Mrs Robinson. He'd only been at Thorp Green for four months when, in May 1843, he boasted to a friend, 'I curl my hair & scent my handkerchief like a Squire – I am the favourite of all the household . . . but my mistress is DAMNABLY TOO FOND OF ME.' He said Mrs Robinson wanted him 'to go to extremities'. He might, of course, have gone to extremities before, and might still have been paying towards the support of his illegitimate child. But this didn't stop him. He'd been signing his poems with an old Angrian pseudonym, calling himself Alexander Percy, Earl of Northangerland, and maybe he really did think he was the cynical, sinister ladykiller of his teenage stories. Thorp Green was just about grand enough to be the setting for one of Northangerland's sexual conquests, and if you squinted a little, which Branwell did, Mrs Robinson could stand in for one of Angria's aristocratic, languishing flirts. In *Agnes Grey*, Anne described her fictional counterpart Mrs Murray as 'a handsome, dashing lady of forty, who certainly required neither rouge nor padding to add to her charms'.

In Philippa Stone's *The Captive Dove*, which is all about Anne and Branwell's time at Thorp Green, Mrs Robinson dazzles Branwell with jewels and silks, and has a way of gazing into men's eyes that she perfected in the mirror when she was fifteen. She tells Branwell she hates her husband, he reads poems to her in the rose garden, and when Anne goes to visit him at his lodgings she sees a hand at his window, a hand that isn't Branwell's, a hand braceleted in gold and *she just knows*. Is that how it happened? Or did it go the way Oscar W. Firkins imagined in his melodrama *Empurpled Moors*, where Anne tries to confirm her suspicions by holding a vigil all night on a rug outside Mrs Robinson's room? Or maybe in the drawing room one evening, Anne looked up to catch a glance that was too intimate, too raw. Maybe she overheard the servants' gossip – Branwell said Mrs Robinson's lady's maid had seen him do enough to get him hanged. Maybe Anne found one of Branwell's love poems. Or maybe Branwell just told her – he was so indiscreet that he sent a friend a lock of Mrs Robinson's hair, saying it had lain all night on his breast and 'would to God it could do so legally!' I think perhaps Anne started to suspect something in church, partly because in both her novels Anne takes a dim view of flirting in church, and also because, around this time, Anne wrote, in the back of her prayer book, in the tiniest, faintest pencil, 'Sick of mankind and their disgusting ways.'

It wasn't just her brother and Mrs Robinson; Anne's eldest pupil, nineteen-year-old Lydia, was also having an affair, with an actor she had met in Scarborough. Henry Roxby Beverley was from a big theatrical family and famed for playing fools. Searching through archives I find an etching of him, wearing cropped red-and-yellow trousers and a massive ruff, his hair streaming wildly out of an absurd plumed hat. There's a print, too, of him playing all nine roles in a farce called *Nine to One or He's Sure to be Done*, from a preening coxcomb to a boxer in exceedingly tight trousers. He does not look like good husband material. If Lydia confided in Anne, she must have remembered reading Hester Chapone, when she was at school, on just this issue. Chapone says if a friend is having a secret love affair, you should try to dissuade her, refuse to be her confidante, and tell her parents. According to Chapone, 'However unkindly she may take this at the time, she will certainly esteem and love you the more for it, whenever she recovers a sense of her duty, or experiences the sad effects of swerving from it.' Which seems optimistic. Anyway, Anne might have sympathised with Lydia. If Mrs Robinson was half as bad as Mrs Hargrave in *The Tenant of Wildfell Hall*, who tries to force her daughters to marry rich men who are old, debauched or both, Anne would have found it hard to support her. Milicent

Hargrave puts a brave face on it; 'our dear mamma is very anxious to see us all well married,' she says, 'that is, united to rich partners. It is not my idea of being well married, but she means it all for the best.' But her younger sister Esther resists. Helen gives her advice Anne might have given the Robinson girls: 'Stand firm, and your mamma will soon relinquish her persecution and the gentleman himself cease to pester you.' But Esther's 'blithe spirit is almost broken, and her sweet temper almost spoiled, by the still unremitting persecutions of her mother in behalf of her rejected suitor – not violent, but wearisome and unremitting like a continual dropping'. Under this kind of pressure, it's easy to see why Lydia might have wanted to escape, and maybe even why she was attracted to an actor, a man skilled at throwing off the constraints of the self.

But Anne must have been doing something to keep both Lydia and Branwell in check, because when she resigned in June 1845, sick of the whole business, it took just weeks for Branwell to get fired, and not much longer for Lydia to elope to Gretna Green.

A month later, back at the Parsonage, Anne wrote in her diary paper, 'I have had some very unpleasant and undreamt of experience of human nature' and 'I . . . cannot well be <u>flatter</u> or older in mind than I am now'. She had lost her financial security and her serenity. Unlike the last time she'd been unemployed, she didn't try to get a new job. Although she felt she had 'escaped' Thorp Green, she also felt battle-weary and listless. Her aunt's legacy (each girl got £300) had bought her some time, so she slumped. And watched Branwell spin out of control.

'We have had sad work with Branwell,' wrote Charlotte that same week; he 'thought of nothing but stunning or drowning his distress of mind'. *Drowning* meant drink, but *stunning* meant drugs; heartache plunged Branwell into a whole new addiction. He swiftly became the scandal of the village, binge-drinking and knocking back laudanum, wandering around wasted, unshaven and depressed, waking the house at night and sleeping all day, lying, dodging debts, and telling everyone that Mrs Robinson was going to leave her husband for him. The barmaid at the Black Bull told Emily's biographer Mary Duclaux that Branwell 'loved to speak about her even to a dog'.

Charlotte found this so embarrassing that she turned her back on her brother. Calling him 'a drain on every resource, an impediment to happiness', she barely spoke to him in the three years between July 1845, when he staggered back from Thorp Green, and his death. She gave up on him, writing as early as August 1845 that 'hope, in his case, seems a fallacy'. At first, Emily was more positive. In their 1845 diary papers, she and Anne echo each other, Emily writing of 'B who I hope will be better and do better, hereafter' and Anne saying 'we hope he will be better and do better in future'. But by March 1846 Emily was calling him 'a hopeless being'. Only Anne seems to have kept hoping he would turn his life around.

Anne was the one who would find him one terrible night in 1848, passed out in a bed that was on fire. Perhaps she was checking on him. Certainly she saved his life. In John Greenwood's account, Branwell had fallen asleep and knocked over his candle. When Anne tried to rouse him, he just muttered, 'Well! Well! We'll make it all right by and by.' Unable to lift him, Anne fetched Emily, who hauled Branwell out of the bed, tore down the blazing bedding, seized a large can of water and quenched the fire.

What do you do when your brother is coming apart at the seams? If you are a Brontë, you write about it. It was Gaskell who first drew a line from Branwell to Heathcliff, Rochester and Huntingdon. When she learned that the sisters had a drunk, disreputable brother, she found it very convenient. She used him to excuse or explain away everything she found dark, churning and unwomanly in their books. Charlotte, Emily and Anne hadn't imagined all this nastiness out of their pretty little heads, she said; they had been 'pressed down . . . for long months and years' by 'hard cruel facts'. Which perplexes me because where exactly, in the roiling tempest of *Wuthering Heights*, are the sweet, ladylike bits Emily is supposed to have come up with on her own? And were Charlotte and Emily really *pressed down* by *hard cruel facts*? Anne told the truth about alcoholism. But when Charlotte and Emily wrote about drunk, chaotic, hurtful men they made them objects of desire.

Maybe the Black Bull isn't the best place to think about Branwell after all. Because what Anne learned about alcohol from Branwell was nothing to what she learned about love. She had worked for and lived with Mrs Robinson for five years, and knew her ex-employer would never give up her easy, privileged life for an odd-looking know-it-all curate's son. She could see that Branwell was confusing fantasy with love. And so was Charlotte.

Charlotte had been back from Brussels for a year and a half, but hadn't secured a job or revived the school scheme because she was obsessed with her Belgian tutor Constantin Heger.

Serious, lofty, quixotic and unavailable, he was all Charlotte's Angrian dreams come to life. In a painting of his family, Heger's wife sits with her children tumbling around her, lit up by sunshine and motherly pride, while Heger stands dramatically in a patch of gloom, head to foot in black, his beetling eyebrows drawn darkly together, ignoring the small daughter who hugs his knees. Charlotte admired Heger's mind but she adored his rages, writing 'when he is very ferocious with me I cry – & that sets all things straight'.

Charlotte explored their sadomasochistic attraction in *The Professor* where the Heger-like Crimsworth says, of his Charlotte-like pupil,

> The reproofs suited her best of all: while I scolded she would chip away with her pen-knife at a pencil or a pen; fidgeting a little, pouting a little, defending herself by monosyllables, and when I deprived her of the pen or pencil . . . she would at last raise her eyes and give me a certain glance, sweetened with gaiety, and pointed with defiance, which, to speak truth, thrilled me as nothing had ever done, and made me . . . her subject, if not her slave.

Charlotte wrote about Heger in *Villette* too, where Lucy Snowe starts teaching at a girls' school and encounters the irascible little despot Paul Emmanuel. He locks Lucy in an attic infested with rats, cockroaches, black beetles and possibly a ghost, and criticises her, for looking at a painting, for wearing a pink dress, for having fun and sometimes just for being English. Lucy just fancies him even more. The moment where she finds 'his olive hand . . . on the most intimate terms with my desk', and realises he has been hiding 'treasures' there, including romance novels which 'smelt of cigars' is 'very shocking' – and not unsexy. Catching him in the act, Lucy exults, 'at last I had him'. She describes the cigar smoke 'curling from his lips' as 'the pale blue breath of his Indian darling', and you don't have to be Freud to have thoughts about that. But I wish Lucy didn't let him hector her. And when she says 'his mind was indeed my library, and whenever it was opened to me, I entered bliss. Intellectually imperfect as I was, I could read little', I want to shout: *be your own library*.

Charlotte's heroines all share her taste for ferocious men who play power games. Shirley believes 'a husband must be able to control me', and when challenged, spits back,

> Did I not say I prefer a *master* – one in whose presence I shall feel obliged and disposed to be good; one whose control my impatient temper must acknowledge; a man whose approbation can reward, whose displeasure punish me; a man I shall feel it impossible not to love, and very possible to fear?

Charlotte's self-abasing letters to Heger are even more depressing to read. Begging her 'master' for 'only the crumbs of bread which fall from the rich man's table', she makes herself poor and small. She worries she is 'raving' and her prose gets overblown and scattered. Heger, who encouraged her to choose and measure her words, must have found the letters' style as alarming as their contents. He tore them up and binned them, but his wife retrieved the pieces, jigsawed them together and stitched them back in place; and who knows what dark night of the soul their marriage went through after that.

Du Maurier said Branwell's tragedy was that he tried to savour 'The rich joys of his infernal world' in the real world. In the summer of 1845 it must have seemed to Anne that this was going to be Charlotte's tragedy too. She found Emily just as reluctant to face facts. They went on holiday – Anne's *only* holiday – and all 27-year-old Emily wanted to do was to play Gondal. Gaskell was wrong. Charlotte and Emily weren't pressed down by facts; they were soaring into fantasy.

Which is why, while *Jane Eyre* and *Wuthering Heights* are terrific on longing, on unrequited love, on thwarted love and on love beyond the grave, they have little to say about having an actual relationship with an actual person who loves you back and is free to do something about it. Cathy and Edgar are married for much of *Wuthering Heights*, but they are not in love. For most of *Jane Eyre*, Jane can't marry Rochester because he is married to someone else. Only Anne allowed her heroine, in *The Tenant of Wildfell Hall*, to marry a man she loved, and who (at first) loved her back, and then explored the consequences. Only Anne went beyond the marriage plot – years before George Eliot did the same in *Middlemarch*.

I only get a sense of how hard it must have been for Anne to write about love so differently from her sisters, how revolutionary it must have seemed, when I leave the pub and walk through the streaming rain to the cottage. I close the curtains, pour a glass of wine, wrap myself in a blanket and put on a DVD. The opening shots of the 1996 BBC miniseries of *The Tenant of Wildfell Hall* could come from any Brontë adaptation: a woman in a sober black dress and white lace collar, a candle guttering, a headlong run through a wild wood, a servant in a homely bonnet, deep mist and a Gothic house sunk in gloom. When Toby Stephens stalks in, I sigh with contentment. I very *much* enjoyed his Rochester. But I sit up, perplexed, when I see that he is playing Gilbert. And Rupert Graves as Huntingdon? The floppy-haired young man of the Merchant Ivory films, all wry irreverence, crinkly smiles and rueful grins, is trying to look devilish, while Stephens, who has pretty much only ever played cads and bounders, is doing his best to stop glowering. It's as if someone mixed up the casting envelopes. Surely Graves would have made a sweet, floundering Gilbert, and Stephens would have been happier as Huntingdon. I can imagine him snatching Helen's paintings, grabbing her hands, stealing kisses, coming in from the hunt 'all spattered and splashed . . . and stained with the blood of his prey', and recklessly hitting the bottle. I feel cheated.

And then I realise the problem isn't the miniseries, but me. I am disappointed because, schooled by years of comfort-watching Brontë dramas, I wanted to succumb to Huntingdon's dark charms. I wanted to fancy him the way I fancied Heathcliff and Rochester. To my chagrin, I have often been attracted to bad men. But Huntingdon is worse than bad. He is not like Jem Merlyn in *Jamaica Inn*, a novel I firmly believe is du Maurier's gift to Brontë fans who have got into trouble trying to find their own Heathcliffs. Instead of making her heroine choose between a bad, irresistible man and a milquetoast, du Maurier gives Mary Yellan a better choice. Just as it looks like she might fall for Joss Merlyn, who's not only a hard-drinking, rotten-hearted, traumatised, wife-beating, murdering ship-wrecker, but also her uncle by marriage, along comes his younger brother Jem, a sexy horse thief, who is also hopeful and kind. However, Huntingdon is not Jem; he's Joss. He's not Angel in *Buffy the Vampire Slayer*, who was once an evil vampire but is now a sweet vegetarian; he's Spike, who enjoys being bad, and who can't be saved because his heart is ice. And yes, I used to fancy Spike.

But I don't any more. I've learned that brutal, selfish men are not *perfectly adorable*, and I think the makers of the miniseries know it too. They cast against type to stop us swooning, to make us think. They also show Huntingdon raping Helen. When this scene was first screened, period-drama fans were up in arms about it, and many online reviewers still are. They find the scene graphic and gratuitous, demand to know why the book has been sexed up, insist Anne would never have written such a thing. But I'm not sure. Anne shows Huntingdon abusing Helen both verbally and physically, and she implies that more happens than she can say. One night, Huntingdon comes upstairs 'sick and stupid', and Helen says, 'I will write no more about that.' It's jarring, because she is usually so searingly honest. As Helen stops short, Anne leaves space for us to think about what a man like Huntingdon, whose evening of drink, violence and humiliation has left him 'sick and stupid', might do once he is alone with his wife. Her silence is also eloquent about how impossible it was to describe marital rape in 1848. There were no words for it. Even twenty years later, John Stuart Mill had no precise term; he had to write about a wife 'being made the instrument of an animal function contrary to her inclinations'. Marital rape didn't become a crime in the UK until 1991. I don't think the miniseries would have surprised Anne. She wanted to show the consequences of fancying violent, self-destructive men like Huntingdon, Heathcliff and Rochester; how awful they are to live with, how hard they are to leave, and how delusional it is to think we can change them. Huntingdon is vile. So vile that *The Tenant of Wildfell Hall* is still shocking. It's still a sucker punch of a book.

The novel is also full of *thinking*. As Anne struggled to understand what was happening to her brother, she dissected all the forces that worked against Branwell, from education to alcohol to the way he pursued love so wrong-headedly. She might have been thinking about how she would pursue love herself, if she had the chance again. After all, at twenty-five, she was not yet an old maid. Her mother had married at twenty-nine, Charlotte would marry at thirty-eight and one of Nussey's sisters would marry at fifty-three. Most of all, I think Anne examined her feelings about Byron. When, as children, the Brontës had pored over Thomas Moore's rollicking *Life of Byron*, Branwell had wanted to be Byron and Anne and her sisters had just wanted him.

Now Anne could see that Branwell's dreams of Byron were destroying him. Because Branwell wasn't a roaring, aristocratic, philandering drunk, wreaking havoc across the fleshpots of Europe, fuelled by claret and champagne; he was mostly just sinking a few whiskies (bought with cash scrounged from his father) with the local stonemason and gravedigger at a pub so near his house that he could have rolled there. You can almost see the Black Bull from the Parsonage. You can walk there in two minutes. Drunk, you can do it in four. (I have checked.) While Byron quaffed gleefully out of a goblet made from a friar's skull, Branwell sheepishly went to temperance meetings and scored his opium at the village apothecary, which is now a retro shop scented with vanilla, and wasn't much less tame then. When the first two cantos of *Childe Harold* were published by John Murray in 1812, Byron woke up famous. No such fanfare greeted the poems Branwell published in the *Halifax Guardian*. And while Byron was a Regency pin-up, Branwell was (said Charlotte) a 'quizzical little personage' with 'a bunch of carroty hair' and (said his friend Grundy) 'almost insignificantly small' with 'a great, bumpy, intellectual forehead' and 'small ferrety eyes', a man who puffed out his chest to make himself look broader, and asked his barber to crest his hair as high as it would go, to give him just one more inch.

It had also become clear to Anne that she didn't want a Byronic hero of her own. From Anne's earliest experiments in Gondal she had questioned whether a Byronic hero was best. Since then, she had surely heard some of the stories Moore left out of his biography of Byron. The poet had died when Anne was four, but his widow, Annabella, was very much alive, living in Leicestershire, and furious with the man who had ruined her life. When they'd first met, she'd been shy, round-faced and rosy-cheeked; 'a cold collation' Byron said, 'and I prefer hot suppers'. Hot suppers like Lady Caroline Lamb who made bonfires of his letters, sent him bloodied ringlets of pubic hair, and (approvingly) dubbed him 'mad, bad and dangerous to know'. But he needed Annabella's money to restore his house. And she was naive enough to think she could reform him. On their wedding night, Byron set fire to a red curtain, paced the gallery with a loaded pistol and hinted at a dark secret. When Annabella discovered that he was sleeping with his half-sister, she wrote, 'My heart is withered away, so that I forget my bread'. She stuck it out for a year, a year in which Byron wore only black, gambled, slept around, smashed furniture and, when she got pregnant, called her ugly and said he hoped she and the baby would die. When she went into labour, he went to the theatre, then came home and shot the tops off soda bottles while she gave birth. Two days later, he forced her to have sex. Deviant sex, she said. Then he kicked her out.

It was 1816, two decades before Caroline Norton, and Annabella knew divorce would be virtually impossible – even if she could prove his incest – and that if the courts deemed him mad, not bad, she'd be expected to stay with him and nurse him. But she knew enough of his secrets to persuade him to agree to a legal separation. After that, gossip drove Byron into exile. He had always written anti-heroes who were haunted by impossible love, and doomed to wander the earth, and now he was living the dream. Eight years later, at only thirty-six, while failing to do much fighting for the Greek war of independence, he caught a chill and died. This didn't make a dent in Byromania. But Annabella kept telling her story, until eventually she found her best listener in the author Harriet Beecher Stowe whose sensational book *Lady Byron Vindicated* did exactly what it said on the tin.

Anne would have been cheered to know that Annabella got some justice, and that the Byrons' daughter, Ada Lovelace, freed herself from her father's legacy to became the world's first computer programmer. Anne knew that living with a man bent on self-destruction wasn't exciting or romantic. Branwell was making everyone unhappy, including himself, and he was forcing his sisters to become his carers; becoming like the drunks in *The Tenant of Wildfell Hall* who have tantrums and demand bottles, and are too immature ever to be good fathers.

The night that ends with Helen unwilling or unable to tell her diary what happens, begins with 'a regular jollification' – a phrase Anne might have borrowed from Branwell who liked to call a boozy night a 'regular rumpus'. Helen's nemesis, the vampish Annabella, tells her husband, Lowborough, who is trying not to drink, that he lacks 'a bold, manly spirit', like his friends, who swear, make uproar, and are so drunk they can't make a cup of tea without spilling everything and spoiling the sugar. They attack Lowborough, and he only gets free when Helen gives him a candle, and he burns his friend Hattersley's hand until he lets go.

That's when Hattersley starts bullying his wife Milicent, and in the most chilling line in the book, she begs him to 'Remember, we are not at home'. It becomes plain what he does when they *are* at home, when he starts 'shaking her, and remorselessly crushing her slight arms in the grip of his powerful fingers'. He hits Milicent's brother when he tries to intervene, and then throws Milicent to the ground.

On another occasion, Helen is assaulted by Milicent's brother, Hargrave. He just wants to be her knight in shining armour, demanding, 'let *me* protect you'. He seizes her hands, he throws himself at her, and he attacks her reputation, taunting her, when someone sees them together, with 'Your fair fame is gone'. He says she may as well submit, and 'say I overcame you, and you could not choose but yield!' She defends herself with her palette knife, rejects him forcefully and makes him clear her name. He slinks away, annoyed that he hasn't been able to cast himself as a roué or a rapist. This was the kind of thing that made the *Literary World's* critic snort that 'If any one choose to study her male characters, it will be found that all that is good or attractive about them is or might be womanish'.

Anne doesn't blame anyone else for Huntingdon's bad behaviour. Helen learns the folly of trying to say it was his mother's fault. Anne was reacting against the way her sisters blamed Mrs Robinson for destroying Branwell. Taking her cue from Charlotte, Gaskell would damn Mrs Robinson as a 'showy woman for her age' who liked hanging out in Mayfair ballrooms and seduced Branwell, causing his death and maybe his sisters' too. Mrs Robinson had lost her husband by then, remarried and become Lady Scott, and did not want her past dragged through the mud. Gaskell's biography came out in March 1857, and by May, Lady Scott's lawyers had forced Gaskell's publishers to recall all unsold copies, and to make a formal retraction in *The Times*. Gaskell found herself 'in the Hornet's nest with a vengeance' and had to rewrite her account of what happened at Thorp Green. Lady Scott's daughters were so upset by the scandal that they refused to show any Brontë biographers their correspondence with Anne, destroying the letters she wrote to them, during the years when they lost their father, fought with their mother and found love. When I scour the Robinson archive I mainly find receipts from York shops. I know the Robinsons bought alcohol at Acton & Co. on Skeldergate, fine wool coats from W. C. Turner, Perruquier, Hair Cutter, and Perfumer, and flour from Thomas Bingley on Davygate. But I don't know any of the things Anne wrote to them about love and life. Of all the bones I have to pick with Gaskell, this is the worst.

If Anne thought her sisters were ready for her unvarnished take on their brother, she was wrong. In his 1932 biography of Charlotte, the Mapp and Lucia novelist E. F. Benson calls *The Tenant of Wildfell Hall* the 'strange harvesting' Anne made of Branwell's 'failings', which seems a bit uncalled for, given how deliciously spiteful his own novels are. He pictures Anne in the Parsonage dining room, ruthlessly 'making copy out of Branwell' while her sisters wish she wouldn't be so 'morbid'. It's an echo of Charlotte calling Anne's motives for writing the novel 'pure, but, I think, slightly morbid', and saying 'She hated her work, but would pursue it'. Which doesn't feel true to the experience of reading *The Tenant of Wildfell Hall*, with its freshness, its wit, its brio. 'When reasoned with on the subject,' said Charlotte, 'she regarded such reasonings as a temptation to self-indulgence. She must be honest; she must not varnish, soften, nor conceal.' Charlotte called her arguments *reasoning*, because she thought she was reasonable and Anne was not. But Anne doesn't sound unreasonable when she says, in her preface to the novel's second edition,

> My object in writing the following pages, was not simply to amuse the Reader, neither was it to gratify my own

taste, nor yet to ingratiate myself with the Press and the Public: I wished to tell the truth, for truth always conveys its own moral to those who are able to receive it.

She knew what she was trying to do, and her confidence is what makes her novel so arresting, urgent and wise. As for her honesty, she argued,

> when we have to do with vice and vicious characters, I maintain it is better to depict them as they really are than as they would wish to appear. To represent a bad thing in its least offensive light is doubtless the most agreeable course for a writer of fiction to pursue; but is it the most honest, or the safest? Is it better to reveal the snares and pitfalls of life to the young and thoughtless traveller, or to cover them with branches and flowers?

Anne was trying to save her readers. She couldn't stop Branwell falling for Mrs Robinson, or drinking, or taking drugs or setting fire to his bed. But she could save him on the page.

Huntingdon does terrible things, much worse than Branwell ever did, and he is saved. Not by love, because Anne didn't think that was possible. Even in *Jane Eyre*, Jane doesn't save Rochester; she has to leave him: he has to let her words and ideals sink in, and has to go through fire, disfigurement and disability before he becomes a better man. In *The Tenant of Wildfell Hall*, too, Helen doesn't save Huntingdon until he is dying, and she comes back to stay with him, to hold his hand at his deathbed, to be kind and indefatigable and to tell him there is

another way to live, or at least another way to die. He cries, at
last, and makes a sort of apology – 'Oh, Helen, if I had listened
to you, it never would have come to this!' – and Helen hopes
he will be saved from hell.

But Anne doesn't make Helen his saviour. In fact, she shows
how naive, how hubristic and how dangerous it is to think you
can save anyone. At first Helen believes,

> There *is* essential goodness in him; – and what delight to
> unfold it! . . . If he has wandered, what bliss to recall
> him! If he is now exposed to the baneful influence of
> corrupting and wicked companions, what glory to deliver
> him from them! – Oh! If I could but believe that Heaven
> has designed me for this!

She thinks she's succeeding when he 'listens attentively' and
even believes it when he says 'that if he had me always by his
side he should never do or say a wicked thing, and that a little
daily talk with me would make him quite a saint'. But this is
never going to happen. At best, she's his 'angel monitress', and
no one wants to be that, a prefect in wings, a traffic warden
holding a zither. Like the Byrons, the Huntingdons are a
marriage of opposites and Helen is the worst possible person
to save her husband. Her strategy is to be cold with him, solemn
and grave, but this only drives him towards the heat of hard
liquor or the warm arms of other women. She never shows him
that alcohol and adultery are false fires, and that, instead, he
could love her, and their son, and books and pictures and fresh
air. Only when she fails does she release herself from the

pressure of trying to be a saviour. 'Fool that I was,' she says, 'to dream that I had strength and purity enough to save myself and him!'

Helen does save her son, by getting him away and then by slipping tartar emetic into his drinks, to make him hate the taste of alcohol. It was a cure the Brontës might have tried on Branwell. Even now, alcoholics are often prescribed disulfiram (Antabuse), which stops the body breaking down acetaldehyde, making the hangover start from the first sip. Helen must have been desperate to put her young son through this, but she didn't want him to end up like his father, or, worse, Lowborough. While Huntingdon is the life and soul of the party, a man who gaily says, 'I like to enjoy my life at all sides and ends,' Lowborough is pale and gloomy, addicted to gambling and laudanum as well as drink, constantly reforming and constantly capitulating; 'a skeleton at a feast', 'silent and grim as a ghost', asking his friends, in genuine terror, 'what you can find to be so merry about. What you see in life I don't know – I see only the blackness of darkness, and a fearful looking for of judgment and fiery indignation!' One night, he contemplates suicide, and in the morning Helen finds a knife thrown out of a window and a razor snapped in two and burned. Lowborough's trouble, again, isn't just alcohol but love. When he separates from his faithless wife, he achieves both happiness and sobriety.

The Tenant of Wildfell Hall is really about bad love versus good love, how to tell the difference, how to get away from bad love and how to get good love instead, how bad love can destroy you, and the joy good love can bring. Which is why Anne didn't end *The Tenant of Wildfell Hall* with Helen escaping

Huntingdon; she gave her heroine the chance to find someone better. At least, *I* think she did. A lot of readers think that when Helen marries Gilbert she jumps from the frying pan into the fire. Are they right? Should I worry about the fact that Gilbert's narrative frames Helen's, so that after Helen gets married we never hear from her again? Perhaps it is as ominous as her silence about the night Huntingdon comes upstairs 'sick and stupid'. The critic Naomi Jacobs even argues that the frame is an act of *'couverture'*, the oppressive system of laws that meant married women had no rights and no voice. As early as 1848, a critic in the *Literary World* was saying Gilbert ought to be 'passed out of the window with a farmyard fork', mainly because he is a 'boor . . . lacking either spirit, generosity or language' to apologise for his vicious attack on Frederick Lawrence.

The attack *is* shocking. Convinced that Lawrence is having an affair with Helen (not knowing that they are actually brother and sister), Gilbert runs into Lawrence on an isolated road. First he is just rude, but then he beats Lawrence over the head with his whip, so hard that Lawrence goes deathly pale, blood trickles down his forehead, and he reels in his saddle and falls off his pony. He lies still. 'Had I killed him?' Gilbert wonders, wavering over whether to help him or whether his 'offences' are 'too unpardonable'. It takes Lawrence some time to recover, not just from the blow, but from the fever he catches while unconscious in the rain. Lawrence is the best man in the book. Which is odd because he is not the romantic lead. When Helen is reunited with the brother she's barely seen since they were separated as children, she has 'very unamiable feelings against my fellow mortals – the male part of them especially'. It is

Lawrence who restores her faith. He's trustworthy, kind and discreet, and they get on very well indeed. In fact, if he wasn't Helen's brother, he would be her ideal man.

Except that he's dull. Gilbert sums him up, devastatingly, as 'a new garment, all very neat and trim to look at, but so tight in the elbows that you would fear to split the seams by the unrestricted motion of your arms, and so smooth and fine in surface that you scruple to expose it to a single drop of rain'. And Helen doesn't want dull. Not after being Huntingdon's 'angel monitress'. She wants to split the seams, she wants to run out in the rain. And it's true that even though she knows Gilbert isn't perfect, she wants him anyway. A woman has needs, and Anne is very frank about female desire. But is it worth the risk? Helen has already advised her friend Esther to 'Keep both heart and hand in your own possession, till you see good reason to part with them' and warned her that 'Marriage may change your circumstances for the better, but, in my private opinion, it is far more likely to produce a contrary result'.

It is sometimes safer to stay single. Which is partly why, before meeting my boyfriend, I was single for six years and like Helen at Wildfell Hall, I was not unhappy. Now, we are moving in together, and I am reading Anne's novel again. I read it as we merge our books, and battle with flatpacks and try to decide whose toaster to keep, as I wonder what the future holds.

My boyfriend thinks Gilbert is a bit of a muppet. Not just because Gilbert attacks Lawrence but because he is not always nice to women. This is a fair criticism. Gilbert treats Eliza Millward shabbily, taking liberties with her, stringing her along, then dropping her. He squeezes her arm so hard that she shrinks into herself with a cry of pain or terror. He gives Helen the silent treatment, resolving, ludicrously, 'to dally with my victim like a cat'. His first response to Helen's harrowing, courageous diary is pique; she's torn out the last pages so he can't read about himself. And yet the more I read *The Tenant of Wildfell Hall*, the more I want to mount a defence of Gilbert.

Gilbert Markham is a decent gentleman farmer who takes his work seriously. He speaks tenderly about 'looking after the wellbeing of my young lambs and their mothers'. He loves his mother. He defends Helen against gossip. He woos her by giving her books. While Huntingdon only picks up books to throw them, in this very literary romance, Gilbert learns Helen's first name by seeing it written in her books. I also feel protective of him when critics say he's smug because he enjoys sitting in his library with 'well-roasted feet'. There's nothing wrong with warm feet. Is Gilbert really a misogynist for saying his friend Halford is more important to him than his wife – or is he just joking? And is sending Helen's diary to Halford an act of appropriation? I'm not sure. Maybe Gilbert got Helen's permission. Maybe there are no secrets in this close-knit, loving family. And anyway, he doesn't just send her diary; he also tells his story, admitting to his violence and his vanity. We only know about his bad behaviour because he tells us. And he does apologise. The *Literary World* critic is wrong. Gilbert's satisfaction at hurting Lawrence very quickly turns to remorse. He bravely goes to Lawrence's house and makes a free and frank apology, and, crucially, he doesn't behave like that again.

What's more, Gilbert is writing with a purpose. Halford is married to Gilbert's feisty sister Rose, who finds it deeply frustrating that their mother is always saying things like

> I'm sure your poor, dear father was as good a husband as ever lived, and after the first six months or so were over, I should as soon have expected him to fly, as to put himself out of his way to pleasure me. He always said I was a good wife, and did my duty; and he always did his – bless him! – he was steady and punctual, seldom found fault without a reason, always did justice to my good dinners, and hardly ever spoiled my cookery by delay – and that's as much as any woman can expect of any man.

Quoting this, Gilbert asks, 'Is it so, Halford? Is that the extent of your domestic virtues; and does your happy wife exact no more?' He seems to think Halford has something to learn about being a good husband, and that he can teach him. And maybe he can. Maybe he has changed. Maybe Helen has changed him. From their earliest conversations she makes him wonder if he was spoiled by his mother, makes him worry about his 'corruption' and inspires him to change. When he thinks he can solve all her problems by marrying her, she asks, 'Are you hero enough . . .?' He learns that there is more to heroism than posturing. He doesn't *start* worthy of her, but he becomes so. *The Tenant of Wildfell Hall* is a very encouraging novel to read when you are trying to change your life. The rash, brutal Gilbert of the past is not the same as the older, wiser Gilbert telling the story.

The best defence of Gilbert is the way he makes Helen feel. With Huntingdon, Helen was prim and miserable, but with Gilbert she is her best self; strong, open and creative. Although it seems counter-intuitive, *The Tenant of Wildfell Hall*, a novel about a marriage falling spectacularly apart, is turning out to be my best guide to ensuring that I am making the right decisions about love. Because Anne makes a sharp distinction between what makes her heroine happy and what turns her into an unhappy ice queen. With Huntingdon, Helen's identity is obliterated; 'I so identify myself with him,' she says, 'that I feel his degradation, his feelings and transgressions as my own.' She loses her moral compass, she feels 'debased, contaminated', and 'indifferent and insensate'. I once wanted love like this, like Cathy saying 'I *am* Heathcliff', declaring love by erasing herself. But now I want love where you still know who and where you are, where you don't feel needy or dependent, the kind of love where you realise you have only been using a tiny corner of your heart before.

Anne must have wanted this too, and hoped for it, or she couldn't have written, in the midst of the coldest, hardest realism, such pure, lyrical romance. As Helen says, 'what the world stigmatises as romantic, is often more nearly allied to the truth than is commonly supposed; for, if the generous ideas of youth are too often overclouded by the sordid views of after-life, that scarcely proves them to be false.' However tough Helen's experiences are, she doesn't stop hoping. Romance is generous, it is brave, and it is worth hanging on to. There is no shame in trying to make a character happy. It might even be a writer's responsibility; if you dream up a character and, as the old storytelling maxim goes, send them up a tree and throw stones at them, perhaps it's also your job to get them down.

Anne did her best to make both her heroines happy. When Weston proposes in *Agnes Grey*, he and Agnes feel transformed, and so does Scarborough with its 'splendid sunset mirrored in the restless world of waters at our feet'. And Helen's proposal to Gilbert is a scene straight out of a medieval romance, even down to the lady presenting her suitor with a rose. But it's not played straight; by this stage in the novel, Anne is having fun. Gilbert hears a rumour that Helen is marrying someone else and races out, breathlessly thinking,

> Oh, I *must* see her – she must know my truth, even if I told it at the church door! I might pass for a madman or an impertinent fool – even she might be offended at such an interruption, or at least might tell me it was now too late – but if I *could* save her! if she *might* be mine! – it was too rapturous a thought!

This is Harry in *When Harry Met Sally*, running, sweating, through New York on New Year's Eve to tell Sally that he wants to spend the rest of his life with her and wants the rest of his life to start as soon as possible. It's ten-year-old Sam in *Love Actually*, zooming to Heathrow Airport to catch Joanna before she crosses the Atlantic. It's Ben in *The Graduate*, driving to Santa Barbara, running out of petrol and sprinting the last blocks to spring Elaine from her wedding. I'm not saying Anne Brontë invented the romcom run, but, wait, did she?

Gilbert covers quite some distance. Anne is at her satirical best describing him on a coach where 'snow heavily clogged the wheels and balled the horses' feet; the animals were consumedly lazy; the coachman most execrably cautious; the passengers confoundedly apathetic in their supine indifference'. They won't help him yell at the coachmen, and unanimously oppose this lovesick madman taking the reins himself. Next, Gilbert tries to get a post-chaise, but the only one in town is being repaired. He dithers over finding a horse, then decides to walk. It's only six miles, 'but the road was strange, and I had to keep stopping to inquire my way; hallooing to carters and clodhoppers, and frequently invading the cottages'. Eventually, harassed, exhausted and dripping sweat, he gets to Grassdale where, to his horror, the bride and groom are already coming out of the church and he strains to see who's in the veil . . . and she's blonde. It's not Helen.

But he still has to tell Helen how he feels. When he sees the size of her house, his heart sinks. And she's not even in. He has to go to her aunt's, which involves *more* forms of transport until, at last, 'I mounted "The Lightning"' – not a knight's steed but another coach. Gilbert's heart is fluttering, his chest is heaving and his fellow passengers keep saying what a fine catch the rich widow will make, and it scares him. Helen has to get him into the house, engineer a tête-à-tête, and give him a rose as proxy for her heart. It's an unlikely rose, a Christmas-rose, blooming when all the other roses are dead, and all the more magical for the glittering snow that dusts its petals.

This is where Anne gave her strongest assurance that Helen will be happy second time around. Helen wants Gilbert to promise that her aunt can live with them after they marry, because once she's vowed to love, honour and obey, her property will be his, and he'll be free to kick out Helen's aunt, and Helen, and her son if he wants to. Why not? It happened to Nelly Weeton. Gilbert's response is groundbreaking: 'do what you will with your own', he says, relinquishing the power marriage will give him. It was the same formula the philosopher and feminist John Stuart Mill would use in 1851, which makes me wonder if he'd read Anne's novel. Mill was appalled when, after years of secret dates at the rhino enclosure at London Zoo, his lover Harriet Taylor was finally free to marry him, and he realised how much power he would have over her. He wrote a 'formal protest against the existing law of marriage, in so far as confer-ring such powers; and a solemn promise never in any case or under any circumstances to use them'. It inspired his and Taylor's famous 1869 essay, 'The Subjection of Women', which argued for equality, and was even *written* equally. When Gilbert says 'do what you will with your own', when he says Helen's aunt must of course live with them, and when he is open-heartedly affectionate with Helen's son, I feel that Helen is going to be safe. This is how you have an equal relationship; you find someone worthy, and you say clearly what you need. I think of all those self-help books that tell women to become doormats to get men. Tracy McMillan's *Why You're Not Married . . . Yet* includes chapters titled 'You're Selfish', 'You're a Mess' and 'You're Crazy'. Helen is not like Cathy and Heathcliff, who can't live without each other. She's not like Charlotte begging for crumbs. She's not like Branwell, so drunk and caught up in a fantasy of love that he talks about it to a pub dog. Helen doesn't commit to Gilbert until she has built a happy, independent life, become a confident mother and a successful painter, and reconciled with her aunt. She isn't going to get lost in a relationship because she knows who she is. She marries on her own terms.

Anne looked at Charlotte trying to turn Heger into the Duke of Zamorna, Branwell imagining he was Northangerland seducing Mrs Robinson, and even at Byron believing the only true love was impossible, taboo and antisocial, and she realised that bad love was a story people got stuck in. In *The Tenant of Wildfell Hall*, Helen sits down at 2 a.m. in her dressing gown to write about her marriage imploding, and feels, 'I have found relief in describing the very circumstances that have destroyed my peace.' Branwell tried to do this too. Hoping, he said, '*to write away my torment*', he started a novel. But he couldn't finish 'And The Weary Are at Rest', about a devilish hero seducing a lady who was bored of her bilious husband, perhaps because Mrs Robinson was conspicuously *not* leaving her husband, however bored she was, however bilious he was. Next, Branwell started a poem about an ancestor of his friend J. B. Leyland, a woman who escaped her father's castle by tying a rope around her waist and throwing out the end so her lover could haul her across a moat. He hoped Mrs Robinson was throwing him a rope when in June 1846 he heard that Mr Robinson was dead, and that the Robinsons' coachman was waiting for him at the Black Bull. The barmaid said he 'fair danced down the churchyard as if he were out of his mind; he was so fond of that woman'. But Mrs Robinson wasn't summoning him to Thorp Green. She was trying to keep him away. And she did it by telling her own stories, getting the coachman to lie that Mr Robinson's will stipulated that if his widow saw Branwell again, she would lose everything. He claimed all Mrs Robinson did was 'kneel in her bedroom in bitter tears and prayers'. Branwell was too tender to see that he was being manipulated. The barmaid found him alone on the floor of the bar parlour. He'd had a fit and was bleating like a calf. Mrs Robinson's stories had left no room for Branwell to write his own. Six months later, he was still blocked: 'if I sit down and try to write, all ideas that used to come clothed in sunlight now press round me in funeral black'. Anne realised the stories she'd been told would make her miserable, if she let them. So she chose to write a different story about love, a story that would help her get past the unhappiness of Thorp Green, and fall back in love with life.

8

PATRICK
or how to change yourself (so you
can change the world)

The longer I spend in Haworth the more good I hear about
Patrick. Many people in the village resent the Brontës for
spawning a tourist industry which has preserved their home in
1840s aspic, but everyone agrees Patrick changed the place for
the better. I used to find him a bit stiff, a bit macho, the way
he shot pistols out of his bedroom window. But now I start to
wonder if there is more to Patrick. Maybe Anne wondered it
too as, at twenty-five, she found herself living with her father
for the first time in five years. She was getting to know him as
a grown-up at the same time as she was turning herself into a
writer whose work would be read outside her family for the
first time.

It was Charlotte's idea to follow their father's example and to
try for publication. In the autumn of 1845, Charlotte 'accidentally
lighted on' some poems of Emily's. At least Charlotte *claimed* it
was an accident. Was she spying? Did she rootle through Emily's
portable writing desk? Charlotte may have found it arousing
when Heger went through *her* desk, but Emily hated snoops,
and judging by the way Agnes and Helen respond to prying,

so did Anne. Agnes is appalled when her pupils rifle through her workbag. And when Huntingdon grabs Helen's portfolio in the early days of their flirtation, she snatches it back. He finds a sketch she's made of him and teases her mercilessly – and she rips it in two and burns it. Later, when Gilbert tries to look at her work without asking, Helen calls it 'great impertinence'. This gives me pause. Is all this digging I'm doing into Anne's life any better than Charlotte prying into Emily's writing? If anyone's guilty of *great impertinence*, I am.

Charlotte wanted to get the poems published. But Emily didn't want anyone reading her poems, not her sister, definitely not the world. Charlotte hadn't even known Emily was still writing; 'we used to show each other what we wrote,' she said, 'but of late years this habit of communication and consultation had been discontinued; hence it ensued that we were mutually ignorant of the progress we might respectively have made.' It wasn't entirely true. Charlotte and Branwell's childhood alliance had dissolved, but the diary papers show that Anne and Emily were still sharing their writing. Now Charlotte did her best to persuade Emily to publish because, she said,

> I knew . . . that a mind like hers could not be without some latent spark of honourable ambition, and refused to be discouraged in my attempts to fan that spark to flame. Meantime, my younger sister quietly produced some of her own compositions, intimating that since Emily's had given me pleasure, I might like to look at hers.

I've read that Anne brought out her poems because she was trying to play peacemaker. But I wonder if instead, as Charlotte fanned the spark of Emily's ambition, it was Anne's that turned into a flame.

Anne's poetry was better than ever, and she knew it; her confidence shines through every word of the poems she wrote that year. At Thorp Green, she'd often written on a Sunday, when church spurred her to go inside herself, or, if the sermon was bad, made her rage on the page. She'd produced some of her boldest, most searching religious poems, including 'A Word to the Elect' and 'The Doubter's Prayer'. Anne's concision anticipates Emily Dickinson. Her poems are limpid, artless, luminous. The critic Derek Stanford admired Anne's economy, elegance and clarity, the way 'Her meaning appears to shine quietly through her verse with a very minimum of loss'. Unfortunately he also thought the poems only worked for readers who shared Anne's religious beliefs. Fannie Ratchford meant to disparage Anne when she called her 'a still small voice of poetry', but perhaps Anne found the passage of Kings where God speaks to Elijah not in a wind, an earthquake or a fire, but in 'a still small voice' useful in finding a voice so different from the Byronic pyrotechnics her siblings sometimes favoured. The humility of her devotional poems has led her to be compared to George Herbert.

She also has a sinewy sureness, in contrast to other Victorian women whose poems were turned into hymns. She didn't ask, like Christina Rossetti, in her 1872 poem 'In the Bleak Midwinter', 'What can I give Him, poor as I am?' Anne always felt she had something to offer, something to say. Dora Greenwell began her famous 1873 hymn 'Redemption' with the admission 'I am not skilled to understand / What God hath willed, what God hath planned'. Anne thought doubt was important, but she believed in her right to write. She wrote with pluck and dash, sometimes with ferocity, and always with grace. Elizabeth Langland has said that Anne's poems make up a sort of spiritual autobiography.

In the months of stasis after coming back from Thorp Green, Anne had been working on 'Views of Life', a long poem about hope versus experience, which she wrote in dialogue so she could argue for both sides, play devil's advocate and wrestle her way to a conclusion. The manuscript is her messiest, her most revised and scrawled-over, as she debated whether to stay true to the hopes of youth or the disillusionment of experience, something she knew all about after the fiasco of Thorp Green. In the poem, hope won in the end – and now, Charlotte's plan for publication was giving Anne some real-life hope: a plan, a scheme.

Charlotte was appealing to the dreams they'd had as children. They'd all, she said, 'very early cherished the dream of one day becoming authors. This dream, never relinquished . . . now suddenly acquired strength and consistency: it took the character of a resolve.' Authorship was not an impossible dream. Two years later, in a survey of 'The Condition of Authors in England, Germany, and France' in *Fraser's Magazine*, the critic George Henry Lewes would assert that 'Literature has become a profession. It is a means of subsistence almost as certain as the bar or the church.' It was one of the only professions women could aspire to. The governess Nelly Weeton had asked, in despair, 'Who would employ a female physician? Who would listen to a female divine, except to ridicule?' But books by women did sell.

Another argument which must have influenced Emily was that they didn't have to use their own names. They had signed their writing with a plethora of names when they were children, pretending to be men of letters jousting in taverns, or shrugging on the robes and coronets of Angrian and Gondal royals, but this would be different. This time they weren't doing it for fun. They were, said Charlotte, 'averse to personal publicity' – at least Emily was. Pseudonyms would also mean they didn't have to tell Branwell what they were up to. Much later, Charlotte would say they didn't tell him 'for fear of causing him too deep a pang of remorse for his own time misspent, and talents misapplied', but no one knows if this was really why they left him out. He didn't tell his sisters he was still writing (and publishing) either. That autumn, the Parsonage was thick with secrets.

Charlotte later said they also used pseudonyms because 'without . . . suspecting that our mode of writing and thinking are not what is called "feminine" – we had a vague impression that authoresses are liable to be looked on with prejudice'. They were right. The more they learned about publishing, the more they realised how readily women could be pigeonholed or patronised.

Maybe they also called themselves Currer, Ellis and Acton Bell because, years earlier, Patrick had taught them the power of pretending to be someone else. Anne was four when Patrick played a game with the children: 'happening to have a mask in the house, I told them all to stand and speak boldly from under cover of the mask'. He doesn't say if the mask was from a play he'd been in at Cambridge, left over from a nativity play at church, or if it was just a mask he kept in his study to put on when he wanted to feel bold, maybe when he was writing his stinging letters to the press, or dreaming up his barnstorming sermons. Anne put the mask on first. When her father asked her what she most wanted, she replied, 'Age and experience.' It's a funny line from a four-year-old. Anne was already fed up with being the baby of the family, already fighting to do more, be more, know more. It makes my heart ache, too, because she died so young, and experienced so little. But I love her avidness, her zest for life, and her courage. She learned then to speak out boldly from behind a mask, and now she was going to become Acton Bell, and do it again.

Like her sisters, Anne wanted a name with the same first letters as her own, but it's not totally clear why she chose 'Acton'. Perhaps she remembered it from her days with the Robinsons; Acton & Co. had been one of the shops they frequented in York. 'Bell' might have been inspired by Patrick's new curate, Arthur Bell Nicholls. The diffident, serious, rather starchy 26-year-old from a farming family in County Offaly, Ireland, had just arrived in Haworth. Maybe Anne and her sisters filched his name for their pseudonym. But the story I like better is that they chose *Bell* because their church had just got three new bells, and they wanted their words to ring out loud and clear. As Anne transformed herself from governess to writer, she had the best example of self-fashioning in her father. One of Patrick's biographies is titled *Man of Sorrow* and the other is *Father of*

Genius, but he was also a shape-shifter, a man who translated himself, by cleverness and sheer force of will, from a labourer in an Irish mud cabin to a Cambridge-educated clergyman.

It sounds like melodrama, but Anne's father really was born in a tiny house made mostly of mud in Drumballyroney, County Down, on St Patrick's Day 1777. In *Cottage Poems*, the slim volume he published in 1810, he called it

> A neat Irish cabin, snow proof,
> Well thatched, had a good earthen floor,
> One chimney in midst of the roof,
> One window, and one latched door.

It reeked of corn because one of the two rooms was taken up by a corn kiln which Patrick's father, Hugh Brunty, used to supplement the money he made as a farmhand, fence-fixer and road-builder. Hugh had the gift of the gab. He told good stories, and despite being a Protestant and very poor, he talked Eleanor – tall, beautiful and (possibly) Catholic – into eloping with him. They had ten children. They lived frugally, on porridge, potatoes, buttermilk and bread, which gave Patrick, the eldest, a lifetime of indigestion. They owned four books, and two were the Bible.

At twelve, Patrick went to work, with a blacksmith, then with a linen-weaver. Three years dragged by. But then a local priest found him in a country lane reading aloud to himself – *Paradise Lost*, doing the voices – and offered to teach him, for free, if he would get up early every morning for lessons, before walking five miles to work. Within a year, Patrick had made such good progress that he became a teacher himself. Inside a book he bought then, he wrote his name over and over, varying the spelling from Brunty to Pruty to Prunty; he was becoming someone else, and he didn't know yet who that person would be.

In 1802, at twenty-five, he set off for Cambridge and called himself Patrick Bronte. (I wish he'd stuck with that, each time I laboriously hit Alt U then e to make the diaeresis.) Maybe he chose it because it means thunder in Greek, or maybe it was because his hero Nelson was made Duke of Brontë after Trafalgar. Patrick loved battle lore, and volunteered for drill in Cambridge's market square, in case Napoleon invaded. Soon after he graduated, he was ordained, and started making a name for himself in Essex, then in Shropshire and then in Yorkshire, where he most wanted to be, at the heart of the Evangelical movement. He still hadn't fixed his name. Mostly he spelled it *Bronté*, but he also flirted with other accents, including, wildly, a breve: *Brontĕ*. He ate plain food, and tramped miles and miles, always carrying a stout stick. He fell for a woman called Mary Burder at his first curacy in Essex, and she may have rejected him for being a poor Irish immigrant, or perhaps (as Juliet Barker suggests) he rejected her because her family were Nonconformists. Either way, he agonised over it, saying, 'Oh! that I could make my God and Saviour, my home, my Father, my all! But this happy state is reserved for better men than I.' This was another thing Anne learned from him: to wrestle with God.

Encouraging his parishioners to examine their hearts – a key tenet for Evangelicals – Patrick constantly examined his own heart too, working out who he was, and how to live out his beliefs in the world. He jumped into a flooded river to save a disabled child from drowning. He got a man freed from jail after he'd been falsely imprisoned. When the Luddite riots started in 1812, he refused to condone violence but also refused to condemn the frame-wreckers who were smashing up the machinery that was being brought in to do their jobs. He was much more sympathetic than Charlotte was when she wrote about the Luddites in *Shirley*, but then, he knew what it was like to be hungry. When one night, he saw fugitives creeping into the churchyard, he let them bury their dead in hallowed ground, and at dawn, he smoothed over the rough graves, so the authorities would never know. This kind of thing could get a man in trouble so he started carrying two loaded pistols everywhere he went, and for the rest of his life, he sewed special gun pockets into each new coat.

This was a red rag to bullish Gaskell. Her Patrick saws off the backs of the chairs, burns his children's red boots for being too colourful, denies his family meat, and rips up his wife's favourite dress, leaving one contemporary reviewer with the impression that Patrick was a 'moody, wretched parson – a man who like a mad dog ought to have been shot, or like a victim of its bite, smothered between two feather beds'. It's horribly unfair, especially as the biography was Patrick's idea. He encouraged Gaskell to be candid – 'No quailing, Mrs Gaskell,' he said, 'no drawing back' – and showed massive restraint in not asking to see the manuscript before it was published. When he asked for (very few) corrections to the next edition, he defended himself, with dignity, saying, 'I do not deny that I am somewhat eccentric. Had I been numbered amongst the calm, sedate, concentric men of the world, I should not have been as I now am, and I should in all probability never have had such children as mine have been.'

Gaskell couldn't see what Patrick's eccentricity did for his children, and she couldn't understand what he was doing for Haworth. Instead, she devoted pages to the hotshot preacher William Grimshaw who had had Patrick's job a *century* before. Grimshaw was an alarmingly confident man who would drive people into church with a horsewhip, or ride all day to sermonise at farmers in their fields, chomping raw onions as he went (perhaps one reason they weren't wild to see him). On his deathbed, he declared, 'I have nothing to do but to step out of my bed into Heaven.'

Patrick never had this certainty. Haworth should have been the place where he settled down. He arrived there at forty-three, happily married, a father of six, looking forward to the solid home that came with the job, which was also solid because perpetual curates were just that, *perpetual*, and couldn't be kicked out. It was a long way from his parents' Irish cabin, and the distance was dizzying. But before he could start to put down roots, Maria fell ill. He felt like 'a stranger in a strange land' as he struggled to get to grips with his new job while nursing her, then losing her, and, *much* too soon, grimly trying to find a stepmother for his children. Anne's godmother (a friend of Maria's) was horrified when he proposed. Another woman jeered at the idea that she'd throw herself away on a poor man with six children. Finally, Patrick tried Mary Burder, the woman he had fallen in love with fifteen years before in Essex, saying he needed a 'dearly beloved friend' to help with his 'small but sweet little family'. She scrawled back a mean reply and even thanked God for saving her from marrying him. But Patrick couldn't let it go. His letters to her are pathetic and humiliated, and hard to read if you like him. Which I now do. Patrick comes across as trapped and panicked, desperate to be understood as he wishes that Burder would have 'other and kindlier views and feelings'. He never did find another person to share his life with.

But he did his best to give his children cleverness, companionship and creativity. He filled the house with books, marking his 'To be retained – semper' (meaning 'always' in his hard-won Latin). Some of the books on the shelves were his own; three years after *Cottage Poems*, he published *The Rural Minstrel: A Miscellany of Descriptive Poems*. His novella, *The Cottage in the Wood, or the Art of Becoming Rich and Happy*, appeared in 1815, and in 1818 came *The Maid of Killarney*, a short novel drenched in nostalgia for Ireland. If Anne read these books again in the months after she returned from Thorp Green, she might have nodded unhappily at Patrick's preface to *The Cottage in the Wood* where he presciently diagnosed what her brother and sisters were going through, warning against 'self-tormenting' by 'creating an imaginary world, which they can never inhabit, only to make the real world, with which they must necessarily be conversant, gloomy and insupportable'.

Patrick encouraged his children to keep pets – including dogs, doves, cats, geese, a pheasant and a hawk – and wrote them letters in their pets' voices. He had a talent for ventriloquism. He liked telling what prim Nussey called 'strange stories' gleaned from visits to his oldest, most isolated parishioners; she said they 'made one shiver and shrink from hearing; but they were full of grim humour and interest'. He always wore a big white silk cravat, for his bad chest, he said, but it really was enormous, going up to his *ears*, some people said; 'white walls of cravat' said Gaskell's daughter; 'choked in yards and yards of cravat' said May Sinclair. His old Cambridge tailor still made his coats, and he wore everything to shreds – and he wasn't embarrassed about it.

In 1845, when Anne returned from Thorp Green, Patrick seemed suddenly old. His cataracts were so bad that he could barely see. He needed everything read out to him, and he stumbled on the cobbles of Main Street.

Patrick had always given his children plenty of privacy – he knew how hard it was to carve out your own space in a crowded house. Now, he didn't push them to apply for work, although he must have been worried about having all his grown-up children under his roof, earning nothing. Charlotte told Nussey that Branwell was making 'no effort to seek a situation' (she wasn't either), and she refused to let Nussey visit because, she said, 'I will invite no one to share our discomfort'. In fact, Branwell was applying for jobs, and that November he had yet another poem published under a pseudonym in the *Halifax Guardian*; in 'Real Rest' he wishes he could swap places with the corpse of a drowned man, because 'cold oblivion' would be better than the turmoil of living and loving. If his sisters read the poem, they didn't realise it was by him, or that he was doing anything but drinking. He spent so much time in the Black Bull, or going on benders in Halifax, that he didn't realise, either, that, fired up by Charlotte's big idea of publishing their poems, his sisters had gone back to the writing routines of their childhood. Anne and Emily would go out on the moors in the afternoons, to get into the 'humour' for writing, and after Patrick went to bed early, stopping halfway up the stairs to wind the clock, all three sisters would put away their sewing and write, reading aloud to each other, and pacing round and round the table. Charlotte said later that the 'readings were of great and stirring interest to all'. Like all good writers' groups, they argued as much as they agreed. Charlotte was frustrated that Emily was not 'amenable' to the 'influence of other intellects' and irked by Anne's 'taciturnity'. As they hammered out their ideas, Anne was working out what she was for, what she could do on the page, which was different to what her sisters were doing, and different to what she had done before.

To put together their book of poems, they chose which to include, alternating one by each of them (with twenty-one of Anne's) and removing all trace of Gondal. It was not a happy process. Emily felt violated, Charlotte felt defensive, and Anne was caught in the middle. It didn't help that things moved fast. Incredibly fast. After trying a few publishers, Charlotte sent a brief note to a London firm called Aylott & Jones on 28 January 1846. She received a reply by return of post. The poems would be published but it would cost the sisters around three-quarters of what Anne had been earning each year at Thorp Green. But publication was publication. They sent off the poems a week later. By mid-March they were correcting proofs, and in May, the book was out. On 7 May, a parcel arrived at the Parsonage. Inside were three copies of a slim volume, neat, elegant, and small enough to fit in a pocket, bound in bottle-green cloth, with *Poems by Currer, Ellis and Acton Bell* spelled out in gilt letters on the cover.

These author copies arrived at a 'house so drear' with 'such gloomy silence', as Anne put it in a poem she wrote about that time, to which she gave the ironic title 'Domestic Peace'. In it, she tries to pin down the 'something gone away' that has made her and her sisters lose their 'mirth', 'love' and, worst of all, their 'peace' – a word she underlines. She's puzzled and devastated that 'Each feels the bliss of all destroyed, / And mourns the change – but each apart.' The book should have bonded them, but it did the opposite. And the pseudonyms created more problems than they solved, provoking the critics. In the first of the (very few) reviews they received, in the *Critic* on 4 July, the critic complained,

> Whether the triumvirate have published in concert, or if their association be the work of an editor, viewing them as kindred spirits, is not recorded. If the poets be of a past or of the present age, if living or dead, whether English or American, where born, or where dwelling, what their ages or station – nay, what their Christian names, the publishers have not thought to reveal to the curious reader.

This was a bit rich because he (or she) was writing anonymously too. Another anonymous critic in the *Athenaeum* assumed the Bells were brothers. It wasn't the most auspicious start.

But Anne didn't care. The book of poems had opened a door, an escape route. Now she was racing to finish the novel she had started a year before. She gave 'Passages in the Life of an Individual' a new title: *Agnes Grey*. Over the previous nine months, since the revival of their writing evenings, Charlotte and Emily had been writing novels too. Charlotte's *The Professor* (its working title was 'The Master') was about her and Heger, although she also drew on some Angrian stories, including one of Branwell's called 'The Wool is Rising'. Emily also went back to her childhood, and *Wuthering Heights* is infused with Gondal. Over the past few years, they had all written prose, and Charlotte had written more than one long novella. But now they each decided to write a full-length novel. Curiously, Branwell had been writing one too, because he thought that 'in the present state of the publishing and reading world a novel is the most saleable article'. But he confided this to a friend, not to his sisters, and, again, they didn't share their ideas with him.

The sisters were so excited about their novels in progress that even before the *Poems* came out, Charlotte had written to Aylott & Jones, in April 1846, grandly announcing that 'C, F, & A Bell are now preparing for the Press a work of fiction – consisting of three distinct and unconnected tales'. Aylott & Jones did not want the novels, so Charlotte started making a list of other publishers to try. On 27 June, she finished her fair copy of *The Professor*. And on 4 July, when the first reviews of the *Poems* came out, the sisters were emboldened to send out their novels, wrapped up, all together, in brown paper.

While Anne began *Agnes Grey* at Thorp Green, she rewrote and finished it at home, and it owes much to the way her father spoke and wrote. After sitting through five years of unsatisfying and unimpressive sermons, Anne was enjoying listening to her father on Sundays, as he spoke without notes, for exactly an hour, using plain, homely language, and trying to cheer on his parishioners, as well as to make them think. Patrick's preface to *Cottage Poems* might have made more sense to Anne now that she was also trying to write with 'simplicity, plainness and perspicuity'. Though her siblings wrote extravagantly, revelling in verbal excess, Anne valued economy. She signed off *Agnes Grey* crisply, even brusquely: 'And now I think I have said sufficient.' Maybe she hoped that working women would read her novel, just as Patrick had addressed *Cottage Poems* to readers who 'turn the sturdy soil, or ply the loom with daily toil'. He had been such a reader himself and he explained that he hadn't come from a literary background but had 'been obliged both to think and speak for himself; and has had recourse, for assistance, only to that Book of Books, the Bible, in which the wisest may learn that they know nothing, and fools be made wise'. Anne also wanted to think and speak for herself, and to use the Bible as a guide to life. Like Patrick, she wanted to balance the 'real, indescribable pleasure' of writing with an awareness of what would 'stand the test of the All-seeing Eye'.

Patrick's own eyes now needed urgent attention. Charlotte and Emily found him a surgeon in Manchester, and in August 1846, Charlotte took him there to have the operation. It was performed without anaesthetic. He bravely said the pain was 'burning . . . but not intolerable', but I don't entirely believe him; it took two people to hold him down while it was happening. Afterwards came a month in a darkened room, and much bleeding with leeches – on the temples *not* the eyelids, he noted, although neither sounds good. Charlotte employed a nurse, which meant that when Anne and Emily forwarded her a letter rejecting their novels, she had time to start a new one. She abandoned the realism she had aimed for in *The Professor*, and went back to 'the wild wonderful and thrilling – the strange, startling and harrowing', beginning *Jane Eyre* in a frenzy, by her father's bedside, in that darkened room. It was lucky that she had trained herself, years ago, to write with her eyes shut. She wrote the first three hundred pages in three weeks.

Back in Haworth, Anne didn't start a second novel, not yet. She was thinking and dreaming, walking the moors, doing some of the housework, and writing poetry. The woolcombers and powerloom workers – the people Patrick had addressed *Cottage Poems* to – went on strike. It dragged on for three months, and the men got poorer, hungrier and many fell ill. When Patrick returned, his sympathies were very much with the workers, not the employers. Anne could have seen why they were striking for herself. Or Tabby could have told her all about it – her father had combed wool, and her brother was still at it. She knew about the combs that had to be kept fever-hot, which made the woolcombers' homes, where they worked, stiflingly hot for them and their families. The average age of death for local woolcombers was just nineteen. It was a hard autumn and a harder winter. In December, a sheriff's officer rapped on the Parsonage door 'on a visit to Branwell', said Charlotte sarcastically, 'inviting him either to pay his debts or to take a trip to York'. York meant court, which meant jail, so his sisters paid up. Anne was coughing at night and could barely breathe; by now, she certainly had asthma, and the cold set it off. Charlotte wrote that 'the sky looks like ice, the earth is frozen, the wind is as keen as a two-edged blade – I cannot keep myself warm', and paid a rare tribute to her youngest sister, saying, 'she bore it as she does all affliction – without one complaint – only sighing now and then when nearly worn out – she has an extraordinary heroism of endurance. I admire her but I certainly could not imitate her'. Even when recognising Anne's heroism, Charlotte put it in the category of 'endurance'.

In the book they had both read at Roe Head School, Chapone defines two different kinds of courage:

> The same degree of active courage is not to be expected in woman as in man; and not belonging to her nature, it is not agreeable in her: but passive courage – patience, and fortitude under sufferings – presence of mind, and calm resignation in danger – are surely desirable.

This obviously made sense to Charlotte. She always put Anne in the second category, of being passively courageous, patient, long-suffering and calm, while she thought Emily was actively brave. Later she would say, 'energy nerved the one, and endurance upheld the other'. The word endurance stuck to Anne like a burr. Her reputation for martyrdom even marks her appearance in a 2011 graphic novel in the *Doctor Who* series, called *The Child of Time*. Far into the future, at a Museum of Lost Opportunities, the Doctor meets all three Brontë sisters, who are gun-toting robots, determined to save the world. I rather enjoy this lethal version of Anne – brassy blonde, impressively bicepped and revealing quite some cleavage as she clutches her weapon in polka-dot gloved hands – until she sacrifices herself to save the Doctor. Of course she does.

As the winter of 1846 dragged on, Anne's novel kept getting rejected, along with *Wuthering Heights* and *The Professor*. Each time the parcel came back, Charlotte crossed off the name of the publishing house, wrote a new one underneath, and sent it off again. This was not savvy; the publishers could see who else had rejected the books, and the manuscripts got tattier and tattier. If Branwell guessed something was going on, he couldn't make himself care. By now he was drinking himself into oblivion, paying for it with money Mrs Robinson sent to keep him away. That April, he had published a poem in the *Halifax Guardian* called 'Letter From a Father on Earth to his Child in her Grave', possibly about his illegitimate daughter. He seems tone-deaf to real grief, imagining if people saw his little daughter's corpse they would shrink from the sight, full of loathing, but 'turn, perchance, with no disgust from me', a bizarre reference to his own appearance. When he digresses to assure the reader that his heart 'aches for its beloved one', it becomes clear that he was writing the poem for Mrs Robinson, and the child was just a pretext. By January 1847, he wrote that he felt, at twenty-eight, 'a thoroughly <u>old man</u>'. Anne must have felt disheartened too. She'd thought she'd turned things around, transformed herself, written a novel she was proud of. But if her book languished unread in the drawer, what was the point?

Then in April 1847, when the rejections had been going on for nine months, Anne had a life-changing encounter with a woman who came to see Patrick.

Mrs Collins was married to the former curate of Keighley, who was a violent alcoholic. Anne listened for two hours as she told her story of years of drinking and abuse, of how her husband abandoned her and their children in Manchester, with nothing to live on, and a hideous disease – probably syphilis – and how she battled to get well and to mother her children. Collins's greatest regret was that she hadn't listened to Patrick when she had visited the Parsonage seven years previously. Patrick had told her to leave her husband. This enlightened, even startling advice would have been difficult to carry out because although, thanks to Caroline Norton, things were changing, it was still almost impossible for women to get divorced, and even harder to get custody of their children. But Patrick's advice revealed that he thought that sometimes doing the right thing meant breaking the law and flouting conventional morality. Anne made this the engine of *The Tenant of Wildfell Hall*.

Now Anne had an idea for her second novel, and a way into writing about what was happening to Branwell, and developing the ideas about men and women she had explored in *Agnes Grey*. She kept writing through the discovery, two months later, that the *Poems* had only sold two copies. *Two!* I could weep. She kept writing as she and her sisters sent the unsold books to their favourite authors, still using their pseudonyms, and attempting to be debonair about how they had 'committed the rash act of printing a volume of poems' which was 'found to be a drug; no man needs it or heeds it'. And then, a few weeks later, a publisher called Thomas Cautley Newby wrote to say he'd take Anne's novel, and Emily's – though not Charlotte's. Anne and Emily would have to pay again, a deal Charlotte called 'somewhat impoverishing to the two authors', advancing Newby fifty pounds to be returned if they sold enough books. Was it 'rash' to jump at this chance? Or was it daring? They said yes.

Charlotte continued gloomily sending out *The Professor* on its own, until she got a rave rejection in July from a London publishing house called Smith, Elder & Co. They asked her to send them her next book, so she sped through the last pages of *Jane Eyre*, and in August they agreed to publish it. They would even pay her. At the same time, Anne and Emily received their proofs from Newby. It all seemed to be going swimmingly, at last, except that Anne was struggling with her new novel. In October, Charlotte wrote to Nussey, who wasn't in on the secret, that Anne 'leads much too sedentary a life, and is continually sitting stooping either over a book or over her desk – it is with difficulty one can prevail on her to take a walk or induce her to converse'. If Charlotte sounds as irritated as she is concerned it's because she was convinced Anne was writing the wrong novel, that 'Nothing less congruous with the writer's nature could be conceived'. Anne shut out her sister's opinions, and stuck to her guns. When Nussey helpfully sent Anne a jar of medicinal crab cheese (a preserve made of crab apples, sugar and butter), she replied politely but firmly, 'The crab cheese is excellent . . . but I don't intend to need it.' She wasn't ill; she was hard at work.

Anne kept writing as *Jane Eyre* was published in mid-October 1847 and became an instant sensation – 'the best novel of the season' said the *Westminster Review* – while her novel languished in her publisher's in-tray. She and Emily had sent their proofs back to Newby months ago and heard nothing. He was a one-man band, who tended to publish writers' first novels but rarely their second. When prolific, popular Fanny Trollope was trying to get her son Anthony published, she went to Newby.

'I expected nothing,' said (Anthony) Trollope. 'And I got nothing . . . I was sure that the book would fail, and it did fail . . . I did not have a word from Mr Newby . . . he paid me nothing.' He took his subsequent books elsewhere. Charlotte asked her editor, William Smith Williams, if Newby was always like this; 'Mr Newby shuffles,' she said, 'gives his word and breaks it . . . My relatives have suffered from exhausting delay and procrastination.' Williams, the literary reader at Smith, Elder & Co., was the first champion of Charlotte's work. A 'pale, mild, stooping man of fifty' (said Charlotte), he was a father of eight, who had known Keats and Hazlitt, and a passionate reader. As he shepherded *Jane Eyre* into publication and as the good reviews appeared, he and Charlotte became good friends. He offered to take over publishing Anne's and Emily's books, but he was too late. Keen to cash in on *Jane Eyre*'s success, Newby had finally decided to do something with the manuscripts sitting on his desk. In fact, he rushed out the books so fast that he didn't bother to put in Anne's and Emily's corrections, and also introduced errors of his own. When the copies arrived, just before Christmas 1847, three volumes bound in maroon, with *Wuthering Heights* taking up the first two volumes, and *Agnes Grey* the third, Charlotte reported to Williams that the mistakes were 'mortifying'. The paper was cheap, Newby had inserted adverts for other books, and the title page didn't even mention *Agnes Grey*.

Newby's delay was especially damaging for Anne. Although she had written *Agnes Grey* first, it came out after *Jane Eyre*, so it looked as though Anne had stolen Charlotte's idea of writing a plain governess, or ineptly copied it. Later, the novelist Harriet

Martineau, who became Charlotte's frenemy, wrote a sort of origin myth for the idea, in which Charlotte

> told her sisters that they were wrong – even morally wrong – in making their heroines beautiful as a matter of course. They replied that it was impossible to make a heroine interesting on any other terms. Her answer was, 'I will prove to you that you are wrong; I will show you a heroine as plain and as small as myself, who shall be as interesting as any of yours.'

Did Martineau invent this, or did Charlotte really tell her this had happened? Either way, readers were left with the impression that *Agnes Grey* was, as *Douglas Jerrold's Weekly Newspaper* put it, 'a sort of younger sister to *Jane Eyre*; but inferior to her in every way'. *Ouch.*

Because *Agnes Grey* was read like this, its complexities were flattened out. Anne had tried to start conversations about more than whether heroines could be plain. Where were the reviews engaging with her takedown of the upper classes? Why was no one joining in the debate about how boys and girls were educated? Even now, if Anne's novel is praised, it is praised for its tidy structure, its neatness, its craft, as if, as the critic Jill Matus has pointed out, Anne is being commended for her good housekeeping, in contrast to her sisters' gloriously messy books. As if *Agnes Grey* doesn't also seethe with violence.

The same critic in *Douglas Jerrold's* admired *Agnes Grey's* realism:

> We do not actually assert that the author must have been a governess himself, to describe as he does the minute torments and incessant tediums of her life, but he must have bribed some governess very largely, either with love or money, to reveal to him the secrets of her prison-house.

While I am pretty offended by the idea of a male novelist bribing a governess *with love* to tell him secrets he can turn into fiction, at least this review recognised Anne's achievement. It was better than the *Atlas*'s review, which appeared a week later, and found *Agnes Grey* 'a somewhat coarse imitation of one of Jane Austin's [*sic*] charming stories'. Anne might have felt – as I do – that if you are going to diss a novel in print, at least get your spelling right.

Anne's novel also suffered in comparison to Emily's, which critics found so 'fearful and repulsive', as the *New Monthly Magazine* said, that 'it should have been called "Withering Heights"'. The *Atlas* found *Agnes Grey*, 'lacking the power and originality of *Wuthering Heights* . . . It leaves no painful impression on the mind – some may think it leaves no impression at all.'

As Anne read review after review, all of which missed the point, she must have thought it was time to put her cards on the table. In *The Tenant of Wildfell Hall* she was much angrier about how teaching boys badly turned them into men who treated women badly. She was much angrier about everything. She used the same intense realism, the same plain style, but her second novel demanded justice and equality. It questioned much of what society held dear.

The Tenant of Wildfell Hall also critiqued her sisters' books, and especially *Jane Eyre*. In Anne's novel, as in Charlotte's, a libertine rejects his wife. Charlotte gave Bertha a classic villain's evil laugh, 'demoniac' and 'strange', and made her unnatural ('She sucked the blood: she said she'd drain my heart,' says her brother, haemorrhaging and horrified), and barely human, calling her a 'clothed hyena', a 'tigress', a 'figure', 'some strange wild animal', a 'goblin', a 'vampire', a 'demon', and even, simply and inhumanly, 'it'. Anne took the libertine's rejected wife out of the attic and put her centre stage. She also took her side. Huntingdon may call his wife 'a very tigress', but Anne doesn't. She even includes a sly parody of Jane in the form of Miss Myers, the governess Huntingdon recruits for his son, who is (just like Jane) a clergyman's daughter and orphan who fancies her boss. In fact, Miss Myers is Huntingdon's mistress. It was a plotline Michel Faber used in his rollicking neo-Victorian novel *The Crimson Petal and the White*, where William Rackham employs his mistress, Sugar, as governess to his daughter. Clever, savvy Sugar is secretly writing a book about the evils of men, and soon joins forces with Rackham's fragile wife and neglected daughter. I think Anne would have got a kick out of that.

Like Sugar, Helen is an outsider heroine. Anne declares her intentions on the title page. Helen is a 'tenant'. She doesn't belong. Although Wildfell Hall was her childhood home she comes back to it as a stranger, not revealing her real name, trailing mystery. She earns her own living, which is unusual enough, and she does it through painting, which is normally the prerogative of men. She is uncompromising and outspoken. She is peculiar. Gilbert's brother jokes that she must be a witch, and Mrs Markham thinks 'there [is] something odd about her' and uses her as a warning, to make her own daughter conform: 'You see what it is for women to affect to be different to other people.' Helen will tell her own story, and when she does, it will become clear that she is an outlaw, a thief. She has had to steal the clothes she is wearing, the paintbrush in her hand, even her son. When Charlotte wanted to allow Jane to leave noble (awful) St John Rivers to go back to a liar, adulterer and would-be bigamist, Charlotte softened the decision by making Jane hear Rochester's voice in the ether, calling her to come. So it's almost duty that makes her go. Except it isn't. It's love and lust, if only Jane could own it. Helen needs no outside prompt to do the unthinkable. She leaves her husband because she knows it is right.

Anne knew it was right because it was the bold advice Patrick had given the beleaguered Mrs Collins. The whole novel is inspired by his refusal to be curbed by convention, his dissident rage. Reading about Patrick I think about my own refugee parents' creativity and resourcefulness. Anne's father had made himself up from scratch, had changed himself so dramatically that he never believed anything had to be the way it was. He felt he could change anything – society, people, the Church – for the better, and it gave him an amazing freedom in the way he thought. Anne saw Patrick baptise illegitimate children when many ministers wouldn't. She saw the way he teased his curate, Nicholls, for his zealous, joyless campaign to get the washerwomen of Haworth to stop hanging wet clothes out to dry on the tombstones in the churchyard in a funny, satirical poem:

The females all routed have fled with their clothes
To stackyards, and backyards, and where no one knows,
And loudly have sworn by the suds which they swim in,
They'll wring off his head, for his warring <u>with women</u>.

Anne saw Patrick oppose capital punishment – he thought most criminals could be rehabilitated and become useful to society. Most of all, she saw him work tirelessly for the poor. He had their houses whitewashed and cleaned to stop the spread of cholera; he had roads repaired and cottages set aside for the worst off. When he opened a school in 1844, he instituted evening classes for child workers who had to fit their education in where they could, just as he had. He fought tooth and nail against the new Poor Law of 1834, which stopped giving out money, blankets, shoes and food in times of hardship or cold, and instead forced the poor into workhouses where their heads were shaved, their clothes were boiled, and they had to do hard labour. Under the new regime, children were separated from parents, men from women, and once you were in a workhouse, it was nearly impossible to get out. It was the law Charles Dickens attacked in *Oliver Twist* – its first instalments came out in 1837, just as the law was being rolled out to Yorkshire. Patrick was horrified by the way the poor were being punished instead of helped, how they were labelled *undeserving*. He called meetings, wrote letters, organised petitions, roared from the pulpit, and grilled election candidates. In *The Times*, he called the new law 'a nose-hewing, finger-lopping quack, a legal deformity, hunchbacked, and one-handed' and urged people to 'obey God, rather than man'. He was calling for revolution, telling his readers,

> We will not therefore submit to go to their bastilles. We will not live on their water gruel, and on their two ounces of cheese, and their fourteen ounces of bread per day. We will not suffer ourselves to be chained by their three tyrannical commissioners; and we will never endure the idea, of men, rolling in affluence and luxury, prescribing to us the most extreme line which can keep body and soul together.

He reassured them that 'God, the father and friend of the poor' would support their protest. It is no coincidence that Anne wrote her most radical book, about a woman throwing off her chains, while living with her father who was urging people to do just that.

In Haworth now, Patrick is honoured at the church as a conscientious parish priest who walked miles every day to tend to his large flock, many of them living in scattered villages and farms. He baptised a child nearly every day of the year, and he performed a funeral nearly every week. To date, he is the longest serving incumbent of Haworth's church, and although it was rebuilt in 1879, and I'm not sure he'd love the plinky-plonk muzak now piped continually through the sound system, I think he'd be proud to be remembered so fondly, and glad to recognise his old communion table, chandelier and memorial tablet, all now corralled into a Brontë Memorial Chapel. Patrick would find the graveyard as sad as ever, and maybe he would pause by the grave built by a local stonemason who buried six of his own small children, and carved a likeness of one child, who died at just a year old, in 1878. The stone child is asleep, his head on a pillow, sheltered by a canopy, and he looks so bereft that tourists sometimes fill his chubby arms with flowers.

If Patrick saw Main Street now, with its perpetual, wind-blown bunting, its Brontë-themed cafes and vintage shops, perhaps he would smile at the poster I see in one window, a parody of the famous wartime propaganda poster, which reads, tartly, 'DON'T TELL ME TO KEEP CALM'; he was always a contrarian. He would have liked the fact that Haworth is still a place where everyone knows everyone else's business, where it is said that you can sneeze at the top of Main Street and by the time you get to the bottom, you'll be asked about your broken leg. Now, as in Patrick's day, Haworth can be a little eerie at night. There are ghost walks, and a surprising amount of drinking, and one evening, after the tourist buses have driven off, a community policeman accosts me to find out who I am. 'We're just here to reassure people,' he says. But about what? Another evening, I go for a curry with my partner (somewhere between thinking about Branwell and thinking about Patrick, I've found myself using the word *partner*) and we are reflected in the kitsch seventies mirrored bar. Later I find out the restaurant is the setting for a whodunnit by the Yorkshire crime writer Robert Barnard called *The Corpse at the Haworth Tandoori*.

The next morning – a Saturday – the archive is closed, so I take my writing to a tea room. The lunch special is a giant Yorkshire pudding with roast beef and seasonal vegetables followed by a Bakewell tart with cream or custard. A sleek blonde in a fur-trimmed parka asks doubtfully if they do a skinny latte, and the waitress laments, 'Everything's skinny here. No one wants real milk.' My breakfast comes topped with a fried slice. Patrick was upset that Gaskell said he denied his children meat, and in fact the diet at the Parsonage was good – and much better than the food he had grown up with himself. Trainspotters in waxed jackets start to arrive for the steam gala, because Haworth's train station is on the heritage *Railway Children* line.

So I up sticks to the Old White Lion, and get so lost in reading over my notes about Anne that I'm startled to look up and find the pub full of people dressed in black. A wake has started around me and I didn't notice. As I leave, I realise that the pub's clock runs backwards, as if taking me back in time, to the 1840s maybe. Back to Anne, just a few doors down, hunched over her anarchic second novel, or pacing round the table with her sisters, arguing that people could change, and sinners could be redeemed, that characters are not fixed, that people are not stuck, that she could change her own life. Hadn't her father done it? Wasn't he changing other people's lives even now? Wasn't she changing her own life, coming into her own, real, angry voice? And wasn't this new novel going to change the world?

Anne's heart must have thudded in her chest as she wrote the scene where Helen confronts Huntingdon, asking,

'. . . will you let me take our child and what remains of my fortune, and go?'

'Go where?'

'Anywhere, where he will be safe from your contaminating influence, and I shall be delivered from your presence – and you from mine.'

'No – by *Jove* I won't!'

'Will you let me have the child then, without the money?'

'No – nor yourself without the child. Do you think I'm going to be made the talk of the country for your fastidious caprices?'

'Then I must stay here, to be hated and despised – But henceforth we are husband and wife only in the name.'

'Very good.'

'I am your child's mother, and *your* housekeeper – nothing more.'

Helen shuts her bedroom door three decades before Nora walked out of her doll's house, slamming the door as she went, in Henrik Ibsen's play. May Sinclair wrote, in 1913, that 'the slamming of Helen Huntingdon's bedroom door against her husband reverberated through Victorian England'.

Helen has dynamited her marriage, and with it the assumption that any marriage is sacred. And later, just as Patrick advised Collins, Helen will leave.

9

HELEN

or how to be the artist of your own life

'Don't you want to be beautiful?' asks a Brylcreemed man on Paternoster Row.

He's trying to sign me up for a day of pampering. I'm annoyed. I've come to this London street because Anne stayed here in July 1848. I don't want to be pampered. If I'd had more presence of mind I'd have quoted Agnes and said, 'It is foolish to wish for beauty.' Although later Agnes refines her position and decides beauty 'though liable to be over-estimated . . . is a gift of God, and not to be despised . . . As well might the humble glowworm despise that power of giving light.' Then there is a curious passage about how if the glowworm didn't glow, 'her winged darling', the fly, would be 'buzzing over and around her; he vainly seeking her, she longing to be found, but with no power to make her presence known, no voice to call him, no wings to follow his flight; – the fly must seek another mate, the worm must live and die alone'. Agnes gazes in the mirror and feels she can 'discover no beauty in those marked features', but she obviously glows for Mr Weston. Maybe there is more than one kind of beauty. And anyway, beauty can be a mixed blessing because, as Helen's aunt says in *The Tenant of Wildfell Hall*, it is 'attractive to the worst kinds of men'.

By the time I've worked all this out, Mr Brylcreem has given up on me. As I walk on, I think about how Anne made the heroine of her second novel a painter, a woman professionally concerned with aesthetics, with beauty.

The Tenant of Wildfell Hall was the first in a flurry of novels with artist heroines, like Dinah Craik's 1850 novel *Olive*. Her eponymous protagonist, 'with her clinging sweetness, her upward gaze, was a type of true woman', falls for a man who makes pronouncements like 'I glory in the wind. It makes me strong and bold. I love to meet with it, to wrestle with it.' It's not a feminist classic. In Charlotte Yonge's 1873 novel *Pillars of the House*, Geraldine (Cherry) Underwood is thrilled that people think her pictures are by a man. Yonge cringingly puns, 'This, the most ambitioned praise a woman can receive, made her indeed Cherry-red.' In these *Künstlerromans*, Anne, Craik and Yonge could theorise about art, anatomise the creative process, reveal the difficulties women artists faced, explore the perils and pleasures of self-expression, and think about how their lives shaped their work and how their work shaped their lives. My friend the playwright Robert Holman says that the energy of a work of art comes from what the artist learns by making it, and that definitely feels true of *The Tenant of Wildfell Hall*, where Anne grappled with her complex feelings about art and life. It was because of what she worked out on the pages of her book that she came to London on 8 July 1848.

She was staking her claim. *The Tenant of Wildfell Hall* had come out a fortnight before. Charlotte was far from producing a second (published) novel (she kept asking her publishers if they would reconsider *The Professor*, and they kept refusing to). If Emily started a second novel, there is no trace of it. Anne had pipped them to the post with *The Tenant of Wildfell Hall* published just six months after *Agnes Grey*. It was selling amazingly well, better than *Wuthering Heights* although not quite as well as *Jane Eyre*. In four more weeks, the first-edition print run would sell out. But Anne's publisher, rascally Newby, thought he could make even more money from a novel by the author of *Jane Eyre*, so he was claiming that Currer Bell had written it. And Charlotte's publishers were annoyed. Had she written *The Tenant of Wildfell Hall*? Was she cheating on them with another publisher? If not, they wrote stiffly, they 'would be glad to be in a position to contradict the statement'. This letter panicked Charlotte. She wanted to go down to London with her sisters and show her publishers there were three of them. Emily wouldn't go but Anne and Charlotte headed south that same afternoon.

It was totally unprecedented. They had never left Haworth without much planning and fretting. They had never popped down to London, a city Charlotte called 'Babylon' and Anne imagined in *The Tenant of Wildfell Hall* as an exhausting, disquieting den of 'corruptions and temptations', so dangerous that early on in her marriage Helen vows, 'I must not let him go to London, whatever comes of it; he will run into all kinds of mischief.' London scared both Anne and Charlotte. But they had to go.

Charlotte urgently wanted to prove she wasn't a liar. In her lively correspondence with her publishers, she'd told them a lot, including her real surname. They were addressing their letters to

> Mr Currer Bell
> Under cover to Miss Brontë
> Haworth
> Bradford
> Yorkshire

and she was signing off as Currer Bell. This was after she'd got herself into a muddle by writing to the publishers of the *Poems* on behalf of the 'Bells' as 'C. Brontë'. Assuming C. Brontë was a man, they replied to 'C. Brontë Esquire', which was fine, until Charlotte found one package with its wrappings torn off. Could Branwell have assumed it was for him and opened it by mistake? He was, of course, the only 'Brontë Esquire' in the house. After that, Charlotte asked them to write to 'Miss Brontë' instead. If Branwell knew what his sisters were up to, he didn't confront them, and after he died, Charlotte was sure he 'never knew what his sisters had done in literature – he was not aware that they had ever published a line'.

But they did tell Patrick. At least, Charlotte told him she'd written *Jane Eyre*, but Anne and Emily didn't say they'd also written novels. So now Patrick knew (but not everything), and Branwell (probably) didn't. As for Charlotte's friends, Taylor had been in on the secret from the start, but Nussey knew nothing. Although she did have her suspicions. In April she had asked Charlotte straight out if she was Currer Bell, and Charlotte had snapped, 'I have given <u>no one</u> a right either to affirm, or hint, in the most distant manner, that I am "publishing" – (humbug!) Whoever has said it . . . is no friend of mine . . . I scout the idea utterly.' Charlotte put her friend in an awkward position, saying if anyone asked, she should say she was 'authorised by Miss Brontë to say that she repels and disowns every accusation of the kind. You may add, if you please, that if anyone has her confidence, you believe you have, and she has made no drivelling confessions to you on the subject.'

Nussey was not cowed, and when, a month later, she read *Jane Eyre*, she felt that 'Charlotte Brontë herself was present in every word, her voice and spirit thrilling through and through'. So she sneakily asked Charlotte what she thought of the novel, and Charlotte rather grandly replied,

> Your naïveté in gravely inquiring my opinion of the 'last new novel' amuses me: we do not subscribe to a circulating library at Haworth and consequently 'new novels' rarely indeed come in our way, and consequently we are not qualified to give opinions thereon.

It was quite the snub.

The truth was that Charlotte liked being able to write freely about real people and places. As it was, clerical Yorkshire was buzzing with gossip that Lowood School was based on the school at Cowan Bridge. If she owned up to being Currer Bell, her freedom was over; 'what author,' she asked, 'would be without the advantage of being able to walk invisible?' So when Emily said they could reveal themselves to their publishers, but no one else, it suited Charlotte.

Charlotte was less interested in proving that Currer Bell was Charlotte Brontë than in proving Currer Bell was not Acton Bell; she told Taylor the London trip was about 'proving our separate identity'. This was an even more pressing issue for Anne. It was *her* novel that was being passed off as another writer's work. Anne and Charlotte disagreed about many things but they were completely united in their desire to get to London as fast as they could. Even when they got caught in a thunderstorm on the way to Keighley, they didn't turn back but travelled all night in wet clothes.

At 7 a.m. they arrived at Euston and went to Paternoster Row, where Anne got her first glimpse of St Paul's. The Row got its name because the medieval monks of St Paul's would walk up it saying their paternoster, timing their 'amen' for Amen Corner and chanting Hail Mary as they went down Ave Maria Lane. Maybe, like Branwell, the cathedral's 'vast expanding roof and glorious dome' made Anne feel she had 'nothing but the sublime to gaze on'. Maybe, like Charlotte, she was exhilarated by the sight of the 'solemn, orbed mass, dark-blue and dim – THE DOME'. The other lure of Paternoster Row was the books. It had been the hub of literary London since Shakespeare's day. Where now I dodge the smell of pumpkin spice lattes wafting out of Starbucks, Anne might have browsed grand, busy bookshops, with publishers' offices at the backs.

The Row's beating heart was the Chapter Coffee House, where Anne and Charlotte were staying; a dark, noisy haunt of writers and publishers, news hounds, convivial doctors who prescribed the Chapter's punch as a remedy for all ills, and bachelors who lingered late over their brandies. Sophisticated Gaskell thought it a 'strange' and 'singular' place to stay, but it was the only place they knew. It was where Charlotte had stayed on her way to Brussels, and Patrick had stayed for his ordination.

It is all gone now. Paternoster Row was bombed in the Blitz, on the night of 29 December 1940, when so many incendiary bombs came down that Londoners said it was a second Great Fire. A hundred and sixty people were killed. On Paternoster Row, five million books were burned. In a series of postcards made soon after, called *London Under Fire*, one is captioned 'St Paul's from Paternoster Row', and while the cathedral still stands, there is no Row, just rubble, debris and emptiness. Now the Row has been reconfigured as a slip road to gleaming, bustling Paternoster Square, home of the London Stock Exchange, and I can't find anything Anne would have seen here, nothing at all.

So I walk down to Cornhill, where Anne and Charlotte went next, to verify their identities to Charlotte's publishers. Anne had come a long way from the time she had been, like Agnes, 'a close and resolute dissembler'. Helen is a very different heroine; a woman who longs to be open and honest. Helen ignores her aunt's warning to 'Keep a guard over your eyes and ears as the inlets of your heart, and over your lips as the outlet, lest they betray you in a moment of unwariness' because she *wants* to be unwary, she wants to fall in love. But once she's married, she finds that when she shows her real feelings, her husband uses them against her. When she cries, he gripes that tears will spoil her beauty and tire out her friends. So she takes her aunt's advice, but she's so wounded that she goes too far. From the nightmare of her marriage, she writes to her aunt 'of course telling her nothing'. Of her diary she says,

> This paper will serve instead of a confidential friend into whose ear I might pour forth the overflowing of my heart. It will not sympathise with my distresses, but then it will not laugh at them, and, if I keep it close, it cannot tell again; so it is, perhaps, the best friend I could have for the purpose.

She sounds so lonely. She doesn't even confide in her friend Milicent, who is going through the same thing, and Milicent is soon conforming to the same code, asking Helen to burn a letter in which she's been too honest about her husband. Anne knew that alcoholics create thickets of claustrophobia and denial around them. She wouldn't have been surprised to learn that a common saying in Alcoholics Anonymous is 'You're only as sick as your secrets'. Helen learns this by living it. Later, when Gilbert goes off in a huff, she admonishes him, 'You should have told me all — no matter how bitterly — it would have been better than this silence.' She does not want to be damaged any more by silence and secrets. Anne also wanted to come out of the shadows, to let go of some of her privacy, to go public.

Helen uses pseudonyms too but she wishes she could stop; Anne used her novel to thrash out the ethics and dilemmas of anonymity. In *The Madwoman in the Attic*, my favourite feminist literary critics, Sandra Gilbert and Susan Gubar, argue that Helen uses her painting to conceal and camouflage instead of to assert and express herself. Which seems a bit unfair because Helen is a runaway wife, and if she revealed herself, the law could force her back to Huntingdon. Her false names are a matter of survival. They are *noms de guerre*. When she is able to, she takes off her mask and tells Gilbert Markham everything, even allowing him to read her diary. What could be more straightforward and candid than that?

On that July day in 1848, Anne must have felt relieved as Charlotte happily told her publisher, George Smith, 'We are three sisters.' They got into trouble for this later because Emily had not authorised them to say that 'Ellis Bell' was a woman or their sister, and Charlotte had to ask Smith, Elder & Co. to go on saying 'Ellis' even in private letters, because, she said, ' "Ellis Bell" will not endure to be alluded to under any other appellation than the "nom de plume". I committed a grand error in betraying his identity to you.' Smith, suave, dynamic and just twenty-four, wanted to reveal his new star writer to literary London, but he had to content himself with taking Charlotte and Anne to dinners, teas, a party, the Royal Academy, the National Gallery and Kensington Gardens under false names. At the opera house, they saw *The Barber of Seville*. Charlotte didn't like it but maybe Anne enjoyed encountering Rossini's effervescent heroine, who finds love and freedom. Charlotte agonised over their unsuitable clothes, but said Anne was 'calm and gentle'. This must have taken some doing. London was daunting. Even Smith scrutinised and judged them. He said, unkindly, of Charlotte, 'I believe she would have given all her genius and her fame to have been beautiful,' and rated Anne condescendingly as 'by no means pretty, yet of a pleasing appearance'. He also said her 'manner was curiously expressive of a wish for protection and encouragement, a kind of constant appeal which invited sympathy'. But maybe she was just dismayed by being coolly assessed by this man about town. London was intimidating in other ways too; the short trip cost fourteen pounds, over half Anne's annual salary at her first governess post.

There is no record of what Anne said to Newby, when (presumably) she went to see him at his office on Mortimer Street. As well as laying down the law, Anne must have discussed the response to her second novel. The day she arrived in London, a poisonous review appeared in the *Spectator*, accusing her of having 'a morbid love for the coarse, not to say the brutal', and calling her characters 'displeasing or repulsive, from their gross, physical or profligate substratum'. That same day, the *Athenaeum* unwittingly referred to Anne's relationship with Charlotte (again!), saying, '*The Tenant of Wildfell Hall* must not hope to gain the popularity of her elder sister *Jane Eyre*.' The review's cheering conclusion that *The Tenant of Wildfell Hall* was 'the most interesting novel which we have read for a month past' was buried in a welter of words about the Bells' 'family likeness' and a warning to all three against 'dwelling upon what is disagreeable'. Anne had recently vowed to defy 'The World's dread scoff'. But published without a real name on it, and without context, her second book had been misunderstood. It had become a *succès de scandale*. When she learned from Newby that a second edition was imminent, she decided to do something about it. In *The Tenant of Wildfell Hall*, Helen declares,

> I would not send a poor girl into the world, unarmed against her foes, and ignorant of the snares that beset her path: nor would I watch and guard her, till, deprived of self-respect and self-reliance, she lost the power, or the will, to watch and guard herself.

Anne decided she wouldn't send her novel out into the world unarmed either. She would write a preface for the new edition.

Anne started writing the minute she got back to Haworth on 12 July. The weather was unusually sultry, and Anne and Emily took their work desks and stools to the end of the garden, and spent the next nine, sunny days, in the shade of the currant bushes, writing. That summer, Branwell seemed worse than ever; Charlotte told Nussey his constitution was 'shattered', and Gaskell said he kept creeping out of the Parsonage while the family were in church to try to buy opium with money he didn't have. He wrote his last letter one Sunday morning that summer, begging his friend, the stonemason John Brown, to get him 'five pence worth of gin in a proper measure'. Anne had her share of what Charlotte called 'sad nights' with her brother. But she kept writing. And by 22 July Anne had finished her preface. It was published in the second week of August.

The preface is succinct – just over a thousand words – and closely argued and very clear, a daring, blistering piece of writing. Even though she signed it Acton Bell, it feels like this is Anne speaking, loudly and boldly, in her own voice. She insisted, 'I would have it to be distinctly understood that Acton Bell is neither Currer nor Ellis Bell, and therefore let not his faults be attributed to them.' The flipside of this, of course, was that Anne didn't want anyone to think she was responsible for the 'faults' she had identified in her sisters' novels.

Anne began by turning her flinty gaze on critics who read her novel 'with a prejudiced mind or [have been] content to judge it by a hasty glance'. She doesn't think artists should respond to their critics, but all the prejudice, haste and 'misapprehensions' have made it a 'necessity'. And then she dives in: 'My object in writing the following pages was not simply to amuse the Reader; neither was it to gratify my own taste, nor yet to ingratiate myself with the Press and the Public: I wished to tell the truth.'

If anything makes me think Anne was never the meek, mild waif she was made out to be, it is this utterly uncompromising preface. Telling the truth 'needs some courage', she says, and a truth-teller will be scorned, just as 'she who undertakes the cleansing of a careless bachelor's apartment [is] liable to more abuse for the dust she raises than commendation for the clearance she effects'. *Cleansing* and *clearance* are her aims; she is trying to help 'reform the errors and abuses of society'. It also makes me laugh that she snidely compares the critics to bachelors who grumble when their friends take the trouble to tidy up their mess.

Nine days is a long time to write a thousand words and perhaps Anne spent some of the time reading and thinking about how other women writers had tackled the dilemma of speaking for themselves while using pseudonyms. She knew she didn't want to do what Emily was doing, jamming her mask on tight, and refusing to take it off. She didn't like Charlotte's way of going about things either, inventing a voice for Currer Bell that sounded a lot like the Angrian heroes she had written as a child. In her letters to the literary world, 'Currer' was ironic, bluff, clubbable, swaggering, a girl's idea of how men talked to men. Anne felt there had to be another way.

Perhaps she read George Sand, whose novels she might first have encountered when Taylor sent Charlotte a bale of French books to read before she went to Brussels. Charlotte ploughed through them, summing them up as 'clever, wicked, sophistical [*sic*] and immoral', and then, endearingly, betrayed her unworldliness by adding 'they give one a thorough idea of France and Paris – and are the best substitute for French conversation'. Sixteen years older than Anne, Sand lived as scandalously as she wrote – and British women were fascinated. Elizabeth Barrett Browning hailed her as a 'large-brained woman and large-hearted man, / Self-called George Sand!', thrilled by Sand choosing her own name, not her father's or husband's. Sand liked her moustache de plume so much that she made everyone call her George, even her lovers, even her children, and she wore men's clothes and hobnailed boots which were 'steady on the pavement. I flew from one end of Paris to the other. I felt as if I could have gone round the world . . .' But Barrett Browning worried that Sand was trying to be something she wasn't. As if to put her in her place, she warned,

> Thy woman's hair, my sister, all unshorn
> Floats back dishevelled strength in agony
> Disproving thy man's name!

Perhaps in the same spirit, Gustave Flaubert called Sand 'a great cow full of ink' – and he was supposed to be her friend. The different prefaces Sand wrote to her first novel, *Indiana*, published in 1832, tell the story of how she shrugged off her pseudonym to speak out in her own voice. Sand wrote the first preface in 1832 in the third person, as 'a young man' pleading for a book he has an 'artless fatherly affection' for. But ten years on, she wrote the second preface in the first person, with no apologies, no disguises, as a woman looking back on her book and feeling that

> my present duty is to congratulate myself on the bold utterances to which I allowed myself to be impelled then and afterwards; bold utterances for which I have been reproached so bitterly, and which would have been bolder still had I known how legitimate and honest and sacred they were.

Anne didn't live to read the third preface, where Sand eviscerated the critics and praised her own novel as 'a very thunderbolt of war'. But even the journey from the first to the second shows a huge gain in confidence. Her novel, she says, comes from 'an overpowering instinct of outcry and rebellion which God had implanted in me, God who makes nothing that is not of some use'. Perhaps Anne took note, because in the Wildfell Hall preface, she wrote,

> Such humble talents as God has given me I will endeavour to put to their greatest use; if I am able to amuse, I will

try to benefit too; and when I feel it my duty to speak an unpalatable truth, with the help of God, I will speak it, though it be to the prejudice of my name and to the detriment of my reader's immediate pleasure as well as my own.

Anne's conviction that she was doing the right thing fortified her against the critics' objection that her work was coarse, brutal, disagreeable. She was upset by the *Spectator's* review, but not so upset that she could not deal swiftly with its argument, writing:

I find myself censured for depicting con amore, with 'a morbid love of the coarse, if not of the brutal,' those scenes which, I will venture to say, have not been more painful for the most fastidious of my critics to read, than they were for me to describe. I may have gone too far, in which case I shall be careful not to trouble myself or my readers in the same way again; but when we have to do with vice and vicious characters, I maintain it is better to depict them as they really are than as they would wish to appear. To represent a bad thing in its least offensive light is doubtless the most agreeable course for a writer of fiction to pursue; but is it the most honest, or the safest? Is it better to reveal the snares and pitfalls of life to the young and thoughtless traveller, or to cover them with branches and flowers? O Reader! if there were less of this delicate concealment of facts – this whispering, 'Peace, peace', when there is no peace – there would be less of sin and misery to the young of both sexes who are left to wring their bitter knowledge from experience.

Anne also had to address the fact that all her reviews were about her gender. Although Anne and her sisters had carefully designed their pseudonyms to be androgynous, many contemporary readers were sure they were women, including the novelist Harriet Martineau who felt that a passage in *Jane Eyre* 'about sewing on brass rings, could have been written only by a woman or an upholsterer' – she never explained why she was so certain it hadn't been written by an upholsterer. The speculation came with a whole series of judgements about what women should and shouldn't write. Like the review of *The Tenant of Wildfell Hall* that appeared in *Sharpe's London Magazine* soon after Anne sent her preface off to Newby, which insisted,

> none but a man could have known so intimately each vile, dark fold of the civilised brute's corrupted nature; none but a man could make so daring an exhibition . . . On the other hand, no man, we should imagine, would have written a work in which all the women, even the worst, are so far superior in every quality, moral and intellectual, to all the men; no man would have made his sex appear at once coarse, brutal and contemptibly weak, at once disgusting and ridiculous. There are, besides, a thousand trifles which indicate a woman's mind . . . Still there is a bold coarseness, a reckless freedom of language, and an apparent familiarity with the sayings and doings of the worst style of *fast* men . . . which would induce

us to believe it impossible that a woman could have written it. A possible solution of the enigma is, that it may be the production of an authoress assisted by her husband, or some other male friend: if this be not the case, we would rather decide on the whole, that it is a man's writing.

Sharpe's claimed that the first critic they'd sent it to had 'returned it to us, saying it was unfit to be noticed in the pages of *Sharpe*' and they were only reviewing it 'to warn our readers, and more especially our lady-readers, against being induced to peruse it, either by the powerful interest of the story, or the talent with which it was written'. This review was unsigned. It might well have been by a woman.

Charlotte's worst review – the notorious piece which would appear in the *Quarterly Review* in December 1848 – was by a woman, Elizabeth Rigby, who wasn't just writing anonymously but was actively pretending to be a man. This made it tricky for her because she wanted to use her superior knowledge of all things feminine to prove Currer Bell was a man. 'No woman,' she said, 'trusses game and garnishes dessert-dishes with the same hands,' no woman would dress Blanche Ingram in a 'morning robe of sky-blue crape', or make Jane put on 'a frock' when woken in the middle of the night. How did a male reviewer know about trussing, garnishing and frocks? Rigby conjured up 'a lady friend, whom we are always happy to consult' on such matters. So here was a woman, pretending to be a man, helped by a (fictional) woman, reviewing a woman who was disguising her identity with an androgynous pseudonym that led most people to think she must be a man. It takes a while to get my head around this and makes me even more sympathetic to Anne's view that all the fuss about who had written what was irrelevant. She was beginning to realise that the Victorian world of letters was deeply dysfunctional and she didn't want to get sucked in.

Like Rigby, Charlotte relished using a male voice. She said once, 'I cannot when I write think always of myself – and of what is elegant and charming in femininity.' For her, writing like a woman meant writing in a corset of gender expectations. But Anne knew that writing as a woman could mean creating dynamic, forceful heroines. It could mean finding her best material in her own experience. It could mean writing from the margins for people on the margins, and writing about disempowerment to empower both her readers and herself. Anne might have thought Charlotte was confusing the question of how she should write with the question of whether she should reveal her identity. For her, the questions were separate, and the answers were different. Anne wrote like a woman, but that didn't mean she had to say she was one. In fact in her preface's stunning conclusion, she attacked the double standard and took on androgyny as a political stance:

I am satisfied that if a book is a good one, it is so whatever the sex of the author may be. All novels are or should be written for both men and women to read, and I am at a loss to conceive how a man should permit himself to write anything that would be really disgraceful to a woman, or why a woman should be censured for writing anything that would be proper and becoming for a man.

Why should she reveal herself and allow the critics to reduce her work to her identity? Why should she gratify the gossips, who she probably felt were no better than the villagers in *The Tenant of Wildfell Hall* who pry into Helen's past, and, in the absence of any real information, make up a 'spicy piece of scandal'. When Gilbert describes the chief gossip, Mrs Wilson, at work – 'the incessant wagging of her head, the frequent distortions of her wrinkled physiognomy, and the winking and malicious twinkle of her little ugly eyes' – his disgust was also Anne's. She didn't want to be talked about.

Anne's preface seems even more astute and gutsy when I compare it to the way Charlotte tried to answer *her* critics. Charlotte was justifiably stung by Rigby's review but didn't do anything about it until August 1849, three months after Anne's death, when she drafted a preface to *Shirley*. A very different sort of preface to Anne's. Charlotte didn't just sign it 'Currer Bell', she wrote it *as* him, pretending to be a bitter 'old bachelor' who complains about his 'invalid-member' (which he says is 'rather an elegant expression – a nice substitute for – gouty foot') and who claims his nastiest comments are 'dictated' by twinges of gout. It was excruciating and Charlotte's publishers refused to print it. They wanted her to write in her own voice, saying who she was, and defending her work, like Anne. But Charlotte said, absurdly, 'it is "Currer Bell" who was insulted – he must reply', and refused to rewrite. Which is why she resorted to attacking Rigby on the pages of *Shirley* instead.

By then, Charlotte had finally put Nussey out of her misery and admitted she was Currer Bell. Her identity was becoming an open secret. Rumours abounded, especially in Yorkshire, where readers recognised people and places in *Shirley*. On another trip to London, Charlotte told some people her real name and made others call her Currer. Then the critic G. H. Lewes, to whom Charlotte had been writing as Currer, did some digging, and met someone who had been at Cowan Bridge school with Charlotte. So he outed her. In a spiteful review of *Shirley*, for the January 1850 *Edinburgh Review*, Lewes revealed that Charlotte was a clergyman's daughter from Yorkshire, and callously referred to her spinsterhood too, saying that if she was a mother she could never have written about Mrs Pryor giving up her child. Pontificating that 'The grand function of woman . . . is, and must ever be, Maternity', he seemed to suggest Charlotte should be making babies not books. (This was before Lewes fell for George Eliot and she taught him to be nice to women who wrote.) The game was up. Just a few weeks later, the *Bradford Observer* revealed Charlotte's name.

So Charlotte panicked and threw up another mask, pretending she was a shrinking violet, a martyr; telling Gaskell stories about stopping writing in the full flow of inspiration so she could sneak potatoes out of the kitchen and peel them, because Tabby was too blind to do it properly, and she didn't want to hurt her feelings. (As if Tabby was shy about asking the girls to peel potatoes.) The biggest casualty of Charlotte's attempt to disguise herself as a good girl was Anne.

Yet I can see why Charlotte clung to her disguises. The late, great literary scholar Carolyn Heilbrun said, in *Writing a Woman's*

Life, that she wrote mystery novels under the pseudonym of Amanda Cross because 'I must have wanted, with extraordinary fervour, to create a space for myself'. A space for oneself is a bit like a room of one's own, and maybe instead of physical space, some women need anonymity, androgyny and peace.

Anne couldn't have written her preface if she hadn't worked out how to handle being a woman artist by writing Helen. Anne had never thought about becoming a painter, but she did work at her drawing, and had to be proficient enough to teach her pupils. She also flouted the convention that women shouldn't make original pictures but should only copy existing works, a convention Charlotte attacked in *Villette* when Lucy Snowe talks of 'copying an elaborate line engraving, tediously working up my copy to the finish of the original', creating 'curiously finical Chinese facsimiles of steel or mezzotint plates' which are 'about as valuable as so many achievements in worsted-work'. The classical heads, flowers and landscapes Anne and Charlotte copied at school, from Roe Head's few fashionable drawing manuals, were just as lacking in worth.

As in her novels, Anne drew from life. All the Brontës were fervent doodlers, and might have got into trouble for it, as Charlotte's hero Wellesley does, in a story she wrote when she was eighteen, where his punishment for having 'drawn a scrawk' in a book is to learn a page of recipes from *The Cook's Guide*, which sounds like something their aunt Elizabeth might have made the children do, if she found them scribbling. But they can't have got into too much trouble; every book they owned is dog-eared, smeared and tatty, in a 'state of dilapidation', like

Cathy's books in *Wuthering Heights*, where Lockwood finds her 'pen-and-ink commentary . . . covering every morsel of blank that the printer had left'. The young Brontës even drew on their nursery walls. Maybe they got licence to draw outside the lines from Thomas Bewick's *History of British Birds*, a book Anne liked so much that she gave it to Arthur in *The Tenant of Wildfell Hall*. Bewick intersperses his faithful pictures of birds with what he called Tailpieces. In these tiny drawings he didn't worry about being ornithologically correct, but indulged his cruel, amoral humour. He drew children building a strangely terrifying snowman; a cunning monkey roasting a chicken over a roaring fire; a boy climbing up to a birds' nest and falling into a river when the branch broke. There were drunks and fools and beggars and boors. From Bewick, Anne learned that marginalia could be powerful. While Bewick's pictures of birds are beautiful, it is his Tailpieces which really bloom in the mind.

Anne was often her siblings' model. In one of Charlotte's studies, Anne, aged thirteen, is half veiled by a cloak, as if her sister was already planning to obituarise her as a woman covered in 'a sort of nun-like veil'. Charlotte also painted Anne dolled up like a society lady, with an extreme wasp waist and wearing a low-cut blue dress, red beads around her swan-like neck. Her curls fall forward, and her eyes are blue-violet, framed by eyebrows that are perfect arches. Her mouth is a rosebud, curving only very slightly at the edges, but not yet into a smile. There's a faint blush on her cheeks, but she is very pale. Her eyes are penetrating and she doesn't smile.

In fact, she doesn't smile in any of her portraits, and in the two Branwell made, the best ones – the ones where he saw something about her that Charlotte missed – Anne is practically scowling. Perhaps she doesn't like the way Branwell has given himself a gun and made himself tower over his sisters. (Was he standing on a box?) It makes an interesting contrast to Emily's drawing of herself and Anne writing, focused, determined and wielding their pens. Anne never looks at her siblings as they paint her. Perhaps she is using the time spent sitting for her portraits to think.

More interesting are Anne's self-portraits. At twenty-two, she sketched herself, looking pretty but cross, and scrawled 'A very bad picture' even more crossly on the back. Maybe she was venting her irritation at not getting the picture right or maybe she was annoyed that she made herself look so blandly beautiful. When I shuffle photocopies of all the pictures of Anne into chronological order, it feels like she was always fighting to stop being gazed at so that she could do some gazing herself. When Anne had just become a governess, in 1839, she sketched a woman (maybe herself) watching the sun rise. She faces away, with her back to us, as if the view overwhelmed her. A year later, something had shifted. In her pencil sketch *What You Please*, she (or her alter ego) is gazing so ardently and seriously that she leans forward, pushing back the branch of a tree to get a better look. By then, Anne was roaming the countryside with a special French sketching block, the very latest thing, designed for going outdoors and drawing from life, in all weathers; one landscape is even splattered with what looks like rain.

At the Brontë archive in Haworth I slip on latex gloves and pull the sketching block out of its layers of acid-free tissue paper. I am lucky to get to see it as it is owned by a local family and only here on loan. I run my hands over the swirly brown leather cover, admiring the black edging. I imagine Anne putting pencils into the loops, using a penknife to slip off the outer sheet of paper, and setting off, like Helen, who spends time 'studying the distinctive characters of the different varieties of trees in their winter nakedness, and copying, with a spirited, though delicate touch, their various ramifications'.

This is Helen at her most confident, an artist who needs to use pseudonyms or else people 'might possibly recognise the style' of her paintings, because, as the critic Antonia Losano has pointed out, she now *has* a style, a voice of her own. She never stops working, either, and has the artist's consciousness, caught between enjoying the world and interpreting it. 'I almost wish I were not a painter,' she tells Gilbert, because 'instead of delivering myself up to the full enjoyment of [nature] as others do, I am always troubling my head about how I could produce the same effect upon canvas'.

She's no longer the young woman who showed Huntingdon what she proudly called her 'masterpiece', a painting which was 'somewhat presumptuous' because she was trying to make something better than she knew how. He interpreted it as a story about 'girlhood just ripening into womanhood', imagining that the girl Helen has painted is 'thinking there will come a time when she will be wooed and won', and asking why she hasn't given the girl her own dark hair. He wants to be doing the gazing, as well as the wooing and the winning, and after they marry, Helen finds that to make him happy she has to 'deck myself out like a painted butterfly'. It is an interesting choice of word. He wants her *painted* not *painting*.

When she realises her marriage is over, she decides, 'The palette and the easel, my darling playmates once, must be my sober toil-fellows now.' She knows she is not yet good enough 'to obtain my livelihood in a strange land, without friends and without recommendation' so she must 'labour hard to improve my talent, and to produce something worthwhile as a specimen of my powers, something to speak favourably for me, whether as an actual painter or a teacher'. She has no illusions. She might not make it as 'an actual painter', but even to teach, she'll need to be better. She isn't aiming for 'brilliant success', but she can't fail because 'I must not take my son to starve'. She is aware, too, that 'I might have to struggle with the indifference or neglect of others, or my own inexperience or inability'. It seems clear that Anne struggled with all these things. Maybe she realised Branwell hadn't worked hard enough at his painting, hadn't studied anatomy with a Bradford doctor like one of his artist friends, hadn't even learned to mix his paints properly. Maybe she remembered how much money had been squandered on his art supplies. To pay for hers, Helen has to find a dealer, sell some of her pictures and her jewellery. While Branwell had a studio to paint in, Helen has to work in the library, in between bringing up her son and entertaining a house full of roaring drunks. Anne also had her writing time squeezed out by obligations and by having to deal with Branwell's bad behaviour. She is at her most deadpan describing Hargrave invading Helen's work space, examining her painting and 'having modestly commented on it, without much encouragement from me, he proceeded to expatiate on the art in general'. However, this scene takes a dark turn when he assaults her.

Later, Huntingdon finds out what Helen is planning and marches her into the library where, says Helen,

My painting materials were laid together on the corner table, ready for tomorrow's use . . . He soon spied them out, and putting down the candle, deliberately proceeded to cast them into the fire: palette, paints, bladders, pencils, brushes, varnish: I saw them all consumed: the palette-knives snapped in two, the oil and turpentine sent hissing and roaring up the chimney. He then rang the bell.

'Benson, take those things away,' said he, pointing to the easel, canvas, and stretcher; 'and tell the housemaid she may kindle the fire with them: your mistress won't want them any more.'

Benson paused aghast and looked at me.

'Take them away, Benson,' said I; and his master muttered an oath.

'And this and all, sir?' said the astonished servant, refer-ring to the half-finished picture.

'That and all,' replied the master; and the things were cleared away.

It is deeply shocking. Huntingdon has always been a philistine, a man who didn't give his new wife time to see one-tenth of the beauties of Rome because he was worried about running into his (many, angry) ex-lovers. But that's not why he destroys Helen's paintings. He does it to show her he can; as her husband, he owns all of it, not just the paint and canvases she has bought since their marriage, but everything she owned before, as well as everything she makes. Caroline Norton's husband even subpoenaed her publishers so he could take her royalties. It's a display of power and brute force. Huntingdon is clearly threatened by the idea of her 'running away and turning artist, and supporting yourself by the labour of your hands'. He wouldn't be so worried if he didn't think she could do it. But, like literature, art was becoming something women could do. The 1851 census counted 548 women artists (to 25,000 governesses), and by 1871, that number had doubled.

Thinking about all this leads me to Tate Britain, one rainy morning, to look at a painting which I am pretty sure was inspired by *The Tenant of Wildfell Hall*. It's by Emily Mary Osborn, who was also a curate's daughter from a big family and who carved out a successful career for herself as an artist. Her paintings often shine a light on women who were less lucky. *The Governess*, from 1860, could be an illustration from *Agnes Grey*, with its plain governess standing accused of something heinous by four fat, spoiled pupils and their velvet-swathed mother. Queen Victoria was so moved by the painting that she bought it.

The picture I've come to see is Osborn's 1857 work *Nameless and Friendless*, which shows a woman in mourning, just like Helen in *The Tenant of Wildfell Hall*. She is trying to sell her paintings in a dark art shop. She is lit like a Virgin Mary, all pathos and virtue, dressed in black and grey, with black hair (another echo of Helen) gleaming beneath her veiled hat. Her son, hopeful in a red scarf, hefts her portfolio. It is almost as big as he is. She fiddles with a piece of string. The portly dealer sneers. If this man doesn't buy her work, she will end up nameless and friendless, and if she becomes destitute, she might have to sell herself instead of pictures – perhaps to the two swells who ogle her from a corner. *Nameless and Friendless* is sentimental but also upsetting. I stand in front of it for a long time.

And then I notice that the pictures that immediately surround it are *all* paintings of women by men. Every last one. There is William Holman Hunt's *The Awakening Conscience*, where a mistress is scared that if she leaves her lover, she'll be discarded like the glove he's chucked carelessly on the floor. There is John Everett Millais's *Mariana*, where a woman in a lonely moated grange longs for the cad who rejected her. There is also his *Ophelia*, and John William Waterhouse's *The Lady of Shalott*, depicting dead or desperate women. I do some counting. It turns out that of the ninety-seven works in the room, just three are by women. One is Joanna Mary Wells's *Gretchen*, a painting which says as much about Victorian women artists as *Nameless and Friendless* or as *The Tenant of Wildfell Hall*. Wells experienced early success like Osborn, but while Osborn went on to travel (and paint) all over the world, and lived to the ripe old age of ninety-seven with, intriguingly, a female companion, Wells died at twenty-nine of complications from giving birth to her third child. *Gretchen* was her last painting, made while she was pregnant, and it is a portrait of the nursemaid who was helping her with her children, and left unfinished. Even the attribution speaks volumes because it says Wells, but she preferred to be known by her maiden name, Boyce.

Angry now, I can see why the suffragettes took meat cleavers and toffee hammers into galleries to slash nudes, why in the 1980s the Guerrilla Girls activists asked if women had to be naked to get into the Met Museum, why Rozsika Parker and Griselda Pollock asked in their 1981 book *Old Mistresses* why there wasn't a female equivalent to the reverential term 'Old Master'. I get angrier still when, a few weeks later, I am researching George Moore, the contrarian, walrus-moustached Irish novelist who championed *Agnes Grey* in the 1920s. Moore called *Agnes Grey* 'the most perfect prose narrative in English letters . . . a narrative simple and beautiful as a muslin dress', a line which has blurbed several editions of the novel. But something about it annoys me, and I can't put my finger on what until I come across Moore's 1893 book *Modern Painting*, where he opines that women's art should be confined to 'amiable transpositions suitable to boudoirs and fans'. Boudoirs and fans! He merrily sums up all women's art, across continents and centuries, as 'charming triflings' and concludes, 'Women have created nothing, they have carried the art of men across their fans charmingly, with exquisite taste, delicacy, and subtlety of feeling, and they have hideously and most mournfully parodied the art of men.'

This was what Anne was up against. Men like Moore didn't believe women could be artists. They couldn't read *The Tenant of Wildfell Hall* and take Helen's story remotely seriously. They certainly couldn't give its author the respect she deserved. Moore called Anne a 'literary Cinderella', an epithet that has stuck. In doing so, he ignores Anne's singular mind, her blazing sense of injustice, her austere, sardonic, demanding prose, and turns her into a passive, pretty object of pity – and of course he turns himself into her Prince Charming.

Moore had views on *The Tenant of Wildfell Hall* too, of course. He didn't like the narrative frame of Gilbert's letters enclosing Helen's diary. In fact, he said, 'almost any man of letters would have laid his hand upon her arm and said: You must not let your heroine give her diary to the young farmer . . . Your heroine must tell the young farmer her story, and an entrancing scene you will make of the telling.' It's staggeringly offensive, the idea that *almost any man of letters* could tell Anne how to write her novel, and the patronising way Moore imagines them laying their hands on her arm. He probably imagines her wearing a muslin dress – and the more I think about it, the less I like his praise of *Agnes Grey*, because I doubt he would compare a man's novel with clothes.

Many critics have got sidetracked into debating *The Tenant of Wildfell Hall*'s frame. But the frame *works*. Anne didn't want Helen to tell Gilbert the story of her life. She didn't want Helen to be 'entrancing'. Instead, Helen gives Gilbert her diary so her words and her story will speak for themselves, just as Anne did when she refused to make her identity part of the story in her preface.

By the end of *The Tenant of Wildfell Hall*, Helen has done what Huntingdon fears: she has succeeded. She loves her studio at Wildfell Hall with its 'professional, business-like appearance', takes pleasure in earning her own living, and when Gilbert visits and Helen grudgingly 'disengag[es] a couple of chairs from the artistic lumber that usurped them', it feels very much as though he is the usurper, and, as he says, Helen's 'heart is in [her] work'. Most of all, Helen has managed to get away from the male gaze. When Gilbert stares at her sketching, admiring 'the elegant white hand that held the pencil, and the graceful neck and glossy raven curls that drooped over the paper', Helen ignores him, and, when he doesn't get the message, tells him to go away. And Gilbert learns. When he looks at Helen's work, he is pleasantly surprised to find it 'strikingly beautiful; it was the very scene itself, transferred as if by magic to the canvas'. In Gilbert, Helen has found the best possible audience for her work.

And as Anne finished writing her preface that hot July day in 1848, perhaps she hoped that she would find the right readers too. And I wonder if she thought back to the self-portrait she had made at twenty-two, and called *A very bad picture*, and felt that in her preface she had finally made a self-portrait that expressed what she wanted to say, and that was, in its own angular, angry way, beautiful.

My partner proposes, in a field, at a festival, while Björk is playing, and everyone is dressed up as pirates and mermaids and jellyfish. When Weston proposes to Agnes, she asks, 'Are you in earnest?' I am just as disbelieving. My partner, like Weston, has to promise he's not joking, that he means it. He asks about five times before I actually say yes. And then we drink champagne and write the date on the cork; and, over the next few weeks, I worry a lot because I am so happy, and because I am terrified that it will all go wrong. Again I find Anne has already said it for me. 'I dare not believe in such felicity,' says Gilbert, when Helen proposes, pressing for a short engagement because, he says, 'the longer I have to wait, the greater will be my dread that something will intervene'. As I plunge into *wedmin* (not a word I've ever felt the need for before) all the tiny choices feel fraught and important because I feel, superstitiously, that if I get this right, the rest of my life will go right too.

I find myself at a dress shop, cajoled into standing on a box and actually twirling, in what feels like a costume for a role I don't know how to play. I've been resisting the marriage plot all my life. I don't want my choice of man to be the last choice I ever make, before I have to vanish from the story. I suddenly feel more sympathetic towards Rosalie in *Agnes Grey*; Rosalie wants 'to . . . coquet with all the world, till I am on the verge of being called an old maid; and then, to escape the infamy of that, after having made ten thousand conquests, to break all their hearts save one'. On her wedding day, she says miserably, 'It's done, my fate is sealed'; all that flirting was a desperate attempt to keep making choices.

But there is more than one way to tell this story. If Anne's taught me anything, she's taught me that. Another minor plotline suddenly feels pertinent, this time from *The Tenant of Wildfell Hall*. It's the story of Eliza Millward's older sister Mary, who causes 'astonishment' when, having gone on plain and unregarded for years, she marries studious Richard Wilson, amazing their friends who thought it 'impossible that the pale, retiring bookworm should ever summon courage to seek a wife, or be able to obtain one if he did, and equally impossible that the plain-looking, plain-dealing, unattractive, unconciliating Miss Millward should ever find a husband'. It's not just because I am embarking on my own late marriage that this moment makes me so happy. It's because Mary and Richard do what everyone thinks is 'impossible'. They surprise the village who had 'long since declared them both born to single blessedness', and their story feels crucial to what Anne was trying to say. Because no one is born to anything. Everyone has the capacity to surprise, and be surprised.

I think about what I'm really trying to do: to build a happy future, to bring two people together, two families, and in our case, two cultures, two religions and three languages. I think about how Gilbert says Mary's (gold-digging) sister and Richard's (gossiping) sister, both end up 'uncomfortable'. His recipe for a happy life includes 'making my wife happy and comfortable', as well as 'harmony' and generosity. Unlike Jane and Rochester who don't even include Adèle in their family circle, Gilbert expands his heart to Helen's aunt and son, making a marriage that is joyous and abundant. This feels like something I can learn.

Helen learns it too. She becomes the artist of her own life. She has spent years being a painted butterfly, years on other people's canvases. She has had to cut her way free using her own palette knife. At Wildfell Hall, paintbrush in hand, she has composed her life like a picture, deciding what to include and what to leave out, shedding abusers and toxic friends, keeping only who and what she needs. Holed up in a crumbling ruin, with nothing to do but walk and paint and mother her son and mystify the neighbours, Helen isn't a painted butterfly any more and she's also no longer the woman who had to use her palette knife as a weapon. She's finally living a more creative life, and as she gains confidence, she starts to let more people into her life, even a new husband. By the end of the novel, she's still painting her own canvas; it's just that now she's using all the colours on her palette.

10

ANNE
or how to take courage

'Gird on thine armour,' Anne commands herself, in 'Self-Communion', the long autobiographical poem she wrote over six months between November 1847 and April 1848. She continues,

> haste, arise,
> For thou hast much to do; –
> To lighten woe, to trample sin,
> And foes without and foes within
> To combat and subdue.

After these stirring lines, the poem drifts into melancholy. Anne tries to urge herself not to let her weary spirit sink, nor to add to the world's evil; to destroy 'bitter poison' and break the 'cruel chain'. But she says tiredly that she isn't getting anywhere, that the way is hard. She is fighting her own doubts ('my worst enemies, I know, / Are those within my breast'), and she longs for 'a rest beyond the grave', although she can't entirely believe it is there. She begs for her 'misty doubts' to clear so she can see

that sunny shore,
However far away!
However wide this rolling sea,
However wild my passage be,
Howe'er my bark be tempest-tost,
May it but reach that haven fair.

I find this impossible to read without remembering that a year later Anne died by the sea.

This is the part of Anne's story where everything happens very fast. Too fast. Painfully fast, so that it feels as though, as Charlotte wrote in *Shirley*, 'The future . . . bursts suddenly, as if a rock had rent, and in it a grave had opened.'

It was around this time that Anne found Branwell in the bed he had set on fire. She must also have seen him have fits, more frequent now, and 'of inexpressible horror', he said. He was making small, spiky, sorrowful sketches of himself; as a corpse next to a hearty, healthy young man; as a martyr at the stake, engulfed in flames; with a noose around his neck. In his last sketch, which he sent in a note to his friend Leyland, like a postcard from the edge, he lies naked in bed, blankets partly over him but not enough to keep warm, clutching the sheets, shutting his eyes and hiding his face in the pillow as he is summoned by death in the form of a looming skeleton.

A few weeks after her formidable, fierce preface was published in August 1848, Anne was cheered by a review in the *Literary World* which, while still mostly awful, concluded, as if the critic couldn't help himself (or herself; this, too, was unsigned), that 'the rich grain of genius . . . freshness and vigour' of Anne's novel 'boldly and eloquently [develops] blind places of wayward passion in the human heart, which is far more interesting to trace than all the bustling lanes and murky alleys through which the will-o'-the-wisp genius of Dickens has so long led the public mind'. What a thrill, to be compared to Dickens, and even judged to be better! Anne couldn't enjoy this triumph for long.

One night in September 1848, Branwell's friend Grundy sent a note inviting him to dinner at the Black Bull. To his surprise, Patrick turned up first. Grundy found Patrick's 'old stiffness of manner was gone'. He spoke 'almost hopelessly' about his son, and when Branwell arrived, Grundy saw why. His friend was unkempt, gaunt, shaking, and his eyes glared 'with the light of madness'. Even a glass of hot brandy didn't help; Branwell looked 'frightened – frightened of himself'. He showed Grundy a carving knife hidden in the sleeve of his coat; reading Grundy's note, he had thought it was from Satan, and had come out intending to stab him. Grundy felt helpless, and at the end of the night 'left him standing bare-headed in the road, with bowed form and dropping tears'.

On 22 September 1848, Branwell went into the village. No one knows where exactly, but on the way back he collapsed on the lane between the church and the Parsonage and was helped home. In the morning he couldn't get up. 'Oh, John, I am dying!' he told his friend the stonemason. 'In all my past life I have done nothing either great or good.' The doctor confirmed that Branwell was close to the end. Anne must have felt, now, that the scenes she wrote in *The Tenant of Wildfell Hall*, where Helen watches at Huntingdon's deathbed, were horribly prescient. Like Helen, she hoped the dying man would find some peace. And Branwell did. As Patrick prayed with his son, Branwell suddenly, out of nowhere, said 'Amen'. It was a moment of calm and mercy and then, as if he had decided that he could go unfrightened into the darkness now, he stood up, and then fell back into his father's arms and died. He was thirty-one. The doctor certified the cause of death as 'Chronic bronchitis – Marasmus'; marasmus is emaciation. But many biographers now think that Branwell's boozing and bad behaviour had masked the fact that he had been wasting away from TB for longer than anyone had realised.

Four days later, at Branwell's funeral, Emily caught a cold. Charlotte was 'very uneasy' about her, and about Anne, whose asthma was worse than ever. Charlotte called Emily's cough and cold 'very obstinate', but this was also what she thought about Emily herself, who refused to see a doctor, and refused to discuss the fact that she was getting more and more ill. Charlotte wrote to W. S. Williams in frustration, saying that 'to put any question, to offer any aid is to annoy; she will not yield a step before pain or sickness till forced; not one of her ordinary avocations will she voluntarily renounce: you must look on, and see her do what she is unfit to do, and not dare to say a word'. Anne could hear Emily's painful, rasping breathing as she insisted on continuing to do the housework, although her sisters begged her to stop. It was clear that she had consumption – perhaps caught from Branwell – and it had reached the awful stage of *galloping*. Charlotte wrote later that Emily 'made haste to leave us'. She desperately said to Nussey,

'I *do* wish I knew her state of mind and feelings.' But Emily shut her out.

At the end of November 1848, Emily had been ill for two months and still refused even to mention her illness. It was at this point that Charlotte did something I find very hard to understand, or forgive. She read aloud the *North American Review*'s savaging of *Jane Eyre*, *Wuthering Heights* and *The Tenant of Wildfell Hall*. Charlotte was tickled by how wrong the critic was about her sisters:

> I studied the two ferocious authors. Ellis, 'the man of uncommon talents, but dogged, brutal, and morose', sat leaning back in his easy chair, drawing his impeded breath as best he could, and looking, alas! piteously pale and wasted; it is not his wont to laugh, but he smiled half-amused and half in scorn as he listened. Acton was sewing, no emotion ever stirs him to loquacity, so he only smiled too, dropping at the same time a single word of calm amazement to hear his character so darkly portrayed . . . How I laugh in my sleeve . . .

Anne got pasted. The critic, E. P. Whipple, said she took 'a morose satisfaction in developing a full and complete science of human brutality'; blamed her for the faults he found in *Wuthering Heights*, and added insult to injury by saying *The Tenant of Wildfell Hall* wasn't as good. He slammed Anne's plotting for 'excessive clumsiness', and declared that 'there is nothing kindly or genial in the author's powerful mind and that, if he continues to write novels, he will introduce into the land of romance a larger number of hateful men and women than any other writer of the day'. That 'if' must have cut Anne to the quick. She wanted to write more novels. She might even have started one – as with so much of Anne's life, it's impossible to be sure. She wasn't trying to write about 'the land of romance' and she didn't think her characters 'hateful', but it would have been hard to believe in herself as Charlotte read the critic's damning conclusion that

> The reader of Acton Bell gains no enlarged view of mankind . . . but is confined to a narrow space of life, and held down, as it were, by main force, to witness the wolfish side of his nature literally and logically set forth. But the Criminal Courts are not the places in which to take a comprehensive view of humanity and the novelist who confines his observation to them is not likely to produce any lasting impression, except of horror and disgust.

Anne must have felt she'd failed. Her book hadn't made this critic think or act more morally. Instead, it had horrified and disgusted him. Did Charlotte really think Anne would find the review funny? She knew Anne had been angry enough about other reviews to respond to her critics in her preface. Charlotte had even told Williams: 'You will have seen some of the notices of *Wildfell Hall*. I wish my sister felt the unfavourable ones less keenly . . . I cannot avoid seeing that her spirits are depressed.' So how could she read the review aloud, for fun? I can't help suspecting that she did it because she agreed with it. She had opposed Anne's second novel from the start. Now she had backup. If Anne guessed this, it would have hurt her even more.

Anne was struggling to follow her own prescription in 'Self-Communion' to 'Press forward, then, without complaint; / Labour and love – and such shall be thy meed.' She repeated this advice in 'The Narrow Way', which was published in *Fraser's Magazine* that December, saying the most important things in life are 'To labour and to love'. While Charlotte had given up writing poetry, and Emily was writing it only for herself, Anne was still sending new poems to editors, but that winter, she didn't write much. She was overwhelmed by grief, and worried about Emily, and battered by the bad reviews. And she was having trouble breathing, and experiencing alarming pains in her side.

But Anne did try to continue to love. She was still corresponding with the two younger Robinson girls, her pupils from Thorp Green, as they navigated the treacherous waters of romance and the marriage market. She probably let them know that Branwell was dead, and maybe that's why they felt able to visit that winter. Charlotte had never liked the Robinsons writing to Anne, never seen why she would want letters from ex-pupils, or to stay in touch with the family of the woman who had ruined Branwell, but even she had to admit that 'They seemed overjoyed to see Anne . . . they were clinging round her like two children'. It must have been some consolation for Anne to know she was so loved.

Especially as Emily didn't seem to want anybody's love. In a last-ditch attempt to rouse her, Charlotte braved the cold to get Emily a sprig of heather from the moors, but it didn't help. On 19 December 1848, Emily got up, tried to comb her hair and dropped her comb in the fire. At midday she finally agreed to see a doctor. It was too late. She died that afternoon. Tabby's nephew William Wood made her coffin. She had wasted away so violently that it measured only sixteen inches across. Emily's dog Keeper followed the coffin into the funeral, three days later. The next day, Charlotte wrote, 'I now look to Anne.'

But Anne was not Emily. She didn't think all doctors were poisoning quacks, and she asked to see a specialist. There are a lot of theories about how she and Emily caught tuberculosis. TB can be latent for years, or forever, and then suddenly become active, as the bacteria 'wake up'. Anne and Emily might have had latent TB since their older sisters died of it, in 1825. Or Anne might have caught it on that whirlwind trip to London, a theory advanced by a professor of obstetrics and gynaecology called Philip Rhodes who undertook 'A Medical Appraisal of the Brontës' in 1972. He thought that 'The whole family was neurotically inturned [*sic*] upon itself and unable to make realistic contacts with the outside world', which left them unable to build up a resistance to TB. It seems too cruel an irony that Anne would catch the disease that would kill her just as she was speaking out for the first time. TB is a disease that makes it hard for sufferers to speak – it would not be possible for a person dying from TB to belt out a song as Mimi does in Puccini's 1896 opera *La Bohème*. The truth is that until drugs were developed to treat TB in 1946, it was everywhere, and Anne could have caught it at any time in her life, and was as likely to have caught it in Haworth as anywhere else.

On 5 January 1849, a Leeds lung specialist called Dr Teale came to the Parsonage. He examined Anne and then, instead of telling her what he had discovered, went to Patrick's study to give him the diagnosis. It must have been agony to wait, but Nussey, who had come to comfort Charlotte, said Anne 'was looking sweetly pretty and flushed and in capital spirits for an invalid'. Nussey obviously thought these were good signs but they send a chill down my spine. I get L. M. Montgomery's 1915 novel *Anne of the Island* off my shelf to reread the pages where Anne Shirley finds her frivolous friend Ruby Gillis as pretty as ever except that 'her blue eyes were too bright and lustrous, and the colour of her cheeks was hectically brilliant; besides, she was very thin'. Ruby is dying of galloping consumption but 'rattling on' as vivaciously as ever. At the Parsonage, Anne walked restlessly about, while the men discussed her fate. When Patrick came in, he only said, 'My *dear* little Anne.' The disease was too far advanced for a cure. All Dr Teale could do was buy Anne time and try to help with the pain.

In *Anne of the Island*, there is a moment where Ruby knows what Anne knew then. She gazes at a moonlit graveyard and shudders because soon she will be lying there, and she shrinks with terror because, she says, 'Heaven must be very beautiful, of course, but . . . it won't be what I've been used to.' She doesn't find the thought of heaven comforting at all. 'I want to live like other girls,' sobs Ruby, and I am sobbing too. Because didn't Anne Brontë also want to live like other girls?

TB hit Anne just at the point where she had found herself as a writer. She was desolate with grief and loss. But she might have lived to write more books – didn't Charlotte? She was only twenty-eight. Before Dr Teale's diagnosis, Anne would have felt she had time.

But she didn't. She met the dark news on her own. She'd lost her confidante, Emily. She and Charlotte never had grown close, and anyway, Charlotte preferred to confide in Nussey. So Anne took to the page. Two days after Dr Teale's visit, she started writing the poem that would be her last.

She wrote the first eight stanzas that day, in pencil, in the small print she'd used as a child, beginning, shatteringly, 'A dreadful darkness closes in.' She begs God, 'Oh, let me suffer and not sin,' and asks for 'courage to resist' the devil and for 'strength'. Line by line, she struggles to understand what is happening to her. Her usual elegant handwriting has deserted her; the words are cramped, the page is blotted. She is angry, too. 'I hoped,' she says, 'that with the brave and strong, / My portioned task might lie.' She is angry with God for not granting her that:

> But Thou hast fixed another part
> And thou hast fixed it well
> I said so with my bleeding heart
> When first the anguish fell.

These are words wrung out like blood.

Over the next few weeks, Anne did everything Dr Teale suggested. She had blisters (hot compresses, supposed to draw the disease to the surface) applied to her side, and took carbonate of iron. She forced down cod liver oil which made her nauseous, and stuck to a tedious regime of rest and quiet. She didn't complain. Charlotte said she was 'as patient as Emily was unflinching'. After three weeks she returned to her poem and added nine more verses, verses which grab at a kind of desperate hope. She vows 'These weary hours will not be lost', and promises to turn to God and serve him whatever her fate might be, 'Whether thus early to depart, / Or yet a while to wait.' A wild hope surges up in her, and she tries to make a deal with God. 'If thou shouldst bring me back to life,' she cries, she'll be wiser, stronger, better. But you can't bargain with God, she knows that. In the last stanza, she promises that she will keep her vow, whether God saves her or not:

> Should death be standing at the gate
> Thus should I keep my vow;
> But, Lord, whate'er my future fate
> So let me serve Thee now.

It is a poem written with bravery, from the tight corner she found herself in. When Charlotte edited it for publication, she called it 'Last Lines' and cut it from seventeen verses to eight, deleting all the anger and despair. Very strangely, she changed the verse where Anne confronts God for having 'taken my delight / And hope of life away' to make it about her own grief: 'Thou, God, has taken our delight / Our treasured hope away'. Where Anne had continued, 'And bid me watch the painful night / And wait the weary day', Charlotte went on, 'Thou bidst us now weep through the night / And sorrow through the day.' It doesn't even make any sense. Some critics think that Charlotte was trying to say that Anne's sadness was all about losing Emily. But this poem is about Anne confronting her own death. It is certainly not about being resigned. Anne was anything but.

Charlotte wrote about Anne, 'her sufferings hitherto are nothing like Emily's'. They were still sharing a room but not a bed – Dr Teale had insisted that Charlotte take some precautions to avoid getting ill herself. Charlotte was glad that, unlike Emily, Anne didn't put the family through 'The agony of forced, total neglect', but she despaired, 'Anne cannot study now, she can scarcely read; she occupies Emily's chair – she does not get well.' Anne had to give up the cod liver oil because it made her too nauseous to eat, and she became dangerously thin. Charlotte couldn't write either, but told her editor, 'Should Anne get better, I think I could rally and become Currer Bell once more.'

Anne's twenty-ninth birthday on 17 January 1849 must have been sombre. If Anne did exercise her right, like Agnes Martin, to destroy her own work, I imagine she did it that grim January. I hope that if she put her papers into the fire, saw each one brown, curl up and turn into ash, she felt like Helen boldly burning the sketch of Huntingdon to stop him teasing her, and wasn't reminded, instead, of the awful scene where Huntingdon puts Helen's work into the fire. In pain, losing weight, coughing, breathless and exhausted, perhaps Anne put her effects in order, knowing this might be her last chance to do anything about her legacy. She must have wondered what would become of her work when she was no longer there to look after it. Perhaps she opened her last diary paper, from July 1845. There, she'd looked forward to writing again in July 1848 'if we are all alive';

'what changes shall we have seen and known,' Anne had wondered, 'and shall we be much changed ourselves?'

At the Parsonage, I examine Anne's sprigged linen handkerchief, which is stained with the blood she coughed up into it. The handkerchief is red and white. The blood has faded to a dull brown. The stains look like islands. It is too horrible to look at for long.

But in February, against the odds, Anne started to get better.

She was wearing the cork soles Nussey had sent, to keep off the chill of the Parsonage's stone floors. And she was taking Godbold's Vegetable Balsam, and thought it was working. Nathaniel Godbold had gone from gingerbread baker to wealthy landowner on the profits of his balsam, which he claimed was 'an infallible remedy for consumptions, asthmas and coughs'. When he died in 1799 his tombstone was even turned into an advert; his epitaph called him the 'Inventor & Proprietor of that excellent medicine The Vegetable Balsam For the Cure of Consumptions & Asthmas'. It was probably mostly sugar, but it couldn't hurt.

Anne could read again, and she chose to read a book that gave her a sense of the things she could do if she got properly well again. Williams had been sending parcels of books, and Charlotte wrote to him that Anne was 'engaged with one of Frederika Bremer's tales'. I wish I knew which of Bremer's books it was. The Swedish feminist was single and proud of it – she told people she was 'betrothed . . . to my pen'. Her novels took an acerbic view of the marriage market, and exposed the ways the legal system was oppressing women. Her hit, *Hertha*, wore its politics on its sleeve and Bremer also included details of several real-life court cases in an appendix so no one could say it was just fiction. The novel triggered the 'Hertha debate' in parliament and the law was changed to give unmarried women new rights. Bremer didn't stop there. She campaigned for women's suffrage, founded an organisation that visited women in prison, and set up a school for deaf and mute children. Anne must have found Bremer's invigorating prose a tonic. As she read, Charlotte managed to get back to *Shirley*, making a fair copy of the first volume and sending it off to her publishers, and daring to hope, 'Oh! If Anne were well, if the void Death has left were a little closed up, if the dreary word *nevermore* would cease sounding in my ears, I think I could yet do something.' Anne also started to hope that she might, after all, have more time. And if she did maybe she could become an activist like Bremer too. Maybe she could write more overtly political novels. Maybe she could put her real name on them. Maybe she could see more of the world, and connect with people who shared her ideals. Maybe she could just *live*.

Anne took action. She said she would like to go to the sea.

Dr Teale agreed that the sea air might help. He even recommended Scarborough – the place Anne most wanted to go, because she had loved it so much when she had spent her holidays with the Robinsons there. The spanner in the works was Charlotte, who felt 'there *must* be some improvement before I can feel justified in taking her away from home'. Unable to flatly refuse, Charlotte dithered. She said Patrick needed her so she couldn't leave the Parsonage. Nussey invited Anne to stay with her family, which was nice but missed the point: Anne wanted to try the sea cure. She didn't want to stay with Nussey's family (whom she didn't know), inland. But Nussey's offer gave her an idea. She needed someone to go to Scarborough with her; perhaps Nussey could be that person? So she asked her. And that's when Charlotte went behind Anne's back and told Nussey to 'write such an answer to this note as I can show Anne – you can write any additional remarks to me on a separate piece of paper'.

By the start of April 1849, Anne still hadn't made it out of Haworth, and she felt impatient and frustrated. Patrick had noted, in his copy of *Modern Domestic Medicine*, that Dr Teale said that 'change of place & climate, could prove beneficial, only in the early stages of consumption – that afterwards, the excitement caused by change of scenes, and beds, and strange company, did harm'. He'd originally thought Anne was in the 'afterwards' but now she had rallied, maybe she was in the 'early stages', in which case time was of the essence. On 5 April, Anne wrote to Nussey again, writing the letter I had read in the Parsonage archive on that blowy May morning all those months ago. She was writing for her life.

'It would be as a companion not as a nurse that I should wish for your company,' she says valiantly, 'otherwise I should not venture to ask it.' She wants to go soon. In May. Yes, Nussey might be hosting visitors then. Yes, it might be cold. As Anne tackles the objections one by one, she sounds like she is pushing a boulder up a hill:

You say May is a trying month and so say others. The earlier part is often cold enough I acknowledge, but according to my experience, we are almost certain of some fine warm days in the latter half when the laburnums and lilacs are in bloom; whereas June is often cold and July generally wet.

She's insisting gently on the evidence of her experience; after all, she knows Scarborough's seasons. And anyway,

I have a more serious reason than this for my impatience of delay; the doctors say that change of air or removal to a better climate would hardly ever fail of success in consumptive cases if the remedy were taken in <u>time</u>, but the reason why there are so many disappointments is, that it is generally deferred till it is too late. Now I would not commit this error . . . I think there is no time to be lost. I have no horror of death: if I thought it inevitable I think I could quietly resign myself to the prospect in the hope that you, dear Miss Nussey, would give as much of your company as you possibly could to Charlotte and be a sister to her in my stead. But I wish it would please God to spare me, not only for Papa's and Charlotte's sakes, but because I long to do some good in the world before I leave it. I have many schemes in my head for future practice, humble and limited indeed, but still I should not like them all to come to nothing, and myself to have lived to so little purpose.

Nussey couldn't refuse that. And anyway, Patrick intervened to say he didn't need Charlotte looking after him; he had Tabby and Martha to do that. So Charlotte couldn't refuse either. Anne paid for everything with a legacy she had just received from her godmother, and she even told Charlotte which lodgings to book. And they were off.

The trouble is: I know what happened next. So I really don't want to go to Scarborough. All week I've been working in Haworth, getting up in the mornings and eating porridge, because that's what Anne had for breakfast, before throwing on my layers to walk up to the Parsonage archive. At lunchtimes, if it's not too wet, I've been on the moors, sitting on a hummock to eat my sandwiches. I've read Anne's letters, held locks of her hair, gazed at a drawing she made of a speckled hen sitting in a basket lined with straw. It all feels very intimate. Anne feels very present. So I don't want to go to the place where she died, where she is buried.

On the morning I am due to leave, I have a sudden urge to run up the moors and get some heather to put on Anne's grave. At first I dismiss the idea because it feels like I might be wallowing in the same schmaltz as the woeful 1930s plays about the Brontës, where there is *always* a scene where Charlotte brings heather to the dying Emily and she's too dazed to recognise it. But as I pack my bags, the thought of the heather keeps tugging at me. So I race up to the Brontë waterfall, pick a suitable sprig – and nearly miss my bus.

When Anne left for Scarborough she was 'more emaciated than Emily was at the very last', wrote Charlotte. She barely had enough breath to go up the stairs, and could hardly sleep, but still, she kept trying to live, even to enjoy herself. 'She is up all day,' wrote Charlotte anxiously, 'and even goes out a little when it is fine . . . but we creep rather than walk.'

Anne wanted to have *fun* in Scarborough, and she wanted to see York Minster again on the way. Charlotte warned Nussey, who was going to meet them at Leeds station, not to be shocked when she saw Anne who had lost so much weight that her arms were 'no thicker than a little child's'. Poor Nussey waited on the platform, but Anne and Charlotte didn't turn up. As the hours went by, she even saw one train stop while two coffins were carried off it, like some kind of ghastly premonition. It got so late that she had to go home for the night. In the morning, she went to Haworth, expecting the worst, but Anne was up and ready to go. She had been too ill to travel the day before but she was still determined to make it to Scarborough.

After that, the journey was plain sailing. Anne's first biographer Gérin writes tenderly about the kind strangers who helped Anne; 'burly-shouldered Yorkshiremen offered their strong arms wherever trains had to be changed, or railway lines crossed; Anne did not have to walk at all; she was carried'. They stopped at York for the night, hired a bath chair for Anne, and went straight to the Minster. Anne was elated. She whispered, 'If finite power can do this, what is the . . .' and never got to finish her sentence because Charlotte and Nussey decided she was getting overexcited and hurried her away. Anne must have been thinking that *infinite* power might do something for her, that it might even make her well. At the shops, they splashed out on bonnets, corsets, silk stockings, gloves and dresses so they would be ready for fashionable Scarborough. Charlotte had thought the shopping would be 'a dreary mockery', but

Anne might have liked returning to the shops she had visited with the Robinsons, especially now she had money to spend. Back on the train, Anne pointed out the landscapes she knew. It was late May, and there were the lilacs and laburnums she had promised, and meadowsweet too, and the fields were starred with buttercups.

Their lodgings were on St Nicholas Cliff, a very glamorous address, overlooking the South Bay. The massive Grand Hotel is there now. It was pretty fancy when it opened in 1867, but is now notorious for outbreaks of vomiting bugs, and for a BBC undercover investigation in which a microbiologist found all manner of filth and bacteria. When I venture in, the Grand seems glutted on its faded grandeur; all sweeping gilt staircases, a circular 'cabaret ballroom', hideous carpets and glitzy chandeliers. But the view is still the view, and it's spectacular: the sea, vast green headlands, the castle and church on the cliffs, the gorgeous perfect curve of the South Bay. This was the spa town's fashionable centre. The medical baths are gone. No one takes the waters any more. The formal French-style gardens are still there, and some of the beautiful Georgian buildings. The Saloon, with its exotic Gothic turrets and sun terraces, is hosting the Last Laugh Comedy Club, a panto and an Elvis impersonator. This might have been where Anne saw Henry Roxby Beverley playing the fool, and watched her pupil, Lydia, fall in love with him. All along the seafront are penny arcades and shops selling dinghies, fudge, surf boards, buckets and spades, sun hats, flat caps, hula hoops, pull-along toy ponies, retro wooden domino sets, beachballs, sunglasses, fluorescent fishing nets.

I go to the Rotunda, which I'm certain Anne visited when she came here as a governess. It would have been the ideal educational outing. The museum was opened in 1829 by William 'Strata' Smith, who founded English geology more or less by himself. By the 1840s, Yorkshire was mad for fossil-hunting, and even women were encouraged to join in, so long as they stuck to conchology (collecting and studying shells), because it involved no unsavoury cruelty and because shells were the perfect ornaments for ladies' boudoirs.

As I tour the Rotunda, I wonder about a pile of shiny pebbles I have seen at the Parsonage. Anne collected them in Scarborough and stored them in her workbox. But were they just pebbles? What if they were more interesting than that? A wild thought comes to me that I could call this book 'Anne Brontë: Dinosaur Hunter', and I show a picture of Anne's pebbles to a geologist from the Rotunda, but they turn out to be quartzite and carnelian. They have no geological significance. At first I am annoyed with myself for trying to make Anne something she wasn't, but now I think maybe what I want is to fix her in stone and bone, to make her legacy more enduring, to make her *last*.

As it gets dark I retreat to my decidedly unglamorous Travelodge, over the road from the Grand, and go to bed with a cup of peppermint tea, an Eccles cake and Gérin's biography of Anne. I want to read again what Gérin says about Anne's time in Scarborough, but I find myself thinking about Gérin instead, about how after she gave Anne her first biography in 1959, she wrote one of Branwell, then Charlotte, then Emily, and then of their biographer, Gaskell. Winifred Gérin came to the Brontës after a very difficult time. She and her husband, the Belgian cellist Eugène Gérin, had spent the war distributing anti-Nazi propaganda in Belgium, fleeing to France (with their cat, Pussy, in a basket) where they turned their Riviera flat into a safe house for refugees, saving as many Jews as they could, and making a dramatic escape to England. There, they were recruited to work on the controversial, top-secret black propaganda campaign, transmitting misinformation to Germany to cause chaos and lower morale. In 1945, Eugène died suddenly. At forty-three, Winifred lost the man she loved, and her work ended with the war. She escaped again – into writing poetry and plays. She channelled her grief about Eugène into a play about Charlotte falling for Heger, her own brooding Belgian, and called it *My Dear Master*. In 1954 she went to Haworth for the first time and fell in love, with the moors, and with a man who was staying at the same bed and breakfast (now the Old White Lion pub, with the backwards clock). John Lock was twenty years younger, charming, slightly directionless and ardent about the Brontës. Soon, they were married, and living in a house on the edge of Haworth which they called Gimmerton, after the village in *Wuthering Heights*. Lock wrote a guide to Haworth and the moors, and then he and their friend, the rector of Haworth, collaborated on a biography of Patrick. Meanwhile, Winifred turned to Anne. She found the detective work of biography thrilling. 'I have followed her everywhere,' she wrote. She felt this was her vocation. Her biographies are tender and sympathetic. Her research is impeccable, and even when she doesn't know something for sure, most of her guesses have turned out to be right. Her work sustained her after Lock left her for their housekeeper. One of her editors teasingly said she didn't need to get quite so weather-beaten in her pursuit of her subjects, but Gérin's enthusiasm and energy are part of the story. And anyway, she didn't want to let Anne and her family go.

I don't either. Anne's birth bicentenary is in 2020; what if I kept on with her until then? What if I moved to Haworth, like Gérin, and my fiancé (yes, I'm even calling him that now) came too, and we wrote matching books and got fish and chips on Sun Street, near the old ducking well, and walked the moors until, like Anne as a girl, I could say, 'We know where deepest lies the snow, / And where the frost-winds keenest blow.' It doesn't seem such a bad idea.

In the morning, I get up early to go to the Sands, remembering the 'solitary ramble' Agnes takes there before anyone else is up, when the tide is out and the sea pulls back to expose the bay. Anne's love for this place inspired her most soaring, stunning prose. Like her, like Agnes, I look out at

> the broad, bright bay, no language can describe the effect of the deep, clear azure of the sky and ocean, the bright morning sunshine on the semicircular barrier of craggy cliffs surmounted by green swelling hills, and on the smooth, wide sands, and the low rocks out at sea – looking, with their clothing of weeds and moss, like little grass-grown islands – and above all, on the brilliant spar-kling waves. And then, the unspeakable purity – and freshness of the air!

The sea is indeed 'foaming and sparkling, as if wild with glee'. For a few minutes, I think, like Agnes, my footsteps are the first on the firm sands, dimpled with pools and streams, but then I see five or six people out with metal detectors, inching along as they move their devices in slow small circles in front of their feet. I hope they find something to make up for ignoring the radiant sunrise. I stride out across the bay. I feel like I could walk right into the sea. Like Agnes, I'm 'forgetting all my cares, feeling as if I had wings to my feet, and could go at least forty miles without fatigue'.

On her last trip to Scarborough, Anne couldn't go *one* mile without fatigue. The morning after they arrived, she went to take the waters. She insisted on going alone, though she fell at the garden gate on her way back. That afternoon, she went to the Sands, where she sent Charlotte and Nussey off for a walk and hired a donkey-carriage. The donkey-boy beat the donkey so she dismissed him and took up the reins. She hated cruelty to the weak and powerless. As she steered the donkey across the bay, she might have remembered writing about Agnes enjoying all this, and feeling she couldn't be any happier – until she recognises her dog, Snap, and then the man she loves, the clever, down-to-earth, gentle curate, who lights up her life 'like the morning star'. At that moment Anne must have wished for health so she could feel Agnes's joy herself, and so she could live to write more scenes of such rapture.

A hundred and sixty-seven years later, Anne feels very near, as a troupe of donkeys arrive, caparisoned in pink, with ribbon bows between their long, silky ears. They are called the Little Rascals. A boy of about four sets off for a ride, half scared, half thrilled. Across from him, a woman deals her dog a sharp blow, and I give her a reproachful look. I walk the bridge across the ravine. I get lemonade, and oranges, as Anne, Charlotte and Nussey did. They also had dandelion coffee, but I can't find any.

The day after her visit to the Sands, Anne wanted to go to church, but Charlotte insisted she rest. That afternoon Anne managed a short walk, and in the evening, she watched the sunset from the window of their lodgings. She told Charlotte she didn't think she was going to live, after all. That evening she realised death was coming, and she began to prepare. She wanted to meet it with grace. First, she asked if they should try to get home, because it might be easier for Charlotte. To Charlotte's great and lasting credit, she said that they should do what Anne wanted: to stay.

The following morning, Monday 28 May 1849, Anne dressed herself but then paused at the top of the stairs from the bedroom to the sitting room, suddenly too scared and too weak to go down. As Nussey helped her, she awkwardly dropped her into a chair, and Anne hugged her and said it wasn't her fault.

They had breakfast, and at eleven, Anne said she felt a change, and asked to see a doctor. This time she spoke to him herself. She told him not to be scared, to be honest, even if the news was terrible, and she asked again if she should try to get home. Taking her hand, he said she was too ill to travel, that she did not have much time. Anne told Nussey to 'Be a sister in my stead. Give Charlotte as much of your company as you can.' All that day, she kept watching the sea, as if trying to see the sunny shore beyond. They moved her to the couch and she didn't take her eyes off the sea. Maybe she did get a glimpse of the sun, the shore, before, at two o'clock, she died.

I could tell you how Nussey makes much of the way Anne died without giving anyone any trouble; 'so little was the house disturbed by the presence of the dying, and the sorrow of those nearly bereaved, that dinner was announced as ready through the half-open door, as the living sister was closing the eyes of the dead'. I could tell you the doctor admired Anne's tranquillity, and Charlotte said Anne 'had had enough of life . . . she laid it down as a burden'. I could tell you that Nussey maintained that Anne 'was very happy and believed she was even then passing out of earth into Heaven'. But Anne hated sentimental deathbed scenes and never wrote one (the death of Huntingdon is the opposite of sentimental; the death of Agnes's father, which Dickens would have gone to town on, happens quietly offstage). There are a lot of words about Anne's death, but her words, the last she said, were: 'Take courage, Charlotte, *take courage.*'

All day I have been dodging signs pointing to Anne's grave. As the sun starts to set, I climb up to St Mary's Church. Weston proposed to Agnes on this hill, too, and I can see why, going up, she took his arm. It's steep. The church's clock has a friendly blue face, and it looks down over the whole town, with its extraordinary view of the sea, which Agnes, in her bliss, called 'the splendid sunset mirrored in the restless world of waters at our feet'. The church is lovely, reassuring, simple and solid. I push at the door and find it's open for 'Messy Church'. Children are splashing paint about in the aisles while a smiling woman dispenses fair-trade tea and biscuits. In one of the chapels, Anne's death certificate is displayed behind glass. Under profession or rank it says 'spinster'. I go out in the cooling air to find her grave.

The churchyard isn't squashed and oppressive like Haworth's, but spacious and open, with a view of the scoop of the bay, and the sparkling sea beyond. It doesn't take long to find the grave. On the headstone is an urn, covered in draperies, sitting on two books. I hope they represent *Anne's* books but then I find books on several graves; Victorian stonemasons deployed them as symbols of faith.

The stone says Anne was twenty-eight when she died; Nussey got it wrong when she registered the death. If she had been buried in Haworth, the stonemason would have been Branwell's friend John, who had known Anne all her life. But here, Nussey and Charlotte were dealing with strangers. When Charlotte returned in 1852 she would be mortified to find no fewer than five mistakes on the inscription. She asked for it to be refaced and relettered. She couldn't face going back to check whether they had got it right second time round. They hadn't. Anne's age is still wrong.

Only three people came to the funeral. The doctor wanted to come, but Charlotte rebuffed him. When she and Nussey arrived, they found Margaret Wooler there too; their friend and old headmistress from Roe Head School happened to be in town, saw the death announced in the local gazette and wanted to mourn the woman she had once taught. Patrick wasn't there. Later, Charlotte would tell Gaskell he hadn't been able to make it because of an 'annual church solemnity' in Haworth, which sounds like a lie because it is. Without asking him, Charlotte rushed the funeral so he couldn't get there in time, because she didn't think he should have to bury yet another of his children. She paid for the funeral out of the legacy Anne had received from her godmother.

In 2009, the Brontë Society decided to do something about Anne's grave, not just about the mistakes but also the wear and decay that was inevitable with a graveyard so high and exposed, with the air so full of salt. A conservator and a senior church buildings officer concluded that the grave couldn't be restored. The society thought about replacing the headstone with a hardier replica or even moving Anne's body to Haworth, but voted to leave her, and her headstone, and to add a plaque at the base of the stone. It is not beautiful, but it is understated, legible and accurate, and while the headstone just called her Patrick's daughter, the plaque says she was a novelist and poet. It strikes me that no grave, however correctly spelled, however attractive, would make up for the sadnesses of Anne's life and the injustices of her afterlife. As for moving her to Haworth, I wonder if independent Anne might have preferred being buried away from home in the place she had dreamed such hope into.

Now I'm finally here, I don't know what to do. I sit on a bench. A middle-aged couple wander over, but don't seem that interested. 'Who was she, again?' she asks him, and he doesn't know. A Japanese tourist appears, clutching a guidebook. He clocks the grave, takes a photo, ticks it off on a checklist and moves on. Then a mother and daughter arrive. They sit on the next bench and the daughter reads a bit of *Agnes Grey* to her mother, who listens, and then says, 'I hope she gives you inspiration.'

I'm on my own now, the sun is setting, and the whole sky is pink and gold.

I look at the grave, misspelled, wrong, neglected, meddled-with, and I can't bear it. I can't bear that she died so young. I can't bear that her life was so hard. I can't bear that she had so few friends at her funeral, not her father, not even her dog, Flossy. I'm glad I brought the heather. I put it on her grave. I pray for her to rest in peace, and vow to try to do her justice. I start to cry as I walk down the hill.

There's nothing that can soften this. Nothing. She didn't even make thirty. She died just as she was finding out what she could do. I think about all the things Anne didn't get to do, of how her life was circumscribed by poverty and misogyny and sheer bad luck. Anne never left Yorkshire apart from that one weekend in London. She never got to be an author out in the world. She never met her fans. She never joined forces with activists like Caroline Norton and Frances Power Cobbe and Frederika Bremer and John Stuart Mill and Harriet Taylor. She never grew old. She never had a proper love affair. She never married. She never became a mother. She never drove with the windows open on the Somerset hills with her friends, as I did, belting out 'Total Eclipse of the Heart' at the tops of our voices. I've already lived eleven years longer than she ever did. I've travelled, I've met many different kinds of people, I've done many different jobs. In the past month, I've probably gone to the theatre more than she ever did in her entire life. I've seen Kate Bush live.

Take courage, take courage, I'm saying to myself, as I go down to the Sands again, tears blurring my vision as the skies darken and the sea comes in. I see a girl, maybe five years old, in a polka-dotted red mac, a pink dress with a ra-ra skirt and glittery wellington boots. She is running into the water, full-pelt, fast as she can, kicking up the waves, and splashing, and squealing with delight. Her mother chases her and she laughs and shrieks and laughs again. And I'm not crying any more. I'm thinking how much Anne would have loved to see that little girl, her pure joy.

In *The Tenant of Wildfell Hall*, Huntingdon returns from a debauched trip to London and taunts Helen: 'I've lived more in these four months, Helen, than you have lived in the whole course of your existence.' But as Anne charts the monotony of all his drunken nights it is clear that he is not really living, he isn't savouring life. Anne's life was sheltered and short, but she took courage and lived it to the full. She showed that you don't have to be privileged to be a writer, you don't have to be happy. You can be a woman, you can grow up in a single-parent family, you can be shunned as an immigrant, so your brother is burned in effigy in the street. You can be so poor that two of your sisters die of neglect at a failing school that doesn't feed them enough or notice they are ill until it's too late to save them, so poor that you ration butter, and paper and postage. You can have just two years of formal education. You can have a recluse for a sister and a drug addict for a brother. You can have debilitating asthma. You can be depressed. You can struggle with your faith. You can be cold almost every day of your life. You

317

can be ignored at work and bullied by your employers. You can be laughed at by other women for your patched and worn and unfashionable clothes. You can be paralysed by such shyness that you barely ever make a friend. You can see terrible cruelty and be unable to stop it. You can be powerless and know that the laws of your country won't help you. And you can still write things that make people cry and laugh and think and feel 167 years after you died young, a hundred miles from home, which, apart from one weekend in London, is the furthest you have ever travelled in your life.

And maybe you can be forgotten, and then remembered again. Maybe. Every year someone sends flowers to the Parsonage on Anne's birthday. They never say who they are. This year I'm sending flowers too.

POSTSCRIPT

Take courage.

I couldn't get the words out of my head. After I returned from Scarborough, I kept thinking about Anne, and, oddly, about a saying by the eighteenth-century Hasidic mystic Rabbi Nachman of Breslov, which I remembered every time I crossed the bridge over Anne's favourite waterfall on the moors. As I gazed down at the seething torrents, I would think about Anne picnicking here, and about Nachman's saying that 'The whole world is a very narrow bridge; the important thing is not to be afraid'. Nachman was a tzaddik, a Hebrew word which literally means a righteous person, but also means a person who is like a superhero or an angel, always on the side of the oppressed. Like Anne, Nachman was a storyteller, writing captivating, weird tales alongside his religious commentary. He told his followers to talk to God outdoors (where 'all the grasses join in his prayer'), but became anxious when God didn't talk back. Like Anne, Nachman died of TB. It occurs to me that his narrow bridge is not so different from her narrow way, and that both Nachman and Anne wanted to inspire courage but knew that courage means nothing without fear. They knew that courage is not easy to find or to hold on to, that you might, at any moment, fall off the bridge and get swept away.

Charlotte almost fell after Anne's death, but she took courage, and forced herself to finish *Shirley*, and did her best to defend her sisters to their critics, and most of all, she wrote her bravest, strangest, most conflicted book. *Villette*, published in 1853, has become my favourite of Charlotte's novels. She had to write it alone, with no sisters to read it, 'no opinion from one living being'. Written 'darkly in the silent workshop of [her] own brain', it has no Gothic melodrama (well, all right, there is a sort of ghost) and no happy ending. Its heroine Lucy Snowe is as angry and as consumed by self-hatred as Charlotte was. The survivor of a tragedy she won't (or can't) talk about, she lies to the reader, she withholds key information, and she tries so hard to crush her desires that she feels like she is driving a tent peg into her own head. *Villette* is constricted, frustrating and unpleasant. That's why it's so good. *Jane Eyre* is an innocent book; *Villette* is by a woman who has lived. In *Villette*, Lucy has to recognise her own ardour; to admit that it can no longer be contained; to try for happiness, at last; and to recognise that there is no closure, that life isn't always fair, that moral choices are muddy, and there are no tidy endings, let alone happy ones.

Charlotte took courage again on a 'dim June morning' in 1854, when she took a leap into the unknown and married Arthur Bell Nicholls, even though she wasn't sure about him, and even though Patrick objected vehemently. Charlotte found that she could and did love Nicholls, and even hoped to have their child. But she fell prey to hyperemesis gravidarum, extreme morning sickness, and nine months after her wedding, her coffin was carried up the same aisle in Haworth's church where she had walked as a bride.

Patrick also took his youngest daughter's last words to heart. After Anne died, he went on the warpath, as if trying to do something his most radical, most humane, most hopeful child would have been proud of. Anne would certainly have admired the rigour and clarity with which her father identified Haworth's biggest problem: bad water. He organised a petition to demand a water supply to every house in the village, so it wasn't just the wealthy who got fresh water. He kept campaigning until, in April 1850, an inspector turned up. Benjamin Herschel Babbage was appalled to find that the average life expectancy was twenty-six, as bad as the poorest, most overcrowded slums of London. In some ways it's a wonder the Brontës lived so *long*. Babbage's report is, jokes Steven Wood, 'Victorian sanitation porn', full of lurid details about how the shortage of privies (and the fact that most had no doors) was 'injurious to health' and 'repugnant to all ideas of decency'; how, because there were no sewers, waste ran down the streets. 'Bad as is this state of things', Babbage agrees with Patrick that 'perhaps the most crying want of Haworth is water'. Worst of all, since the graveyard didn't have proper drainage, the corpses were literally seeping into what water there was.

Because Babbage closed down the churchyard, and put an end to burying people inside the church, when Patrick died at eighty-four, on 7 June 1861, his parish had to get special permission from the Secretary of State to bury him with his family (apart from Anne). Even then, his coffin had to be embedded in powdered charcoal and entombed separately from the others in brick or stone. For all that this was troublesome,

Patrick might have been glad. He had got what he wanted. He'd changed his world.

Nicholls took courage too, when he proposed to Charlotte. In fact, he had to keep taking courage because she rejected him at first, and because he had to defy Patrick, who didn't want them to marry. After Charlotte died, the two men became friends, but poor Nicholls found that Haworth's board of trustees didn't want him to succeed Patrick. He had to sell up quickly, auctioning off everything, including the table where Anne had written her two novels. In a grand and devastated gesture, he had Charlotte's bed destroyed. He returned to Ireland, where he said he had buried his heart with Charlotte but managed to marry a very understanding cousin. (There is a story about the famous portrait of Charlotte by George Richmond, which hung above their sofa, falling on his new wife's head while she was having a nap, and stunning her. It might be apocryphal but it *feels* true.) Nicholls was badgered by Brontë fans for the rest of his life.

As for the question Anne articulated for me, 'What, Where, and How Shall I Be When I Have Got Through?', I have been trying. Though she no longer appears in my dreams, I have been trying to grasp the thorn. To find my narrow way and stick to it. To write a new story when I don't like the one I'm given. To expand my heart. To take courage.

On honeymoon in Ireland, we take a detour to Banagher, in County Offaly, where Charlotte spent her honeymoon. It is February, very cold and pretty bleak, and almost everything is closed, including the Friends of Asthma charity shop, and a multi-purpose establishment called William Lyons which seems to be not just a 'Lounge Bar' but also a wool buyer and seller of fishing rods and firearms. Nicholls's old house is now a bed and breakfast called Charlotte's Way. In the churchyard, we try and fail to find Nicholls's grave. I remember Charlotte writing to her friend Margaret Wooler from Banagher to say, 'My dear husband . . . appears in a new light in his own country.' Having been so wary of marrying him she now feels glad she has made 'what seems a right choice'.

As we leave Banagher, the sun breaks through for a moment and the River Shannon gleams gold in the twilight, and I can see how Charlotte would have been happy here. But then the clouds come down again, like the lid on a saucepan; sleet falls, and on the motorway, deep fog descends. We can only see a few metres ahead, just beyond the beam of the headlights. The sun is setting; soon it will be dark. My new husband is driving, I am navigating. And all we can do is keep going, hope that more of the road will become visible, hope to get to where we're going, hope we like it when we do, and try to be brave.

And now, to quote Anne, I think I have said sufficient.

SELECTED READING

When quoting from Anne Brontë's books I have used the following editions:

The Poems of Anne Brontë: A New Text and Commentary by Anne Brontë, edited by Edward Chitham (Macmillan, Basingstoke and London, 1979)

The Tenant of Wildfell Hall by Anne Brontë, edited by Stevie Davies (Penguin, London, 1996)

Agnes Grey by Anne Brontë, edited by Angeline Goreau (Penguin, London, 2004)

For her sisters' work, I have used:

The Professor, Tales from Angria, Poems etc by The Brontës, edited by Phyllis Bentley (Collins, London, 1966)

Jane Eyre by Charlotte Brontë (Norton, New York, 2001)

Shirley by Charlotte Brontë, edited by Andrew and Judith Hook (Penguin, London, 1994)

Villette by Charlotte Brontë, edited by Sally Minogue (Wordsworth, Hertfordshire, 1993)

Wuthering Heights by Emily Brontë, edited by David Daiches (Penguin, London, 1965)

The Complete Poems by Emily Brontë, edited by Janet Gezari (Penguin, London, 1992)

When quoting from the letters, I have used *The Letters of Charlotte Brontë: with a selection of letters by family and friends*, edited by Margaret Smith, Volumes 1–3 (Oxford University Press, 1995–2004). However, the Brontës' spelling and punctuation are famously haphazard, so, following the example of some previous writers on the Brontës, I have clarified it where I can.

The reviews of Anne and her sisters' works are all from *The Brontës: The Critical Heritage*, edited by Miriam Allott (Routledge & Kegan Paul, Oxford, 1974).

I owe much to Juliet Barker's impeccably researched group biography, *The Brontës* (Abacus, London, 2010), to Lucasta Miller's *The Brontë Myth* (Vintage, London, 2000) which dismantles some of the oldest, hoariest stories about the family, and to *The Art of the Brontës* by Christine Alexander and Jane Sellars (Cambridge University Press, 1995) which rewards their art with the close attention that has been paid to their writing.

It's impossible to write about the Brontës without grappling with Elizabeth Gaskell, who got there first, in *The Life of Charlotte Brontë* (London, Penguin, 1998). I found Ann Dinsdale's book with Mark Davis, *In the Footsteps of the Brontës* (Amberley, Stroud, 2013), very helpful in getting a sense of place. I also found *The Brontë Cabinet: Three Lives in Nine Objects* by Deborah Lutz (Norton, New York, 2015) very useful in thinking about the Brontës' things.

On Anne specifically, Winifred Gérin's *Anne Brontë: a Biography* (Penguin, London, 1976) is indispensable, and Elizabeth Langland's *Anne Brontë: The Other One* (Macmillan, Basingstoke and London, 1989) is a fantastic short overview of the life and work. Other useful works on Anne are: *A Life of Anne Brontë* by Edward Chitham (Blackwell, Oxford, 1991); *Anne Brontë – Her Life and Work* by Ada Harrison and Derek Stanford (Methuen, London, 1959); *Anne Brontë: A New Critical Assessment* by P. J. M. Scott (Vision, London, 1983); and *Anne Brontë: her life and writings* by Will T. Hale (Indiana University Press, 1929).

In the **Introduction**, I used *Louisa May Alcott: Her Life, Letters and Journals*, edited by Ednah Cheney (Roberts Brothers, Boston, 1889), and *Little Women: an annotated edition* by Louisa May Alcott, edited by Daniel Shealy (Harvard University Press, Cambridge, Massachussets, 2013). I learned about the marginalia in Anne's Bible from 'Contextualising Anne Brontë's Bible' by Maria Frawley, in *New Approaches to the Literary Art of Anne Brontë*, edited by Julie Nash and Barbara A. Suess (Routledge, Oxford, 2001); Anne's Bible is in the Morgan Library & Museum in New York.

In **Chapter 1, on Maria**, Hermione Lee's *Virginia Woolf* (Vintage, London, 1997) helped me think back through *To the Lighthouse* by Virginia Woolf (Penguin, London, 1992). 'The Advantages of Poverty in Religious Concerns' by Maria Brontë is reprinted in *The Brontës: Life and Letters* by Clement Shorter (Hodder & Stoughton, London, 1908). I read Caroline Norton's letter to Queen Victoria at http://digital.library.upenn.edu/women/ norton/alttq/alttq.html, and found Diane Atkinson's biography,

The Criminal Conversation of Mrs Norton (Preface, London, 2012), very useful, as well as Norton's novel *Lost and Saved* (Hurst & Blackett, London, 1863). For a startling overview into how all the mothers in Gothic novels are dead or imprisoned, I was fascinated by 'The Missing Mother: The Meanings of Maternal Absence in the Gothic Mode' by Ruth Bienstock Anolik, in *Modern Language Studies*, Volume 33, Number 1 (2003). Laura C. Berry's 'Acts of Custody and Incarceration in *Wuthering Heights* and *The Tenant of Wildfell Hall*' in *NOVEL*, Volume 30, Number 1 (1996) helped me understand the trap Norton finds herself in. *Mary, a fiction; and The Wrongs of Woman* by Mary Wollstonecraft, edited by Gary Kelly (Oxford University Press, 1976), is a liberating read.

In **Chapter 2, on Elizabeth**, I looked at May Sinclair's intense *The Three Brontës* (Hutchinson & Co., London, 1912). 'The Brontës' by Marianne Thormählen, in *The Blackwell Companion to the Bible in English Literature*, edited by Rebecca Lemon and others (Blackwell, Oxford, 2009), was very helpful in thinking through Anne's beliefs, as was *The Brontës and Religion* by Marianne Thormählen (Cambridge University Press, 1999). For an alternative view, I was usefully challenged by 'Exiled and Harassed Anne' by Ernest Raymond, in *Brontë Society Transactions*, Volume 11, Issue 4 (1949), and 'The Drug-Like Brontë Dream' by Margaret Lane, in *Brontë Society Transactions*, Volume 12, Issue 2 (1952). Jonathan Raban's wonderful *Passage to Juneau* (Picador, London, 2000) was very useful in thinking about Cowper; the true story of the storm is in *A Voyage Round the World* by George Anson (Heron Books, Geneva, 1923).

Jeanette Winterson's story about *Jane Eyre* is in her memoir, *Why be Happy When You Could be Normal?* (Vintage, London, 2012).

In **Chapter 3, on Tabby**, I was lucky to be able to benefit from Steven Wood's extraordinary scholarship on Haworth and the moors; his latest book, *The Real Wuthering Heights: The Story of the Withins Farms* by Steven Wood and Peter Brears (Amberley, Stroud, 2016), is a useful corrective to many of the myths about Top Withins. *The Moor: Lives, Landscape, Literature* by William Atkins (Faber & Faber, London, 2014) was very helpful on the bog burst. Of the many guides to Haworth and the moors, I enjoyed *The Perfect Companion: The First Authentic Guidebook to Bronteland* [sic] *in the History of the Yorkshire Dales* by Frank Thompson (Frank Thompson Classic Publications, Haworth, 1978), *A Springtime Saunter: Round and About Brontë Land* by Whiteley Turner (Halifax Courier, 1913), and Halliwell Sutcliffe's essay 'The Spirit of the Moors', in *Brontë Society Transactions*, Volume 2, Issue 13 (1903). It was a huge pleasure to reread *The Secret Garden* by Frances Hodgson Burnett (Heinemann, London, 1976). *The Grasmere and Alfoxden Journals* by Dorothy Wordsworth, edited by Pamela Woof (Oxford University Press, 2002) is fabulous, as is *The Ballad of Dorothy Wordsworth* by Frances Wilson (Faber & Faber, London, 2008). 'From Simianized Irish to Oriental Despots: Heathcliff, Rochester and Racial Difference' by Elsie Michie, in *NOVEL: A Forum on Fiction*, Volume 25, Issue 2 (1992), was useful on Victorian racism towards the Irish. 'Tabitha Aykroyd' by C. Mabel Edgerley, in *Brontë Society Transactions*, Volume 10, Issue 2 (1941), was helpful on Tabby (although some of her conjectures have now been challenged) as was Ann Dinsdale's very clear and up-to-date *At Home with the Brontës* (Amberley, Stroud, 2013). Florence White's *Good Things in England* (Persephone, London, 1999) is a joy.

In **Chapter 4, on Emily**, Stevie Davies's *Emily Brontë: Heretic* (The Woman's Press, London, 1994) hugely influenced my approach. *Tales of Glasstown, Angria and Gondal: Selected Writings*, by the Brontës, edited by Christine Alexander (Oxford World's Classics, Oxford, 2010) is fantastic. For attempts to synthesise the Gondal stories, *The Brontës' Web of Childhood* by Fannie E. Ratchford (Russell & Russell, New York, 1964), *Gondal's Queen: a novel in verse* by Emily Jane Brontë, arranged, with an introduction and notes by Fannie E. Ratchford (University of Texas Press, Austin, 1955), and *An Investigation of Gondal* by W. D. Paden (Bookman Associates, New York, 1958), are all interesting. Rebecca West's essay 'The Role of Fantasy in the Work of the Brontës', in *Brontë Society Transactions*, Volume 12, Issue 64 (1954), is very powerful. *The Brontës Went to Woolworths* by Rachel Ferguson (Ernest Benn, London, 1931) is both fun and fascinating. I relied on *Becoming Queen* by Kate Williams (Hutchinson, London, 2008) to find out about the early life of Queen Victoria, and also on *The Adventures of Alice Laselles* by Alexandrina Victoria (Royal Collection Trust, London, 2015). Virginia Moore's *The Life and Eager Death of Emily Brontë, a biography* (Rich & Cowan, London, 1936) is a revealing read. Antonia Forest's *Peter's Room* (Faber, London, 1978) is a joy. Stassa Edwards's 'The Animalistic Emily Brontë' is at http://the-toast.net/2014/06/10/the-animalistic-emily-bronte/ For the stories from John Greenwood, I consulted Albert H. Preston's

'John Greenwood and The Brontës', in *Brontë Society Transactions*, Volume 12, Issue 1 (1951). The story of the woman inspired by Anne's novel to leave her marriage is 'Abuse inside Christian marriages – a personal story' by Isabella Young in the *Sydney Morning Herald*, 2 March 2015. To learn more about Ellen Nussey, I read 'Reminiscences of the Late Ellen Nussey' by William Scruton, in *Brontë Society Transactions*, Volume 1, Issue 8 (1898), as well as Nussey's own 'Reminiscences of Charlotte Brontë' in *Scribner's Monthly* (1871). 'The Brontës and the Conmen' by Mark Bostridge, in the *TLS*, 30 September 2015, clarified much about Shorter and Wise. For more on the formidable Mary Taylor, read *'More Precious than Rubies': Mary Taylor, Friend of Charlotte Brontë, Strong-Minded Woman* by Joan Bellamy (Highgate of Beverley, 2002). Mary Taylor's novel *Miss Miles, or a tale of Yorkshire life 60 years ago* (Remington & Co., London, 1890) is also excellent.

In **Chapter 5, on Charlotte**, I loved *Charlotte Brontë: A Passionate Life* by Lyndall Gordon (Virago, London, 2008). On Anne's hair, 'Bad Hair Days for the Brontës' was published on the BBC website on 24 April 2008, while the critic who was depressed by the controversy was William H. Pritchard, writing in *The Hudson Review*, Volume 49, Issue 2 (1996). *Letters on the Improvement of the Mind* by Hester Chapone (J. Exshaw, Dublin, 1773) is fascinating. 'The Rescue: James La Trobe and Anne Brontë' by Margaret Connor, in *Brontë Society Transactions*, Volume 24, Issue 1 (1999), gave useful context. Some works by critics who were less than enthusiastic about Anne are: *The Key to the Brontë Works: The Key to Charlotte Brontë's Wuthering Heights, Jane Eyre and her other works, Showing the method of their* *construction and their relation to the facts and people of her life*, by John Malham-Dembleby (Walter Scott Publishing, London, 1911); 'At the Grave of Anne Brontë' by Percy C. Standing in *The English Illustrated Magazine* (August 1897); *The Essence of the Brontës* by Muriel Spark (Carcanet, Manchester, 2014); and Margaret Oliphant, in *Women Novelists of Queen Victoria's Reign* (Hurst & Blackett, London, 1897). Mary Ward's preface to *The Tenant of Wildfell Hall* is in the Smith, Elder, London, 1898 edition of the novel. *The Crimes of Charlotte Brontë* by James Tully (Constable, London, 2013) is fascinating. The Brontë plays I read were *Moor Born* by Dan Totheroh (Samuel French, New York, 1934), *The Brontës of Haworth Parsonage* by John Davison (Frederick Muller Ltd, London, 1934), *Wild Decembers* by Clemence Dane (William Heineman, London, 1932), *Branwell* by Martyn Richards (Longmans, Dorset, 1948). *Withering Looks* by Lip Service Theatre is sadly not published but there is information about it at www.lipservicetheatre.co.uk/shows/withering-looks. I don't recommend *Devotion: the book of the film* by Warwick Mannon (Hollywood Publications, 1946). My thoughts on *Shirley* were influenced by 'Private and Social Themes in *Shirley*' by Professor Asa Briggs, in *Brontë Society Transactions*, Volume 13, Issue 68 (1958). I found G. D. Hargreaves's essays, 'Incomplete Texts of *The Tenant of Wildfell Hall*', in *Brontë Society Transactions*, Volume 16, Issue 2 (1972), 'Further Omissions in *The Tenant of Wildfell Hall*' in *Brontë Society Transactions*, Volume 17, Issue 2 (1977), and 'Smith, Elder's 1857–60 Edition of the Brontë Life and works', in *Brontë Society Transactions*, Volume 29, Issue 1 (2004), crucial to understanding Anne's publication history and the variant texts. *Their Proper Sphere: a study of the*

Brontë sisters as early Victorian female novelists by Inga-Stina Ewbank (Edward Arnold, London, 1966) is heartening. *A Book for Her* by Bridget Christie (Century, London, 2015) tells the story of how she developed her show *A Bic for Her*.

In **Chapter 6, on Agnes**, I learned about Victorian governesses from *Other People's Daughters: The Life and Times of the Governess* by Ruth Brandon (Weidenfeld & Nicholson, London, 2008) and *The Victorian Governess* by Kathryn Hughes (Hambledon Press, London, 1993). *Journal of a Governess* by Nelly Weeton, edited by Edward Hall (Oxford University Press, London, 1936–9) is searing. *The Governess* by Marguerite Gardiner, Countess of Blessington (London, 1839), is the opposite. I learned about Anne's ghost in 'Spooky tale of "haunted" staircase from Blake Hall in Mirfield with Brontë links – which has turned up in New York' by Martin Shaw, *Huddersfield Daily Examiner*, 29 December 2014. '"Hapless Dependents": Women and Animals in Anne Brontë's *Agnes Grey*' by Maggie Berg, in *Studies in the Novel*, Volume 34, Number 2 (2002), was very useful, as was *Save the Cat! The Last Book on Screenwriting That You'll Ever Need* by Blake Snyder (Michael Wiese Productions, Studio City, California, 2005).

In **Chapter 7, on Branwell**, I began with Daphne du Maurier's wonderful *The Infernal World of Branwell Brontë* (Penguin, Harmondsworth, 1972). For fictional treatments of Anne's time at Thorp Green, Philippa Stone's *The Captive Dove* (Robert Hale, London, 1968) is intriguing; Oscar W. Firkins's play *Empurpled Moors*, in *The Bride of Quietness and other plays* (University of Minneapolis Press, 1933), is less so. There is good thinking about

Huntingdon in 'The Villain of *Wildfell Hall*: Aspects and Prospects of Arthur Huntingdon' by Marianne Thormählen in *Modern Language Review*, Volume 88, Number 4 (1993), and '"Imbecile Laughter" and "Desperate Earnest" in *The Tenant of Wildfell Hall*' by Juliet McMaster, in *Modern Language Quarterly*, Volume 43 (1982). Deborah Lutz's *The Dangerous Lover: Gothic Villains, Byronism and the Nineteenth-Century Seduction Narrative* (Ohio State University Press, 2006) is also very good on the allure of bad men, as is *The Female Romantics: Nineteenth-century Women Novelists and Byronism* by Caroline Franklin (Routledge, London, 2013). I relied on Edna O'Brien's *Byron in Love* (Orion, London, 2009) and Fiona MacCarthy's *Byron: Life and Legend* (Faber & Faber, London, 2003) for the poet's story. I found 'Angel or Sister? Writing and Screening the Heroine of Anne Brontë's *The Tenant of Wildfell* Hall' by Aleks Sierz, in *Sisterhoods: Across the Literature/ Media Divide*, edited by Deborah Cartmell, I. Q. Hunter, Heidi Kaye and Imelda Whelehan (Pluto, London, 1998), very useful in contextualising the miniseries. *Charlotte Brontë* by E. F. Benson (Longmans, London, 1932) was helpful on Anne's treatment of Branwell. I'm indebted to 'The Art of Comparison: Remarriage in Anne Brontë's *The Tenant of Wildfell Hall*' by Nicole A. Diederich, in *Rocky Mountain Review of Language and Literature*, Volume 57, Number 2 (2003), for insight into the risks Helen takes in marrying again, and for the comparison with John Stuart Mill. In worrying about Gilbert, and the narrative frame, I also found Rachel K. Carnell's 'Feminism and the Public Sphere in Anne Brontë's *The Tenant of Wildfell Hall*', in *Nineteenth-Century Literature*, Volume 53, Number 1 (1998), very useful, as well as Naomi Jacobs's 'Gender and Layered Narrative in *Wuthering*

Heights and *The Tenant of Wildfell Hall'*, in *The Journal of Narrative Technique*, Volume 16, Number 3 (1986), Tess O'Toole's 'Siblings and Suitors in the Narrative Architecture of *The Tenant of Wildfell Hall'*, in *Studies in English Literature, 1500–1900*, Volume 39, Number 4, (1999), and John Sutherland's 'Who is Helen Graham?', in *Is Heathcliff a Murderer? Puzzles in 19th Century Fiction* (Oxford University Press, 1996). Penny Gay's essay, 'Anne Brontë and the forms of romantic comedy', in *Brontë Society Transactions*, Volume 23, Issue 1 (1998), helped me defend Gilbert.

In **Chapter 8, on Patrick**, I enjoyed both *A Man of Sorrows: The Life, Letters and Times of the Rev. Patrick Brontë 1777–1861* by John Lock and W. T. Dixon (Nelson, London, 1965) and *Patrick Brontë: Father of Genius* by Dudley Green (Nonsuch, Stroud, 2008). Terry Eagleton's *Myths of Power: A Marxist Study of the Brontës* (Macmillan, Basingstoke, 1988) is illuminating on the Brontës, class and immigration. *Doctor Who: The Child of Time* by Jonathan Morris and others (Panini UK, Tunbridge Wells, 2012) is surreal. Jill L. Matus's *Unstable Bodies: Victorian Representations of Sexuality and Maternity* (Manchester University Press, 1995) was very interesting on reviews of *Agnes Grey*. The *Report on a Preliminary Inquiry into the Sewerage, Drainage, and Supply of Water, and the Sanitary Conditions of the Inhabitants of the Hamlet of Haworth* by Benjamin Herschel Babbage (General Board of Health, London, 1850) is not for the faint-hearted. Nor is *A Corpse at the Haworth Tandoori* by Robert Barnard (HarperCollins, London, 1998).

In **Chapter 9, on Helen**, Antonia Losano's excellent essay, 'The Professionalization of the Woman Artist in Anne Brontë's

The Tenant of Wildfell Hall', in *Nineteenth-Century Literature*, Volume 58, Number 1 (2003), helped me think through Helen's journey, as did 'Art and the artist as heroine in the novels of Charlotte, Emily and Anne Brontë' by Jane Sellars, in *Brontë Society Transactions*, Volume 20, Issue 2 (1990), and 'The Artist in her Studio: The Influence of the Brontës on Women Artists' by Jane Sellars, in *Brontë Studies*, Volume 30, Issue 3 (2005). For a different view, try *The Madwoman in the Attic* by Sandra Gilbert and Susan Gubar (Yale University Press, New Haven and London, 2000). *Old Mistresses* by Roszika Parker and Griselda Pollock (Routledge & Kegan Paul, London, 1981) is very good on the need for a new word to describe women artists. I don't entirely recommend *Olive* by Dinah Craik (Macmillan, London, 1893) or *Pillars of the House* by Charlotte Yonge (Macmillan, London, 1888). Carolyn Heilbrun's insight about pseudonyms comes from her groundbreaking *Writing a Woman's Life* (Norton, New York, 1988). Meghan Bullock's essay, 'Abuse, silence and solitude in Anne Brontë's *The Tenant of Wildfell Hall'*, in *Brontë Studies*, Volume 29, Issue 2 (2004), helped me think through the silence of the abused women in Anne's novel. For a survey of the way gossip works in the novel, 'Gossip, Diary, Letter, Text: Anne Brontë's Narrative Tenant and the Problematic of the Gothic Sequel' by Jan B. Gordon, in *ELH*, Volume 51, Number 4 (1984), is excellent.

In **Chapter 10, on Anne**, I reread *Anne of the Island* by L. M. Montgomery (Puffin, Harmondsworth, 1983). I learned about Gérin from Helen MacEwan's *Winifred Gérin: Biographer of the Brontës* (Sussex Academic Press, London, 2016).

ACKNOWLEDGEMENTS

This book would not have happened if Ann Dinsdale hadn't shown me Anne Brontë's last letter. I'm also hugely grateful for her expertise and scholarship, and for help from her colleagues at the Brontë Parsonage, especially Sarah Laycock, Amy Rowbottom and Charissa Hutchins. Also in Haworth I would like to thank Steven Wood for walking me across the moors and for patient and detailed responses to my many questions since. Thanks also to Julie Akhurst and Steve Brown for showing me around their home, Ponden Hall; to Jennifer Dunne and Pete Rawson at Scarborough Museums Trust for enlightening me about Anne's pebbles; to the Reverend Christopher Parkin for letting me have a look at the Holy Trinity Church, Little Ouseburn; to Ben Butler-Cole for sailing lore; to Robert Freeman at Craven Museum and Gallery Skipton and to the staff at the British Library and the London Library for tracking down manuscripts and secondary sources.

My wonderful agent Judith Murray believed in this book from the start, as did my brilliant editor Becky Hardie, who is the perfect mix of encouragement and rigour. Also at Chatto, huge thanks to Charlotte Humphery, Kris Potter, Mari Yamazaki, Katherine Fry, Charlotte Knight and Louise Court.

Thank you to Robert Holman for letting me quote him (again!). And thank you to all the people I've had useful and illuminating conversations with about Anne over the past two years, especially: Naomi Alderman, Sam Baker, Marina Benjamin, Lucy Caldwell, Maddy Costa, Lyndall Gordon, Paul King, Robert Macfarlane, Helen McColl, Shane Morgan and the cast of his production of *The Tenant of Wildfell Hall*, Amy Rosenthal, Héloïse Sénéchal, and of course my staunch and stalwart writers' group – Robin Booth, Nick Harrop, Matt Morrison and Ben Musgrave. And thank you to my late aunt Anne Ellis, who first gave me *The Tenant of Wildfell Hall*.

Lastly, thanks – and love – to my parents and my brother, and to my friend Emma Ayech. And most of all, to Jude Cook, for enduring many hours of driving and tramping about Yorkshire, and many nights of reading drafts, and for helping me to take courage and to expand my heart.

INDEX

Index

Index

Index

Index